BIG BLUE
WRECKING CREW

Also by Jerry Barca

Unbeatable

BIG BLUE
WRECKING CREW

SMASHMOUTH FOOTBALL, A LITTLE BIT OF CRAZY,
AND THE '86 SUPER BOWL CHAMPION NEW YORK GIANTS

JERRY BARCA

St. Martin's Press ⚏ New York

To BD2000,

You know what it takes to make it happen.

www.stmartins.com

Designed by Meghan Day Healey

The Library of Congress Cataloging-in-Publication Data is available upon request.

ISBN 978-1-250-07153-8 (hardcover)
ISBN 978-1-4668-8267-6 (e-book)

Our books may be purchased in bulk for promotional, educational, or business use. Please contact your local bookseller or the Macmillan Corporate and Premium Sales Department at 1-800-221-7945, extension 5442, or by e-mail at Macmillan SpecialMarkets@macmillan.com.

First Edition: August 2016

10 9 8 7 6 5 4 3 2 1

CONTENTS

PART THREE
Identity

PART FOUR
Giant Football

PART

The End to Pure Mayhem

ONE

1
THE FUMBLE

NOVEMBER 19, 1978

Playing at the Meadowlands beneath a sky of scattered clouds on a slightly breezy autumn day, the New York Giants took a 17–6 lead into the fourth quarter.

The Philadelphia Eagles mounted a rally, closing a 13-play, 91-yard drive with a one-yard Mike Hogan touchdown run. With less than four minutes to play, the Giants' lead had been cut to 17–12. Typical of the Giants' ineptitude, three New York penalties, two pass interferences, and a roughing the passer accounted for 49 yards on the drive.

Thirty-five seconds after the Eagles scored, Giants running back Doug Kotar fumbled, handing the ball back to Philadelphia. Quarterback Ron Jaworski and the Eagles' offense took over at the Giants' 33-yard line.

With under two minutes to play, Jaworski dropped back to pass. He pumped. Then he pulled his arm back again and let the ball fly. The pass slipped through the hands of a leaping Hogan and dropped into the chest of Giants rookie defensive back Odis McKinney.

The Giants had the ball inside their own 20-yard line. The Eagles were out of time-outs. There was no way for Philadelphia to stop the clock. The game was over. The Giants would win. Somehow, they had recovered from Kotar's miscue. Now, all they had to do was snap the ball a few times and let the time run out. That's it.

A win would snap a three-game losing streak. The Giants would be 6–6. They would be in the play-off hunt with four games remaining.

"I wanted to fall on the ball three times and, just like, go home. Let's have a cold one. It's Miller time," said Giants quarterback Joe Pisarcik.[1]

That didn't happen.

On first down, Pisarcik took the snap, backed up three yards, and fell to the ground. Eagles linebackers Frank LeMaster and Bill Bergey shot through the Giants' offensive line. LeMaster drove a blocker and himself over a prone Pisarcik. Eagles and Giants players pushed and shoved each other after the play.

Perched above the field in a coach's box, Giants offensive coordinator Bob Gibson decided his unit would answer the rough play from Philly. He sent in Pro 65 Up. It was a run.

In the huddle, when Pisarcik called the play, he heard the chatter from his teammates questioning the rationale of running the ball rather than just falling on it and letting the clock run down. In recent games, Pisarcik had changed a few of Gibson's calls, and Gibson laced into him for it. This time, Pisarcik felt compelled to follow the directives.

The play went off smoothly. Pisarcik used a reverse pivot to the right to mislead the defense. Then he handed the ball off to Larry Csonka for an off-tackle run to the left. Csonka clenched both arms around the ball. He muscled through the left side for 11 yards. It was now third down and two. By the time the Giants snapped the ball, the game clock would have ticked below thirty seconds. All they had to do was snap it, fall on the ground, and the game would be over.

The Giants didn't do that. Gibson made the same play call. He sent it down to an assistant coach on the sideline. The assistant relayed it to second-year tight end Al Dixon, who shuttled Pro 65 Up to Pisarcik.

"That's crazy," one lineman said when he heard the call.

"It was very distinctive coming from the sideline," said Brad Benson, an offensive lineman who was in the huddle. "I guess he was proving a point to Pisarcik: 'Hand the ball off.'"

Maybe Gibson had read the newspaper that morning, the article with anonymous players ridiculing his play calling, saying the team would be better off with Pisarcik calling the shots.

Before the Giants broke the huddle, CBS started rolling the credits—that thick, yellow-block font moving up TV screens. This was the ultimate sign that the outcome had been decided. *Rolling credits meant the game was over.*

It was just the formality of snapping the ball. On the field, though, the offensive and defensive linemen started chatting.

"Usually, when the quarterback is just going to fall on the ball, we tell the other team to take it easy and not bury him," said Giants center Jim Clack.[2]

Eagles nose tackle Charlie Johnson asked Clack if he should go easy.

"No, we're running a play," Clack told Johnson.

The same exchange went down the line.

"We're going," Brad Benson told the Eagles.

"Are you serious?" he heard back from the other side.

"Here we go," Benson said with disbelief as he bent into his stance.

Clack hiked the ball to Pisarcik. Things went bad. The ball came up to the right. It danced up Pisarcik's forearm. The quarterback reverse pivoted. Barely controlling the ball, he turned and swung the ball into Csonka's hip as the back charged into the line. The ball squirted backward off Csonka. Pisarcik moved to fall on it. The ball bounced off the Astroturf, between his hands.

The clunky awkwardness of the Giants was met with an equal amount of grace and ease from Eagles defensive back Herman Edwards. He swooped in. Snatched the ball in stride and ran to the end zone, spiking the ball for good measure when he scored.

Pisarcik raised his head from his prostrate position and watched Edwards lead the flurry of bodies to the end zone. The Eagles won the game 19–17.

By that day—November 19, 1978—there had been plenty of New York Giants losses. This one was number 130 since the Giants fell to the Chicago Bears in the 1963 championship game, the last time the NFL's flagship franchise had taken a whiff of play-off football.

This was special, though. This was a how-could-that-have-happened, bewildering defeat, one that lives in eternity in the Hall of Football Stupidity. In Philadelphia, they call it the Miracle of Meadowlands. In Giants' infamy, it is The Fumble.

It is the Giants' crowning bumble, the most public humiliation of a proud organization's fifteen-year swoon.

The Fumble is the bookend across the shelf from the image of a helmetless, bloodied Y. A. Tittle kneeling on the field. He had just thrown a pick six to the Steelers in the second week of a two-win 1964 season, the first year of the Giants' downward drift.

While it may be hard to think of it this way, The Fumble, on its own, is one stupid play call executed with a mix of bungling and bad luck. A team can recover from feeding the blooper reel, but the stigmata comes from what the Giants were as an organization when it happened. As unpredictable as it is that a team could invent a way to lose a game, it hurt even more because with the Giants, The Fumble wasn't all that unpredictable.

"When I heard about The Fumble, at first I laughed, then I thought how ironic that it happened to the Giants. Then it became understandable," said Fred Dryer, a former Giants defensive end, who was now part of the NFC West–dominating Los Angeles Rams.[3]

The Giants franchise was in disarray, marred by amateur-level talent, embarrassing personnel moves, no locker room leadership, a recalcitrant front office, and ownership infighting that would soon become very public.

With The Fumble, anybody—from fans to players to coaches—could point to a physical manifestation of how bad things had become for the organization. Yet it would get even worse.

THE BOOKMAKER'S TEAM IN A PAINFUL PERIOD

At the dawn of the twentieth century, Tim Mara's turf ran along Broadway from Wanamaker's department store on Tenth Avenue up four blocks to Union Square. The teenager hustled on the streets as a newsboy.

Born in 1887 to policeman John Mara and the former Elizabeth Harris, Timothy James Mara grew up poor on Manhattan's Lower East Side.

While working his newspaper route, Mara couldn't help but notice that bookies, a legal profession at the time, dressed the best and worked the least of anybody he saw. He soon began running bets as a messenger. Mara would deliver the newspaper to hotel guests, take their bets, and run them to a bookie. When the hotel guest lost a bet, Mara received 5 percent of the wager.

With an entrepreneurial sense, he stopped being the middleman. He took his own bets and grew his gambling business. Later, he set up shop in the enclosure at Belmont Park racetrack. He became one of the city's "most respected 'wagering commissioners,'" *The New York Times* wrote.

In 1925, NFL officials knew the sustainable course for the league meant establishing operations in New York City. Those officials also knew bookmakers might go for a risky investment, a gamble. Mara didn't see it that way. He figured the small amount he paid to establish the team was worth at least the most worthless business in Manhattan, an empty store or shoeshining operation, he would say.

Mara purchased the Giants for what is recorded in history as either $2,500 or $500. Either figure means it cost a pittance to land a pro sports team in the Big Apple. A common practice at the time, the football team took the same name as the local baseball brethren, who—like Mara's football team—played at the Polo Grounds.

The story goes that Mara had never seen a football game when he bought into the NFL. "The Giants were founded on a combination of brute strength and ignorance. The players supplied the brute strength. I supplied the ignorance," he said.[1]

The Giants started in hard times. It wasn't so much issues on the field as it was getting people to the field. Back then, nobody paid much attention to pro football.

The same year the Giants came into existence, Harold "Red" Grange, a.k.a. "The Galloping Ghost," signed a contract to play for the Chicago Bears. He was the type of sports legend the NFL needed to boost its popularity. In college, Grange averaged more than 209 yards from scrimmage per game. In a twenty-game career at the University of Illinois, he scored 31 touchdowns, more than a quarter of the time reaching the end zone from 50 yards or farther away. His play, spectacular on its own, became bronzed in the poetic mythmaking prose that colored the nation's sports pages. "A streak of fire, a breath of flame / eluding all who reach and clutch" is how famed sportswriter Grantland Rice described Grange. When Grange signed with the Bears, a contract for nineteen games barnstorming across the country, his stardom was so great his compensation included a percentage of the ticket sales.

Professional football was a lower-grade option than its college counterpart, and even further behind boxing and baseball. Pro football teams were regional squads that might exist one season and then go away the next. With Grange in the fold, the five-year-old NFL had a superstar it could market.

Mara attempted to replicate the Grange recipe in an effort to draw crowds to the Polo Grounds. The Giants signed multisport legend Jim Thorpe. The contract stipulated that Thorpe only had to play half of each game. The deal didn't bring in the crowds. Thorpe, long past his prime, was released after three games.

Nothing seemed to work financially. Aside from visits from Grange and the Bears, the Giants were losing money every year. They won championships in 1927, '34, and '38, yet they continued to lose money.

After the stock market crash in 1929, Mara, in an effort to keep the team and protect it from creditors, gave ownership to his sons, twenty-two-year-old Jack and fourteen-year-old Wellington. The father remained as the chairman of the board.

During this period, the league was a fledgling enterprise, and Tim Mara became a devout pioneer. On more than one occasion, he led charges to stave off competition posed by football leagues that could have threatened the NFL. Even though it meant using less talented players and forcing the odd situation of the Philadelphia Eagles and Pittsburgh Steelers playing as one team, he pushed to keep the NFL operating during World War II. It was during this stretch that the Giants began to lead the league in attendance.

A few years later in 1955, the Giants' attendance slipped to ninth in the league. The Mara sons now ran the operation. An undisclosed group offered to buy the team that year for $1 million. The Maras turned it down. A year later, in 1956, the team moved from the splinter-bestowing wooden-floor showers of the Polo Grounds to the tiled bathrooms of Yankee Stadium. They added another championship that year, trouncing the Bears 47–7.

Then it happened: the 1958 NFL Championship. The Baltimore Colts played the Giants at Yankee Stadium. It was a great confluence of events—a widely consumable TV broadcast, a great New York team, a Colts squad loaded with future Hall of Famers, and sudden-death overtime.

An estimated forty-five million viewers watched the Colts jump out to a 14–3 lead. The Giants came back to take a 17–14 lead in the fourth quarter, but Baltimore tied the game on a 20-yard field goal with seven seconds left.

Led by Johnny Unitas, the best quarterback of the era and one of the greatest of all time, the Colts bested the Giants 23–17 in overtime. It has been dubbed "The Greatest Game Ever Played." Probably an overstatement for a contest with seven turnovers, but its impact on the growth of the NFL can't be exaggerated. That game left a mark on America's pop culture consciousness, and the NFL has become bigger, and bigger, and bigger ever since.

After the 1958 championship, the NFL mattered in the sports landscape. The fulfillment of what it meant to have a New York franchise started to happen, too. The Giants lost that game, but the players became celebrities. Madison Avenue took note of the strapping, handsome Giants and turned them into product-selling stars.

Defensive back Dick Nolan endorsed cigarettes. An image of him in uniform puffing Camels spread across a billboard on Forty-Fourth and Broadway—Times Square. In 1961, after his playing days ended, Charlie Conerly, the quarterback who had never ridden a horse, became the Marlboro Man. Sam Huff pushed the "full-flavored smoke" of Marlboros, too. Huff, a barreled-chested linebacker, had deals for print ads of Afta aftershave and Brookfield suits.

Huff was the subject of a groundbreaking film. He had been miked for sound in practice and an exhibition game. In 1959, Walter Cronkite, the preeminent TV journalist, narrated the final product, *The Violent World of Sam Huff,* a thirty-minute CBS TV special. That same year, Huff became the first professional football player on the cover of *Time* magazine.

The boys in the Giants uniforms were big-time, and no one was bigger than the dark-haired, blue-eyed running back with movie star looks, Frank Gifford. He did print ads for sportswear and TV commercials for Vitalis V7 hair product. He was a guest on the popular TV program *What's My Line?,* and he even had his own show.

Tim Mara established the Giants as a family operation. It was run on the principles of honesty and selflessness. In the 1950s, Tim Mara's grandchildren could be seen floating around the locker room after games. When the Great Depression leveled New York City, Mayor Jimmy Walker called out for help. Mara answered, hosting a postseason exhibition in 1930 between the Giants and a Knute Rockne–coached all-star squad of players from the

University of Notre Dame. The pros won the game easily, and four days later, Mara gave all the revenue—$115,153, the modern equivalent of $1.6 million—to the city.

On February 16, 1959, the seventy-one-year-old team founder died of a heart attack in his home at 975 Park Avenue. The family-oriented, league-first stamp he put on the franchise remained. With his sons, Jack and Wellington, in charge, the Giants were poised to cash in on the CBS TV contract in 1960. The New York franchise stood to make more than four times the amount of a small-market team like the Green Bay Packers. The Maras declined the larger payout in favor of sharing the TV money equally.

"You had to think league first and that the league is only as strong as its weakest partner," Wellington Mara's son John said of his father and the family's approach. "If you had too big a revenue disparity among teams, then you wouldn't have a very successful league in the long run. That was his core belief for as long as I can remember, and that was something that he preached all the time, and that's why he felt so strongly about equal sharing of TV revenues."

More than fifty-five years later, the NFL earns about $3.2 billion in TV broadcast rights. The revenue-sharing move is viewed as the financial backbone of the NFL's success.

In June of 1965, the Giants' team president, fifty-seven-year-old Jack Mara, died of cancer. His younger brother, Wellington, succeeded Jack as president. When the Giants' top brass reorganized, Jack Mara's son Tim became vice president and continued to serve as team treasurer. The ownership split had been fifty-fifty between the sons of the founder. It remained that way with Wellington owning half and the surviving side of Jack's family owning half as well. When the restructuring occurred, the general manager position was left vacant. It remained that way until about three months after The Fumble.

The losing started the season before Wellington's brother Jack died. The Giants fell 14–10 to the Chicago Bears at Wrigley Field in the '63 NFL Championship. They followed that with the worst season in team history, a 2–10–2 campaign. Well, the worst season until two years later when the team went 1–12–1. Aging stars and injured players interrupted the inertia of success. Brilliant coordinators—Tom Landry on the defensive side, and Vince Lombardi on offense—departed New York to build their legends as head coaches in Dallas and Green Bay, respectively.

From 1954 to 1963, the Giants fielded a winning team every year. They only won one championship, but they played in the championship game six times. They ingrained themselves in the fabric of the city, and they built an ultraloyal fan base along the way. During the fifteen-year drought from 1964 through The Fumble, the Giants had two winning years. On seven occasions, they fielded teams that produced ten or more losses in a season. This is a team that went from making routine trips to the championship game, having a heartthrob running back with a TV show, and a defensive back puffing smoke on a Broadway billboard to an organization that won a measly 35 percent of the time it played. The legendary brand upon which the NFL built much of its popularity had become an embarrassment. Fans started serenading the head coach about his impending departure.

"That period was a painful period in our history and for our family, too," John Mara said.

On a mid-September morning in 1969, Wellington walked into the kitchen at the family's home in White Plains, New York. John was getting ready for school. Wellington told him he was going to make a change at head coach. In the Giants organization, Allie Sherman was loved, but it was time for him to go. Sherman had coached the Giants to the NFL Championship game in each of his first three seasons, 1961–63. But those glory years were a relic now. When Wellington spoke to John that morning, the Giants had just finished a winless preseason with a final game against the Pittsburgh Steelers in Montreal. In Yankee Stadium, where the Giants played their home games, the fans had been singing "Good-bye, Allie" for a while. In Montreal, they sang it in French, "Au revoir, Allie."

Wellington fired Sherman. He hired one of Sherman's assistants, Alex Webster, who had also played running back for the Giants from 1955 to 1964. The head coaching change didn't change the results all that much. In five seasons, Webster posted a 29–40–1 record. He had two winning seasons but never made the play-offs.

In 1973, it was clear the Webster era was coming to a close. By this point, eighteen-year-old John Mara would occasionally be on the sidelines during games. At halftime, during the final game of the season, Webster came up to John in the locker room at the Yale Bowl. The coach was in tears. He put his arm around the team president's son and apologized.

"I'm so sorry I couldn't bring you a winner. I did the best I could," John remembers the coach telling him.

"It was a painful, painful period. But again, he didn't have the organization behind him, feeding him the talent he needed," Mara said.

3

PURE MAYHEM

The Giants needed a quarterback. To be a winner, you need a quarterback, and not just any quarterback. The Giants had to search quickly for that star because there was a new team in town. As those dreary years commenced, the G-Men had to compete for popularity with the upstart New York Jets from that upstart American Football League. Those Jets, they had a quarterback. And that quarterback held the city in his hand. Joe Willie Namath, a mink coat–wearing, Super Bowl–win-guaranteeing playboy whose bravado was matched by his film study, toughness, and rocket arm.

By the time Namath led the Jets to a Super Bowl win in January 1969, the Giants had already made a trade with the Minnesota Vikings for Fran Tarkenton. The blue team gave the purple team a couple of first-round picks for the scrambling future Hall of Famer, and it almost worked out. With Tarkenton, the Giants treaded water. After missing the play-offs with a 9–5 record in '70, Tarkenton figured his team would draft the defensive help it needed to push them into the postseason.

With the eighteenth overall pick in the first round, the Giants passed on defensive back Jack Tatum and defensive end Jack Youngblood, an all-American out of Florida and a future Hall of Famer. New York went for offense instead. They plucked an unknown running back from an unknown school, Rocky Thompson of West Texas State. He started one game in the pros and played mostly as a kick returner before exiting the NFL after three nondescript seasons.

Tarkenton eventually had a falling-out with Wellington Mara during contract negotiations. "They told me take it or leave it," Tarkenton said. "So I left. That was a terrible thing from their standpoint."[1]

Tarkenton stayed home, skipping an exhibition game. He was traded back to the Vikings a few months later. The Giants received journeyman quarterback Norm Snead and draft picks, one resulting in hulking linebacker Brad Van Pelt. In return, Minnesota got a quarterback who started three Super Bowls.

In 1978, as Tarkenton wrapped up a career that set all-time NFL passing records for completions, yards, and touchdowns, he took time to take shots at the Giants.

"I just didn't think the Giants had the organization capable of putting together a team that would win consistently. Too many ex-Giants had jobs in the organization. There weren't enough fresh new outside ideas. Another thing was, I never felt there was a clear-cut line of authority."

Tarkenton's words had truth and an extra sting because after his departure, the Giants could never find a quarterback to lead them back to prominence. Snead was already thirty-three years old when he became the starter. He was a smart player, but the personnel department hoped Randy Johnson would develop into a marquee guy. That never happened. Johnson had a string of injuries, threw the ball carelessly, and had bad practice habits.

The Giants missed on drafting Dan Fouts and Ron Jaworski in 1973. They made a deal for Jim Del Gaizo. He was *the* diamond in the rough. The left-hander was an undrafted free agent who had spent time with the Miami Dolphins. Understand that the early 1970s Dolphins were similar to the '60s Packers, the '80s 49ers, and '00s Patriots. They had already won two Super Bowls, and Don Shula had coached them to a perfect season in 1972. Teams looking to improve chased the Dolphins' formula for success. In Del Gaizo's case, the Green Bay Packers gave up two first-round picks for a backup signal caller who had played well in games of no consequence. The Giants, chasing that formula, had hired Dolphins defensive coordinator Bill Arnsparger as their head coach in 1974. He was the defensive genius of the era. Arnsparger pressed to acquire Del Gaizo. The Giants sent a third-round pick to the Packers. Then, after the trade, Giants brass watched Del Gaizo throw the ball. "I knew at that moment we had made a grave error," said Andy Robustelli, the Giants' director of operations.[2] In '74, Del Gaizo started one game and appeared in three others. For the season, he completed 12 of 32 passes and threw three interceptions and no touchdowns. After that, he never played in another NFL game.

Midway through Arnsparger's first season, the Giants traded for the big arm of Craig Morton. Morton had started Super Bowl V for the Dallas Cowboys, but he was mostly a backup to superstars Don Meredith and Roger Staubach. Morton had signed with the Houston Texans of the World Football League, but he never played for them because of the trade.

Arnsparger's handling of Morton reinforced the idea that he was a great coordinator but unfit to be a head coach in New York. Arnsparger made rules. One was that if players were late for the team bus or plane, the team would take off without them. Arnsparger never mentioned that the rule didn't apply to Morton.

Before one road trip, Arnsparger found himself standing up in front of the team's filled charter plane.[3]

"Craig had an emergency," he said before delaying the plane to wait for Morton's arrival.

"Biggest act of hypocrisy I have seen in my life," said defensive end George Martin. "'We will make no exceptions for anyone.' You institute that rule, make a definitive statement, and the first-string quarterback has been out all night—we knew what he was doing—plane is held up, bus is held up. Arnsparger lost all credibility with us."

Morton wasn't all that bad. He had the talent to lead a team, just not the Giants. The year after he left New York, he started in the Super Bowl for the Broncos. Befitting the Giants, the trade to acquire Morton from Dallas was made exponentially worse because one of the draft picks New York gave the Cowboys resulted in Dallas taking Hall of Fame defensive tackle Randy White, the co-MVP of the Super Bowl in which Morton played for the Broncos.

During this quarterbacking debacle, the Giants even had a field general go AWOL. Carl Summerell, a fourth-round pick out of East Carolina in '74, looked ready to challenge Morton for the starting spot in '76. Summerell played the entire preseason game against the Patriots, completing 13 of 18 passes in an overtime loss in early August. Then he was gone. He went back to Norfolk, Virginia, to address some family issues, and he never returned to pro football.

The woeful play can't be entirely blamed on the quarterbacks. There were other failed personnel moves. The offensive line played at a semipro level. Highly touted linemen turned out to be too inconsistent or too fat to play.

"It took a lot of courage to take a snap as a quarterback there during a football game," said offensive lineman Brad Benson.

Larry Csonka signed a three-year, $1.2 million deal to play in New York. An aging fullback, used mostly as a blocker, meant Csonka earned $892.85 per yard for his time, and it actually cost the Giants even more. Wellington Mara's combined approaches of old-world NFL and honorable business had the Giants send two third-round picks to the Dolphins even though they signed Csonka as a free agent out of the defunct World Football League.

The bright spots on the 1978 roster weren't necessarily strokes of brilliant talent evaluation. Defensive end George Martin came in as an eleventh-round draft pick out of Oregon. Linebacker coach Marty Schottenheimer had to argue with personnel staffers for the team to take Harry Carson out of South Carolina State. Carson played in a three-point stance at defensive end in college. Schottenheimer saw a player who, if he played standing up and away from the line, would make a great linebacker. The young coach was right, and the Giants took Carson in the fourth round of the '76 draft.

The Giants' mess wasn't confined to just football. Teammates had shoving matches on the sidelines of a game. During another game, Schottenheimer received word that his car was being towed. He thought it was a joke. It wasn't. He parked in a spot that wasn't assigned to him, and management had it towed.

"You walk in the locker room, guys are sitting there smoking. Their facilities were absolutely hideous. Horrendous. Horrendous," Martin said.

Martin shared a locker with another player during a period when players had one practice uniform and it wasn't laundered during the day. During two-a-day practices in training camp, he would come off the field and hang his sweat-laden gear. "You see how putrid that is and you come back in the afternoon and you have to put the same stuff on."

Martin came to the Giants already married and with a daughter. He made $500 a week in training camp and almost immediately became disillusioned. Part of it was the lack of talent, the uncoordinated teammate with the man boobs. Another player, Martin said, couldn't walk and chew gum at the same time.

"This can't be pro ball," he said.

A couple of years in, the environment hadn't changed.

To save money, players shared hotel rooms on the road. On one road trip, Martin went out for dinner on his own. Walking back, he thought about how lucky he was to be in the NFL. The team was losing, but he was providing for his family. He came back to the room a little earlier than his roommate expected. He opened the door and saw his roommate and a group of teammates huddled around a pile of cocaine on a glass table.

"The moment I see it, I froze."

Martin knows he's a square, a family man, a Christian, a country boy. He's pretty much everything that would have nothing to do with a pile of blow in a hotel room the night before a game.

"They start laughing and poking fun. Somebody says, 'Dude, haven't you ever seen $5,000 worth of s-h-i-t before?' I'm sweating. I do a reversal. I walk out of the room."

Martin returned to the room shortly before curfew. His roommate, the others, and the cocaine were gone.

The next day, he went to a coach and said he would never have another roommate again. The coach never gave him any pushback.

"He knew exactly what I was talking about," Martin said. "That's the kind of things that were going on in those early years. That wasn't an exception. That was kind of like the rule. For those guys on that fringe, doing that, it was commonplace."

Toward the end of the 1977 season, Brad Benson arrived at the Meadowlands.

One of the first guys he met was "the Commissioner," a man whose dour voice fit seamlessly with the steely, smelly strip of New Jersey Turnpike landscape in Elizabeth, near Newark International Airport.

The Commissioner—or Commish, as he was also called—picked up new players at the airport, drove cut players to the airport, and shuttled players in and out of Manhattan to the team doctor. According to the team's media guide, his real name was Julius "Whitey" Horai, and his title was administrative assistant.

"Get in the car. We're taking you for a physical," the Commish gargled at Benson at the team facility.

"So what are you doing here?" the Commish asked as the drive in the Pontiac station wagon began.

"I'm trying out for the team," said Benson, who had driven from his home in Western Pennsylvania.

"Oh, yeah," said the Commish. "Good luck with that.

"Yeah, it's a waste of time, driving guys over. They never make it. Waste of time," he continued, needing little interaction to keep the conversation going.

"Where are you from?"

"Altoona, Pennsylvania."

"Never heard of it. What are you, a hillbilly?"

The talking stopped. Maybe the Commish had talked himself out, or maybe he'd found something else to be annoyed at. When the Giants reached out to Benson, he had been teaching sixth-grade math in Altoona. Now, he sat quietly with one thought: *What the fuck did I just get into here?*

Benson had been a stowaway with the Patriots. New England selected the six-foot-three, 260-pound Penn State product in the eighth round of the 1977 draft. He was never officially on the roster, but he was on the team.

Benson and another rookie dressed and showered in a separate area. New England paid them by having the pair take out personal loans from a local bank. The Patriots cosigned the loans with the agreement that the players would never have to pay them back. The Patriots repaid the loans, and therefore no trace of these salaries showed up on the team's books. The other rookie got called up to the big boy roster. He signed a new deal and had to pay back the loan. At this point, Benson headed home to Pennsylvania.

For Benson, sports and football were serious things where he grew up. He was a state champion wrestler in high school. His football team traveled two hundred miles by train to play in Masilon, Ohio. They played in front of crowds of thirty thousand fans. This was Western Pennsylvania football. Its 1970s fraternity brothers included Joe Montana, Tony Dorsett, and Dan Marino. When Benson left Altoona, he played under the rigor of Joe Paterno at Penn State.

He joined the Giants in the organization's second season at the Meadowlands, the paved-over Jersey swampland just outside New York City. Like George Martin's experience, what greeted Benson was nothing he could have imagined was professional football.

"It was culture shock," Benson said. "It was just pure mayhem. Pure mayhem in the locker room, on the field."

Players meandered from drill to drill in practice. God forbid somebody played hard. That guy was immediately ostracized.

After morning meetings, some guys preferred liquid lunch. They skipped out of the facility and headed to spots on Route 17 to grab some beers and cocktails.

Back at Giants Stadium, those who stuck around grabbed food that was set up on tables in the weight room next to the two adjacent racquetball courts, further deemphasizing strength training.

"It was like a health club," Benson said. "It wasn't really an NFL team, and it wasn't going to be either."

4

FUMBLE FALLOUT AND THE FAMILY FEUD

On the morning of The Fumble, that sacrosanct levee dividing the public and the locker room became breached. An article in *The New York Times* quoted unnamed players railing against assistant coaches.

"The first thing I tell any rookie is not to listen to the coaches," said one veteran.

The players had no faith in offensive coordinator Bob Gibson.

In the face of the criticism and an apparently divided squad, head coach John McVay talked about his 5–6 team making a five-game run and finishing at 10–6. Then The Fumble happened that afternoon, and any thought of keeping the season or team together disappeared.

"That's the most horrifying ending to a ball game I've ever seen," McVay said after the loss.[1]

He could've stopped it. McVay could've overruled Gibson's play call. On the sideline, he picked up a headset to listen in, but it wasn't working.

Wellington Mara, the team president, and Andy Robustelli, the director of operations, moved swiftly through the postgame locker room to get to Gibson. They met with him away from the players. After the conversation, Gibson walked out of the meeting and the Giants' locker room. The fifty-one-year-old never called another play in his life. He had been fired on the spot. He receded from the sports world, living on Sanibel Island on Florida's west coast. He opened up a bait shop, a liquor store, and a restaurant.[2] He never spoke publicly about why he called Pro 65 Up.

Fearing reactions from upset fans, Pisarcik, with dried blood under his middle fingernail from where he bobbled the snap, used a police escort to go from the locker room to his car in the parking lot. The quarterback was granted time away from the team. He headed to his home in Fort Lauderdale, Florida.

Lying on the beach, catching some rays, maybe he could leave the mess behind. Some guy stood over him, interrupting his tranquility.

"Aren't you Joe Pisarcik?"

The mustachioed signal caller with a '70s bowl cut nodded.

"What happened on that play? Why didn't you just fall on the ball?"[3]

He rejoined the Giants later that week. The team's unraveling had gained momentum. Instead of using the collective pronoun *we*, McVay now referred to the team's future with the distant *you*. He knew the end of the season would be the end of his time with the Giants.

Third-year linebacker Harry Carson had one thought after The Fumble: *Get me outta here.*

He wore a California Angels baseball cap to give management a hint as to where he wanted to be traded. He started taking different routes to drive to work just to experience a change of scenery.

Other players grew more vociferous. "Sooner or later, everyone who passes through here gets screwed up," said starting defensive tackle John Mendenhall.[4]

The Giants' loyal fans, who amazingly had the team leading the NFL in attendance, used The Fumble as a rallying point.

Ron Freiman, a season ticket holder for twenty-three years and the owner of a printing business, placed a classified ad in *The Star-Ledger*. He asked fellow Giants fans to send him their tickets for an organized burning in the stadium parking lot.

Before the Giants lost to the Rams in early December, Freiman burned more than one hundred tickets in a urinal marked with the name Wellington Mara. He then mailed the ashes to Mara.

"He was well aware that we needed to make some changes by that point in time. But he was a human being, too. To see yourself hung in effigy, with your family in the stands watching, that was not a very happy period of time for us. He suffered through that. He took the losses harder than any-body. Felt it was on his shoulders to try to do something about it. This was his life. This really affected him very deeply," John Mara said of his father, Wellington.

The night of The Fumble, Michael Spielberg called his father, Morris, a Newark furniture store owner. Michael told his father the blunder was a sign from God to do something.

The older Spielberg responded by organizing the Committee Against Mara Insensitivity to Giants Fans. The group of lawyers, doctors, construc-tion workers—all season ticket holders—had its sights on getting a court injunction to halt the sale of season tickets and instead release them on a game-by-game basis.

"We, the fans, are getting together to force the Maras into either get-ting a football man to run the organization or to sell the team," Spielberg said.[5]

Arthur Milne, a dentist from Basking Ridge, had the idea for the plane. He was so fed up he was going to do it by himself, but the Committee Against Mara Insensitivity to Giants Fans subsidized the cost.

A week after the ticket burning, the group met for a three-dollar con-tinental breakfast at the Ramada Inn on Route 3 in Clifton, a few miles west of the Meadowlands. There they unveiled the plan: during the game, a plane would leave nearby Teterboro Airport and fly over the stadium dragging a banner that read "15 Years of Lousy Football—We've Had Enough." Spielberg and Co. instructed the breakfast crew to distribute fly-ers in the parking lot, directing fans to chant "We've had enough!" when the plane made its appearance.

The temperature fell below freezing, and wind whipped through the stadium that was one-third empty, the largest no-show crowd of the sea-son. The Giants had a 10–0 lead on the Cardinals when the plane appeared in the third quarter. On cue, the chant began: "We've had enough! We've had enough! We've had enough!" The Giants won the game 17–0, but it didn't matter.

A week later, they lost at Philadelphia to close out a 6–10 season. Within a couple of days, McVay officially got the ax. Among a plethora of names thrown out as his replacement, three stood out. Penn State's Joe Paterno came in at the top of the rumor list. He was busy getting ready to play Alabama and Paul "Bear" Bryant for the national title. Stanford head coach Bill Walsh, a former Bengals offensive coordinator, had a relationship with the Giants. While at Stanford, Walsh traveled cross-country to conduct clinics for the Giants' coaching staff. The Dallas Cowboys had the hottest name among NFL assistant coaches, Dan Reeves. The thirty-four-year-old offensive coordinator had traces of Giants lineage since he worked and played under Tom Landry.

Although Paterno spoke to Wellington Mara about the position, he publicly, emphatically, and repeatedly declared he had no interest in coaching the team. In early January, the Giants could also cross Walsh's name off the list. He took over as the head coach of the San Francisco 49ers. McVay, the fired Giants coach, found a job with Walsh. He joined San Francisco's front office and left the team years later with a fistful of Super Bowl rings.

Days and weeks dragged on, and the Giants had no coach. The search looked like a bumbling mess.

Wellington Mara interviewed Reeves privately. When Wellington's nephew Tim Mara heard about it, Tim called Reeves. The confused young assistant coach had been asked by Wellington to keep the meeting confidential. Reeves told Tim he had been looking at oil wells in Texas. Eventually, Tom Landry had to step in to protect his assistant coach and get him out from in between the Giants' co-owners.

Small flecks of the feud between the Maras had begun to show, but the uncle and nephew had been battling for years.

Andy Robustelli, the director of operations, who really acted as a general manager, had given his resignation before the '78 season, but he promised to stay until his replacement was hired. That search went nowhere, too.

Robustelli was in the middle of the family tension. Like many in the organization, Robustelli was a former Giant. He came back to the team after initial overtures from Tim Mara's side. Early in his front office tenure, the Hall of Fame defensive end began to despise the younger co-owner because he realized Tim Mara wanted to use Robustelli to minimize Wellington.

"I discovered after a while he would do almost anything to get Well out of a decision-making position," Robustelli said.[6]

Tim Mara ran the business side. Wellington Mara ran everything else. Wellington was well intentioned, but the place was loaded with old Giants and lacked the innovative operations that had come into the NFL. Decisions had been made based on loyalty, not on football.

"The club was literally run by one man for a decade," Robustelli said in reference to Wellington.[7]

John Mara remembered the familial dispute started percolating when lucrative contracts were given to Larry Csonka and Brad Van Pelt. Tim didn't like the money being spent on these two, and Wellington went through with the deals. As the losses mounted, the relationship worsened.

"It became a complete disaster, which is a shame. It never should've happened," John Mara said. "If I have one regret in my professional life, it's that I wasn't mature enough at the time to have acted as a mediator to try to keep them both together and try to keep that from getting public. I was in law school at the time and was pretty hotheaded and took my father's side with everything, and there were some things I could've done differently to have prevented all that."

In early 1979, the initial public argument was minimized to an impasse over hiring a coach and general manager, as well as which position to fill first. The fight was really about power and control of the team. A decade earlier, the NFL made a rule requiring a majority owner, but the Giants' fifty-fifty split was grandfathered in, and it left the Maras in a stalemate. Ultimately, the principal had to be called in to help select a general manager.

NFL commissioner Pete Rozelle intervened. He asked each Mara to submit four names to fill the general manager position. That process furthered the spat. Tim wrote his names in alphabetical order. Wellington listed his in order of the most to least desirable candidate. Only one name appeared on both lists: Jan Van Duser, personnel director for the NFL. He turned down the gig, twice.

This taking place in New Jersey meant that in the midst of this clash, some politician had to step in with a vociferous but altogether toothless plan. Governor Brendan Byrne told a North Jersey luncheon crowd he had contacted the New Jersey Sports and Exposition Authority to see if the agency could step in to resolve the dispute. "I have not excluded the possibility of a public or private buyout of the Giants to solve their ridiculous disputes," Byrne said.[8]

While the family infighting had been trickling out since the end of the '78 season, it finally erupted in the basement of Giants Stadium. In early February, after the initial mediation with Rozelle failed, Wellington called an impromptu and awkward press conference. In a room used by reporters during the week and players' wives on game day, the Maras took turns. Wellington, reading from a statement, said the only serious disagreement was on hiring a director of operations. Wellington planned to move ahead with hiring the coach and "as president I have the final decision-making responsibility."

When the Giants came into existence, Wellington was a nine-year-old ball boy. Named after the Duke of Wellington, the players nicknamed him "The Duke." In 1941, Wilson Sporting Goods Co. named the official NFL football "The Duke" after him. The move came at the suggestion of Chicago Bears owner and coach George Halas. It was a nod to Wellington's father, who helped orchestrate the deal for Wilson to be the league's official football supplier.

Now, the sixty-two-year-old father of eleven who had lived through every moment of the Giants' existence left the room.

Tim Mara, the forty-three-year-old jet-setter in his second marriage, took the stage.

"I just want to have a winner. Well wants a winner his way. But Well's way has had us in the cellar the last six years."[9]

Tim said if Wellington acted, he would bring legal action to stop it.

Wellington reentered the room after being asked to return.

He wondered if it was time for rebuttal. He offered the obvious and unreachable solution: "I just wish my father, God rest him, had given 51 percent to either Jack or myself."[10]

Chris Mara, Wellington's third-oldest child and the team's senior vice president of player evaluation, was in school at Boston College at the time. He didn't realize the family's internal fight had gone public until it interrupted one of his daily routines. Each morning, he started his day by grabbing the New York City newspapers. "Sure enough, one morning I went down there, and there was the front page of the *Daily News* and *New York Post,* and it's splattered all over," he said. "I knew there were things happening, but it kind of took me by surprise a little bit."

5

THE COMPROMISE CHOICE

The Miami Dolphins personnel director picked up his office phone and heard some oddball crooning.

"East Side, West Side, all around the town," said Bob Patzwall, singing the lyrics of "The Sidewalks of New York."

"What the hell are you talking about?" George Young snapped at his broker.

"I'm just getting you ready to go to New York," said Patzwall, who had also played high school football for, and coached under, Young.

"For God's sake, stop that. I've got a job."

In Baltimore, where Patzwall was calling from, word was that Young was headed to the Giants as the new general manager. Baltimore knew George Young, and Young would always know Baltimore. His roots were in the city. Though he moved to a couple of other places, he always returned to visit friends and host parties.

George Bernard Young Jr. grew up in Baltimore's Tenth Ward, a tough Irish enclave in an era when Catholic parishes dictated boundary lines between neighborhoods. Born in 1930, Young lived at the corner of Ensor and Preston Streets, above the bakery owned by his mother's family and across the street from the Stag Bar operated by his father.

Like most pub owners at the time, George's father took betting action at the bar. When George Sr. knew the police were headed to the Stag, he'd hide the wagering slips under George Jr.'s bedcovers. George Young Sr. was also known to have bet the family's insurance policy on a horse. It didn't work out. Nor did the marriage between George's parents. They divorced.

George's mother, Frances, remained a strong influence throughout his life, as did the Catholic education he received. After being educated by Marianists, and playing the fife in the fife and bugle corps at St. James grammar school, George went to Calvert Hall for high school. There, at the school run by Christian Brothers, George was an honor student, baseball pitcher, basketball team manager, and a football player.

George graduated from Calvert and went to Bucknell in Lewisburg, Pennsylvania. Dispatched about 140 miles away from home, he didn't like it. He wanted to go back to Baltimore. He called his mother. She refused to let George act on his homesickness. She told him to stay put. He did, and that's about the time the single-mindedness developed. He studied in school, but studying was something he always did, something he was always going to do. He even incorporated studying into this great focus—football.

Young trained with unusual intensity for the time. He lifted weights. Now an obvious practice, but this was the late 1940s. He became so strong he could bend a horseshoe five inches. He worked out so often, his roommates forced him to put his smelly, sweat-drenched clothes in the hallway.

He ran to build up his endurance. Back in Baltimore, on college breaks, he ran around Lake Clifton Reservoir in a rubber suit. The running kept Young in shape, and this was a must in order to offset other habits. The beefy six-foot-three, 270-pounder could easily finish a bag of Oreos and a six-pack of Pepsi-Cola in one sitting.

In 1951, Young served as cocaptain of an undefeated Bucknell team. The defensive tackle made the Little All-America team, and the Dallas Texans picked him in the twenty-sixth round of the 1952 NFL draft.

Young didn't make the squad. He was a last-round pick with terrible eyesight. Young refused to wear glasses while playing. The story goes that at one point he pounced on what he thought was a fumble only to come off the turf with another player's helmet in his grasp. In his brief time with the Texans, he did make a lifelong friend in fellow defensive tackle Art Donovan. Midway through the 1952 season, the Texans' ownership turned the team over to the NFL. They became the Colts and started playing in Baltimore the following season.

Young and Donovan continued their friendship in Charm City, Donovan embarking on a Hall of Fame career and Young coaching football and teaching history at the high school level. The duo socialized together. Some of Young's players spotted him and Donovan stage side at the end of high school dances because the grown-ups were dating two girls in the band the Queens of Rhythm.

Young was not a partier, nor was he a ladies' man. He never drank or smoked. He had seen enough of that from his view on Ensor and Preston Streets. "I grew up around drunk Irishmen all my life," he said.

He attended every coaching clinic he could throughout the Northeast. A lot of times these clinics were football in the daytime and carousing conventions at night. Ahead of the big convention in Atlantic City, head coaches warned their assistants about staying away from the whores who came in droves from the coal region knowing the testosterone-filled clientele had to be good for business.

In the evening, Young's hotel room hosted a different type of get-together. After attending seminars and lectures all day, Young broke out the 16mm projector with the Bausch & Lomb Cinemascope lens. Somebody else brought the screen. It was film-watching time. Guys might drink a few beers and smoke some cigarettes, but the main attraction was reel after reel of grainy football films. Coaches sat around, studied schemes, exchanged ideas, and showcased their stars, looking to find them a place to play in college.

Young brought all this knowledge back to the Calvert Hall Cardinals and the City College Black Knights. He coached at his alma mater, Calvert Hall, for five years. He posted a 16–22–5 record, grabbing the 1957 Maryland Scholastic Association championship, Calvert Hall's first in twenty-two years. In 1959, he became the head coach at City College, which, contrary to its name, was an all-boys public high school. In nine years with the Black Knights, Young guided a powerhouse, going 60–11–2 and notching five MSA championships.

Young had a thorough, meticulous nature, and it came through in his coaching. In June of 1954, Young sent letters to the students playing for Calvert Hall. The typed, single-spaced, 855-word message opened with a manifesto on why the team would implement the "Sliding T" and not the "Split T" offense. Each letter ended with the sign-off "Cardinally yours." The postscript, in Young's near-flawless Palmer method penmanship, added a personal note about specific training for each player.

When players first met Young, they were intimidated. He was a towering, round figure, a quiet man in gray sweats, behind the thick black half-frame spectacles. Soon enough, his reputation for rigorous practices preceded the actual introduction, making him even more fearsome.

"If you don't want to sacrifice each and every day between now and Thanksgiving, leave the room," Young would tell his troops. "Neither rain, nor sleet, nor dark of night will keep us from practicing every day."[1]

At City College, Young mandated that his players wear jackets, ties, and shined shoes on game days. "That was not merely symbolic. It had occurred to me that never once had I seen a boy, standing in line to see the vice-principal to be disciplined, who was wearing a coat and tie."[2]

Young prepped his team with plays he drew up on his overhead projector, the same one he used to teach history. He had every minute of practice mapped out on one side of a three-by-five index card. He ran drills over and over again. Players repeated assignments so often, fifty years later some of them can still rattle off their roles on specific plays. When a player went offside or drifted mentally, that player headed to the kissing tree. Young sent them on a run to a distant tree where they had to pucker up to the bark and then run back. Young never had a playbook. His teams used five or ten plays to the left and then reversed them for five or ten plays to the right.

"Straight up and very simple," said Ed Novak, who was an assistant to Young at City College. "There weren't any big things. You just did the small things well, and things worked out."

While the playbook was nonexistent, Young compiled reams and reams of notes on strategy and scouting. He traveled to watch future opponents, and he pored over game film searching for flaws and tells.

"He would tell us, 'If the right guard has his right arm down, it's a run. If he has his left hand down, it's a pass.' Little things like that," said George Petrides, who played on two of Young's championship teams at City College. "'If the receiver has his left foot back, it's going to be this route. If he has his right foot back, it's going to be this route.' All those little tiny things, he had details for everything . . . He was as thorough as you can be."

This approach extended to academics as well. Young would get ahold of his players' report cards before their families. He squeezed into a desk he placed at center court in City College's basketball gym. One by one, he met with each of his players and went over their grades.

He made sure his kids who had the grades for college went there. He did that for Bob Patzwall, who ended up being his broker. No one in Patzwall's family had ever been to college. When Young asked him what he planned to do after graduating from Calvert Hall, Patzwall told the coach he was headed to the beach town of Ocean City for a week and then he'd start working at the American Can Company. Patzwall's grandfather, father, uncle, and cousin had all worked for the can shop. "It supported my family, and I was next," he said.

"You're good enough to play somewhere. You ought to go somewhere," Young told him.

"I can't afford it," Patzwall said.

"Well, how about we try to take care of that."

Patzwall sat in the passenger seat of Young's brown Chevy Impala as the coach drove his player to Williams College, Gettysburg College, and nearby Johns Hopkins. None of the schools seemed to be a fit. One final road trip worked. The pair ended the visits at Young's alma mater.

"He literally delivered me to Bucknell, personally," Patzwall said.

After an undefeated championship year in his junior season at City College, quarterback Kurt Schmoke had the attention of recruiters from Big Ten schools.

Young heard about this. The coach didn't buy into it. Staring at Schmoke with his hand on his chin, Young addressed his quarterback.

"Let me tell you something."

"What's that, Coach?"

"You're not that good."

It could have crushed a kid's confidence. It didn't. Young's players knew if he was anything, he was honest and direct.

"Look, for a lot of the guys out here, playing football is going to be part of their life going forward, but for you, every year after you leave high school, football is going to become less and less important. So let me give you another set of schools you ought to apply to."

Young was right. Schmoke went to Yale. He played football for a few years in New Haven. He was the defensive back who got beat in the famed 29–29 tie with Harvard. But of greater note, in 1987, Young's former state championship quarterback became the first African American mayor of Baltimore.

Somewhere between scouting teams, teaching history, coaching football, and carting players to college visits, Young found the time to marry a teacher, the former Kathryn Mary Love "Lovey" Reddington. The only reason his assistant coaches knew of the nuptials is because they asked why Young had washed his car.

Going to school at night, Young earned a master's degree in educational administration from Loyola College. He continued taking graduate-level courses at Johns Hopkins, studying Russian, Latin American, and Chinese histories while securing a certificate of advanced studies in education.

With all this going on, Young crammed in some time to help the ball club that played across the street from City College at Memorial Stadium, the Baltimore Colts.

Colts head coach Don Shula and his assistants had to staff the Pro Bowl in Los Angeles in 1968. At the same time, Shula needed someone to evaluate college players for the upcoming draft. He asked Young if he had time to do it. Young obliged. Shula gave him the keys to his office so the high school coach could access film on the players. Young made it through every one of them. He prepped notes, and when the Colts' coaches returned, Young was ready with his overhead projector.

"He got up in front of our staff, and he gave the best report on why we should either accept or reject a player. It was just outstanding, the way it was organized, and the study he had put into it. So, I said, 'I've got to have that guy working for me,'" Shula said.

That's how Young made the jump from high school to the NFL. It wasn't easy. Initially, he didn't cut ties with teaching; he took a sabbatical. "My nature is student or teacher," he said. "When I was a high school teacher, and a student myself at night, that was when I had the best of both worlds."[3]

He started with the Colts in '68 as a personnel assistant. That's when he started saying *fuck*. Never a screamer, and merely a casual profanity user, it was when he made the leap to the NFL that Young began using the F-word.

Young moved in and out of different positions with the Colts. He was the offensive line coach for the Super Bowl V champs. Even though the Colts beat the Cowboys in that game, Young and Ernie Accorsi, the public relations director at the time, both noticed something different about the Dallas players. They were big, strong, and athletic. The Cowboys had developed a system of drafting talent, and Young and Accorsi had witnessed it working. Standing on the field during warm-ups, Young and Accorsi knew what they saw in the Dallas players was the future of the NFL.

Young moved to scouting for the Colts. He tracked college players and opponents. He became the director of personnel.

Young was working on scouting reports at nine o'clock one night in 1972 when a fire broke out in the team offices. Everyone ran out of the building. As they gathered out on Howard Street, nobody could find Young. Accorsi went back for him. He found Young taking his time walking toward an exit, both arms full of notebooks.

"Fuck the fire. I was thinking about my notes. I worked very hard on them and didn't want to lose them," Young said.[4]

He became the Colts' offensive coordinator in 1973 under Howard Schnellenberger. After a dismal '74 season, the Colts cleaned house. Young was out of a job. He had to leave Baltimore. Shula, who at this point was the head coach of the Dolphins, hired him in Miami. Young became his right hand.

In Miami, Young continued to scout opponents and evaluate college and pro players. Now, he added handling contracts to his responsibilities.

"He made sure he covered all the bases. He was never in a race against time. He made sure he took the time necessary to do the best job he could do," Shula said. "He worked hard, and he had his own convictions after a lot of study and a lot of research. Then he would stand by his convictions. He wouldn't cave to somebody else if he felt a certain way about a player."

Before Young's arrival, Shula coached Miami to the only perfect season in the Super Bowl era, making the Dolphins a revered organization; however, the facilities did not match the mystique.

"Our lockers were two-by-fours with wire in between, and then a nail was pounded into the two-by-four to hang your equipment on, and that was it," Shula said.

The weight room was a little building next to the main offices. It had one Universal Gym, forcing offensive linemen Jim Langer, Bob Kuchenberg, and others to stand around and take turns to get a lift in.

An old, mostly converted maintenance barn housed the main offices. A tractor and wheelbarrow often sat near the entrance. When it rained, buckets caught the drips of water that fell through the roof. The offices flanked one long hallway. Shula had the biggest one, but it couldn't accommodate his entire staff. During game-planning sessions, the offensive and defensive staffs took turns swapping spots in the hallway for places to stand in the office.

Young's office was about one-third the size of Shula's. It was stuffy and hot, and this was the place where Young settled contracts with the players. Young sat unfazed as sweat dripped down his face. It was a test of will in the negotiation. On one occasion, cornerback Tim Foley went straight to

Shula after meeting with Young. "He said, 'Give me the contract. I'll sign anything. I don't want to sit in that office any longer,'" Shula recalled.

Young was in that office when Patzwall called, teasing Young about heading to New York. Young had already turned down a job offer to work with Bill Walsh in the 49ers' front office.

Young's name did not appear on either of the lists the Maras had submitted to Pete Rozelle. After things came undone at the family feud press conference, Wellington put forth Young to Rozelle. Wellington feared if Tim Mara thought Young was Wellington's pick, the hire wouldn't happen. Publicly, the suggestion had to come from Rozelle, and it did.

At 11:00 A.M. on February 13, Wellington called the Dolphins, looking for owner Joe Robbie. He wasn't available. Shula took the call. The coach gave the go-ahead for Young to interview. The next day, Valentine's Day, Young flew to New York. Both Maras interviewed him in Rozelle's Manhattan office. Later that night at Gallaghers Steakhouse in New York City, dubbed as the compromise choice, George Young was introduced at a press conference as the general manager. A man who was just about ten years removed from being a high school football coach and teacher was now charged with righting the direction of the New York Giants.

"He, almost single-handedly, made us a much more professional organization that could compete with other teams in the league," John Mara said.

Young's arrival signaled the end to the pure mayhem that had splintered the franchise. It wouldn't be gone immediately, but Young announced his authority quite quickly.

"I don't care who gets credit for anything, as long as we're going in the same direction. That's more important than any ego trips," he said the night he took the job.[5]

The next day, he flew back to Miami, grabbed his toothbrush and some fresh shirts, and headed on a five-day, nine thousand–mile trip to interview head coaching candidates. He interviewed four men, all NFL offensive coordinators. Three of them—Dan Reeves of the Cowboys, John Idzik of the Jets, and Jerry Rhome of the Seahawks—had been candidates before Young's arrival. The fourth candidate was Ray Perkins, the San Diego Chargers' offensive coordinator. Perkins hadn't been a Mara candidate, but Young had his eye on him from their days together with the Colts.

Young, who was coaching the offensive line at the time in Baltimore, never forgot Perkins coming up to him, asking him how his unit planned to handle the blitz packages one week. It just wasn't something a receiver asks the offensive line coach.[6]

Perkins had an impressive pedigree. In college, he won two national titles and garnered all-American honors playing wide receiver at Alabama under coach Paul "Bear" Bryant. With the Crimson Tide, he caught passes from Joe Namath and Ken Stabler. In the NFL, he had Johnny Unitas as his quarterback. After his playing days ended, Perkins was an assistant at Mississippi State. He broke into the NFL as a wide receivers coach with the New England Patriots before taking the job in San Diego for one season.

After the '78 season, Perkins interviewed with Al Davis for the Oakland Raiders' job left vacant by the retirement of John Madden. During the interview, Perkins realized he wasn't getting the job, and if he did, he'd turn it down. He knew his personality wouldn't gel with Davis's style.

After that interview, Young called him. The new Giants GM wondered if Perkins would fly to New Jersey to interview for the head coaching job.

"I sure would. I'd give anything to be in an organization with you," Perkins told Young.

That night, Perkins went to a mall in San Diego. He bought a briefcase to get ready for his trip. He flew out the next day. Using a false name, he checked into the same hotel as Young, the Sheraton in Hasbrouck Heights.[7] The interview lasted a couple of hours. Then came the press conference. Nine days after Young became the general manager, he selected Perkins as the next head coach of the New York Giants.

"George believed in him. I remember George's quote: 'He will make it uncomfortable for them to lose,'" John Mara said.

Perkins hadn't been on the radar of either Mara, but he was needed for the culture change that was about to take place.

"He had a strange personality," John Mara said. "He was just different. But he was the right guy for us at the time, extremely disciplined."

Bear Bryant had been asked to evaluate Perkins as a player. The coach smiled. "He wasn't big, 170 or so," Bryant said. "But he wasn't bashful about hitting somebody. He didn't come from Peaceful Valley."[8]

After picking a head coach, Young settled in at the Giants' facilities. He placed his office in between the hallways separating the Maras. It was symbolic and pragmatic: all Giants football now went through Young.

Perkins began hiring his staff. The first call he made was to twenty-six-year-old Ernie Adams, the quality control coach he had worked with in New England. When Perkins left the Patriots for the Chargers, he told Adams, "I'm going to be a head coach one day, and you are going to be the first guy I hire."

Even though he had never played the position, Adams became Perkins's quarterbacks coach.

About a month later, Perkins had to travel back to San Diego to take care of selling his house and other personal business that goes with moving from one coast to another. Before he left New Jersey, Adams made sure to have a conversation with Perkins.

"There's one guy that I can think of that you need to talk to," Adams told Perkins.

"Well, who is it?"

"A guy named Bill Belichick."

"Where is he?"

"He was at Baltimore for a year doing quality control. Then he left there after the first year and went to Detroit, and he was there for two years. He went from there to Denver. He's in Denver right now."

Adams had known Belichick since high school. They were football teammates at Phillips Academy in Andover, Massachusetts, an elite New England boarding school.

Perkins told Adams to get Belichick a flight from Denver to San Diego. He'd interview him there.

Perkins and Belichick met for nearly four hours in a San Diego airport hotel room.

"He didn't view the kicking game as a token phase of the game. He wanted to make plays to win games in the kicking game, and that was absolutely my goal," Belichick said.

Perkins said he would be so involved in the offense, he would serve as a support to the young coach, but the head coach wouldn't be devoting time to the special teams game plan. That would be on Belichick.

Perkins was impressed with how the twenty-six-year-old responded. "He was not going to back down from anything. If he didn't know it, he was going to find out about it. And he's going to teach it, and he's going to coach it."

Before leaving the hotel room, Perkins hired Belichick.

As he continued to fill out his staff, Perkins looked for a college linebackers coach. Rather than go with an experienced NFL coach, Perkins wanted to break in a college coach. He called Steve Sloan, another one of Perkins's quarterbacks at Alabama.

"Parcells. Bill Parcells," Sloan said without hesitation.

Parcells had coached college linebackers for more than a decade. He worked for Sloan at Vanderbilt and Texas Tech.

At this point, Parcells had just finished 3–8 in his first year as the head coach at Air Force. He wanted out of Colorado Springs, but he couldn't find a job worth taking. He had returned from a recruiting trip in California when Perkins called him.

They hardly knew each other. They had met once at Texas Tech. Perkins was there scouting a college all-star game, looking at Oregon—and future Patriots—tight end Russ Francis.

When Perkins called Sloan, he said he knew Parcells was who he was looking for. He just wanted the confirmation.

Parcells was relieved to get the call. He had no problem returning to New Jersey, his home state, for an interview.

"I would have walked," Parcells said.[9]

As more assistants were added, the next order of business was the draft. The Giants had the seventh pick in the first round. They needed a quarterback—badly—and Young and Perkins had to make the pick.

PART

LT, Simms, Parcells

TWO

6

FINDING WHITEY

Phil Simms kept a board next to his telephone in his Morehead State dorm room.

The phone rang. It was a quick conversation, a scheduling call. He'd hang up, and on the board, he'd jot down the date, time, and team coming to watch him throw a football. More than twenty NFL teams called to send representatives to Morehead, Kentucky, to evaluate "Whitey" Simms, the blond, six-foot-three, 216-pound quarterback.

Simms scrawled the NFL home cities in a list.

Kansas City
Green Bay
San Francisco
Pittsburgh

"I had visitors every day," he said.

In January 1979, the Steelers had won the Super Bowl, the team's third in a five-year span. Their quarterback, Terry Bradshaw, had been named the game's MVP and the NFL MVP that year. Chuck Noll still made a trip to see Simms in the lead-up to that spring's NFL draft.

"Didn't say a word," Simms said. "He brought down his coaching staff, and I threw for him, and I threw the ball great when they came."

Morehead State, an Ohio Valley Conference school with an enrollment of 7,200 students, wasn't a football power. The Eagles weren't even a winner. In the history of the NFL draft, only six players from Morehead State had ever been taken. None had been selected higher than pick number 147.

Of the half dozen players who had been picked, just one ended up playing in the league; defensive tackle Dave Haverdick played eight games for the Detroit Lions in 1970. Giants tight end Gary Shirk was the lone active NFL player from Morehead State, a free agent, who first played pro ball in the short-lived World Football League.

With Simms under center, Morehead State never won more than three games in a season. He wasn't a national name. The school, obviously, was an unknown, and yet Simms knew the attention from the pro level was coming.

The quarterback ended up on the NFL radar because of a conversation that happened seventy miles away at the University of Kentucky. A pro scout was visiting the Southeastern Conference school. Though the Wildcats posted a 4–6–1 record that year, seven of their players would be taken in the 1979 draft.

The scout who eyed talent at Kentucky had Morehead State on his list of schools to check out. He asked a Kentucky assistant coach if it was worth his time to make the trip to the small college.

Kentucky's defensive line coach Bill Glaser told the scout to go. He said the quarterback at Morehead would catch his eye.

Glaser knew Simms from high school. Glaser coached at St. Xavier in Louisville, the same city where Simms attended Southern High School. Glaser had also seen Simms up close in college. In 1976, before moving on to Kentucky, Glaser spent a year as the defensive coordinator at Morehead State.

The scout made the trip from Lexington to Morehead. He watched film of Simms. He watched him throw live on the school's football field. During the passing session, the scout asked Simms to throw one as far as he could. He launched a 72-yard pass. The scout had seen enough.

Before he left Morehead State, the scout told head coach Wayne Chapman the campus would be flooded with NFL personnel as the draft approached.

"When I put out the word about your guy, you're going to have people here every day. So, I want you to get the coffee ready. Be alert. You know this is coming."

Phillip Martin Simms was born to William "Willie" Simms and the former Barbara Ann McConnell. For the first few years of his life, Simms lived with his family on his paternal grandfather's farm in Springfield, Kentucky. His grandfather owned the land, but Simms's family farmed it. A smattering of cattle, hogs, chicken, and sheep lived on the hundreds of acres, but tobacco plants were the most prominent crop.

There were also eight Simms children. Phil was the fifth oldest in a split of five boys and three girls.

Willie Simms had played baseball, dabbling in the Southern League, playing for teams in South Carolina and Georgia. Willie taught the children how to throw, starting with Dominic, the oldest. Soon the older children supplemented Willie's initial tutorials, teaching their younger siblings the basics, too.

Baseball was Phil's first love, and it was a family thing. His parents' honeymoon was spent at a Cincinnati Reds' home stand.

Saturday night was baseball night on the farm. For hours the family would play in a hayfield. "That's why baseball was such a big deal," Phil said. "They were farmers, and baseball was where it's at."

They'd play football, too. The children battled it out in the mud with games ending, or pausing, for bloody noses or cries of "Mommy, he hit me."

Phil started playing in these games at about three years old. Even then, Dominic Simms remembers his younger brother showing a competitive side. "He always had that bulldog mentality. I can't run as fast as you, but I'm going to hurt you or do something to make the game even. That's the way you have to play."

Phil Simms's grandfather saw the little boy's big hands and gave the future quarterback his first nickname—Yogi, after Yogi Berra, the New York Yankees' catcher.

"His hand's bigger than a catcher's mitt," Dominic recalled his grandfather saying.

When Phil was about five years old, the family moved off the farm and to the city of Louisville.

Willie and Barbara took factory jobs. Willie started in a cabinet factory. They both worked for General Electric before settling in for a long period of employment at Brown & Williamson Tobacco, makers of Kool and Pall Mall cigarettes. When Brown & Williamson moved to Georgia, Willie worked as a janitor at St. Rita's, the Catholic grammar school. Barbara did odds and ends to make money.

In Louisville, the Simmses rented a small three-bedroom house before buying a three-bedroom Cape Cod for the family of ten. Pretty soon thereafter, the boys had jobs.

Each night before they went to sleep, the Simms brothers laid out their clothes for the next day. The alarm rang before 5:00 A.M. There was no fuss, just the shuffling sound of changing clothes and shoes slipping onto feet. When they left the house, they sprang into a run toward a delivery point. There they picked up their newspapers. They counted them out, making sure they had the right number before putting them in their sacks. With sacks slung over their shoulders, they took off delivering the news.

"Why we worked? If you wanted something, we had to work. You know, eight kids," Phil said. "I don't remember my mom ever buying any of us anything. We bought everything. School supplies and clothes—we all did it ourselves."

The news business doesn't have days off, and neither did the paperboys. The Simms boys delivered *The Courier-Journal* in the morning and *The Louisville Times* in the afternoon.

"Rain or snow. Shine or cold, it didn't matter," Dominic said.

One morning, when he first had the route, Dominic mentioned the rain to his father. "Put a coat on," was the lone response Willie offered.

On Saturdays, the coupon and special sections that beef up the Sunday editions piled up at the Simmses' house, where the boys assembled the inserts with the regular sections.

"The front of our house, it was incredible how much stuff had to be delivered," said Phil, who was about nine years old when he started delivering papers.

Sitting in his home office decades later in Franklin Lakes, New Jersey, Phil doesn't engage—and hasn't ever, really—in the idea that this is some poor man's tale. This was his family's life, the only one they knew.

There were Christmases without gifts. When there were presents under a tree, it was one per child, pants or gloves.

"Well, one year we got a bike. I got a bike. They gave it to me, my two other brothers," Phil said. "That was unbelievable."

The year of the bicycle, that story still lives on when the brothers get together.

The Simmses had a driveway covered in rocks. That's where Dominic, the oldest, took the two-wheeler for a spin on Christmas morning. Phil rode the handlebars.

"About halfway down, we wrecked," Dominic said.

Phil's chin hit the ground. The skin split against the rocks. Blood flowed everywhere.

"I carried that little bastard all the way back up to the house because I was scared to death he was going to die. I didn't know any different then," Dominic said.

Regardless of Dominic's fear, there were no tears from Phil, just a few Christmas Day stitches to close up the gash.

Before he could play organized sports, Phil would plant himself at the Okolona Little League field on Blue Lick Road, just off Preston Highway. He'd watch Dominic play, his eyes glued to the games, yearning to take the field.

"I'm just thinking how cool it was to go watch him play," Phil said.

When he did start playing, Phil was one of those kids who could strike everybody out, and he could hit, too.

"Baseball came easy to me. It was natural. I grew up in that environment," he said.

In one Little League game, Phil went 3 for 4 with three home runs. He was so proud of himself. When he got home, he told his parents how he played.

Willie Simms wasn't impressed. He snapped at Phil, telling him there was no need to be so happy. If he hit three home runs, he should've hit four.

Stunned, Phil said nothing.

A few years later, he had become a known guy in the area—Whitey Simms, the kid with the longish blond hair. His youth league stardom made him a target for opponents. During a Babe Ruth game, an opposing pitcher struck him out and laughed at Simms as he walked back to the dugout. Phil didn't react. He kept his head down and took a seat.

"Next time he came up, he hit one so fucking far," Dominic said.

As Phil went around the bases for the home run, he locked eyes with the pitcher and laughed at him.

"It was like, 'Okay, you got me once, but I hurt you worse,'" said Dominic, who watched the incident play out.

During his junior year of high school, Phil was going steady with one of the seven Tutwiler girls, a family on the Simmses' paper route. A boy from cross-city rival DeSales High School wanted to date the girl. That didn't sit well with Phil. The teenagers handled it the way you handled such a thing in Louisville in the early 1970s. They met up for a fight on Dee Road in front of the Tutwiler house. The boy from DeSales brought a pal. One of Phil's brothers went down to Dee Road with some friends to make sure the fight would be fair.

As the combatants sized each other up, Phil turned to his backers and told them they could leave.

"Yeah, y'all go back to your party. It won't take long," he told them.

One by one, Phil handled both boys, and that settled everything.

He left the fight with some of their blood on his shirt and his white pants. A few weeks later, he broke up with the girl.

Truth is, there were other things more important to Phil than girls and the typical high school social scene.

"I loved sports my whole life, and I was embarrassed a lot of the time how much I liked it. I couldn't really express sometimes my desire to do more," he said.

When his friends talked about going out on Friday night and heading to a party or meeting up somewhere to hang out on the weekend, Phil wanted to go to the park and play basketball. Too uncomfortable to voice his unorthodox nightlife ideas, he kept his thoughts to himself.

On a few occasions, he and his pals would play sports on a weekend night. After, they'd have a beer and some laughs.

"I loved those nights," Phil said.

In high school, it was clear Simms could throw the football well. It started with his first pass playing full-pads tackle football. That was in sixth grade at St. Rita's, a 60-yard touchdown bomb to David Grakul.[1]

College football recruiting was decades away from becoming an over-done nationwide industry. It was regional, and while Simms's arm strength was there, he didn't have the makeup for the offense of the era. Colleges weren't looking for big-armed throwers in the early 1970s. They wanted quarterbacks who could run the wishbone and veer-option offenses.

Vince Semary, an assistant coach at Morehead State, spotted Simms at the 1973 state championship game between Simms's Southern High School and Trinity, the Catholic football powerhouse.

Southern was no match for the defending state champs. Trinity won 16–0 to claim the title. Even though his team didn't put a point on the board, Semary couldn't shake his impression of the losing quarterback.

"This kid was just hanging in there pitching that ball. It was unbeliev-able," Semary said. "He was taking a beating. They couldn't protect him. But he stood back in that pocket and threw the ball. I said, 'Geez, this kid's got a lot of courage, you know.' He was a tough kid, had great throwing technique."

After the game, Semary stood outside Southern's locker room, waiting for the team to disperse. He stopped Simms when he saw the quarterback walk out. Semary conducted some fact-finding. He couldn't believe what he discovered. Simms had generated hardly any interest from college programs. Seeing his opportunity, Semary went for it: "Well, I'd like you to come to Morehead."

Simms's older brother Dominic had attended Morehead State for a couple of years, playing baseball there. So Phil had some familiarity with the school.

"It wasn't a big recruiting job. I wish I could say it was. But he didn't have many offers," Semary said.

Simms redshirted his first year in college. In 1975, he started at quarterback. The team went 3–7 scoring just 88 points in ten games.

Steve Walters became Morehead State's offensive coordinator in Simms's sophomore year. In an era in which offenses focused on running and utilizing the option, Walters was a radical. He wanted to throw the ball on just about every down. After one season at Morehead, Walters left to become an assistant at Tulsa. He would eventually become an NFL assistant coach for more than twenty years, but the one season he spent with Simms never left the quarterback's mind.

"He really taught me so much in my sophomore year that it carried me through my junior and senior years," Simms said. "If he'd stayed there, we would've been a prolific offense by the standards of those days."

In his junior year, Simms aired it out (by the standards of those days). He completed 134 of 367 passes for 2,041 yards. He threw 13 touchdowns and 15 interceptions. He led the Ohio Valley Conference in passing for the second consecutive season and was named conference player of the year.

Simms could've parlayed being the award-winning quarterback into a rock star lifestyle on campus. He didn't, though. It wasn't him.

"If you had a daughter, you'd want her to date him. He's such a nice guy," said Buck Dawson, the track-and-field coach at Morehead who tried—unsuccessfully—to lure Simms into throwing the javelin.

Simms also kept working throughout college. He laid blacktop. He painted houses for $100 a house. He loaded liquor for a Kentucky distiller. The summer before his senior year, he thought he hit the jackpot. He made between seven and eight dollars an hour putting trucks together at the Ford Motor Company plant. He installed steel cables in the chassis and bolted them down. He'd work sixty hours a week and make about $500 before taxes, "which I thought was all the money in the world," Simms said.[2]

With a slight change, his social life in college followed a similar pattern as in high school. At Morehead, he found a group of friends who wanted to play sports on weekend nights. They broke into the weight room and worked out. They snuck into the gym to play basketball until midnight. Afterward, they grabbed something to eat and then went to any party that might be going on.

In Simms's senior year, Morehead State posted its third consecutive two-win season. Simms didn't repeat as conference player of the year, nor did he lead the league in passing. He didn't even make first-team all-conference.

In four years, his team never finished any higher than second-to-last place in the Ohio Valley, but once word spread about his ability to throw the football, the scouts kept coming.

At the family's home in Louisville, Willie Simms called a brief meeting of Phil's siblings and the family's close friends. It was clear Phil was headed to the NFL, and Willie wanted to address how the inner circle would respond to the attention.

"Here's the rules from now on: we do not talk about this anymore outside of this circle of friends right here in this house," Willie said.

"Why?" asked Dominic, the oldest Simms child.

"Just keep your mouth shut."

Later that day, a sports reporter called looking to talk to the family about Phil. Willie fielded the interview request and said he had no idea NFL teams were looking at his son.

Dominic was happy for his brother, but that came with the customary big-brother bemusement. "I beat on this kid my whole life, and he's going to play pro football?"

Dominic had to leave work early the day the Green Bay Packers came to the Simms home. His little brother needed someone to catch passes. The Packers had the fifteenth pick in the draft. They sent Zeke Bratkowski, an assistant with Green Bay who had won three NFL championships and two Super Bowls as a player with the organization.

Phil threw passes to Dominic in an open field. After the football work-out, the Simmses and the Green Bay staffers drank coffee and ate some of Barbara Simms's homemade pie.

"It went great. They were another one. I'm sure they were going to take me if I was there," Phil said.

Simms even had a quick throwing session back at Morehead State with Joe Gibbs. The future Washington Redskins head coach had just taken over the San Diego Chargers' offensive coordinator spot left vacant by new Giants coach Ray Perkins.

One visiting coach left a distinct impression. Bill Walsh, the new San Francisco 49ers coach, was an outlier. He visited Simms twice.

"It was pretty cool. He was so different from the rest. He was just different. Football coaches were, '*Rah-g, erggh, rah-g, erggh,*'" Simms said, imitating the stereotypical tough-guy coach demeanor. "Bill, you could see, was a thinker. It was much more. I guess the best word—he was pol-ished. Just so cool."

When Simms threw passes for Walsh, the coach stood in a pensive pose. His right arm crossed to inside his left elbow. His left hand raised so his fingers could gently rest against his face.

"I don't think I threw one ball that wasn't a perfect spiral, right on tar-get the whole workout. And he kept talking to me as I was getting ready to throw."

'Throw it easier," Walsh said in a soft voice as he continued to give Simms various instructions on technique as the quarterback dropped back and tossed the ball.

"As I was listening to him, I was like dreaming, and the more he talked to me, the better it got. It was unbelievable."

Simms never thought Walsh would actually draft him. Simms figured Walsh would take Steve Dils because Dils played at Stanford, where Walsh had just been the head coach.

"Well, not necessarily. Steve Dils doesn't have your talent," Walsh said.

"Oh," Simms said, halted by the compliment.

"We are going to draft you. And when we draft you, I want you to fly out the next day because we are going to get to work on you being the quarterback. You are going to lead the NFL in passing next year as a rookie."

"He says all this to me, just like that. And he goes: 'You don't believe me?'

"'Oh, yeah, I believe you, Mr. Walsh.' Who wouldn't be enamored with that?"

Meanwhile, in New Jersey, new Giants head coach Ray Perkins asked the team's scouting staff to compile a list of the top quarterbacks in the draft. Perkins wanted to visit each of them himself.

The Giants already had a file on Simms. The team's first scout to see him had unparalleled investigatory training. Ed Rutledge had been a special agent in J. Edgar Hoover's FBI. While on assignment performing a security clearance on a professor in California, Rutledge found a book on coaching football. It was a life-changing moment. He switched professions and eventually became an assistant coach on Blanton Collier's star-filled staff at the University of Kentucky. There, Rutledge's fellow assistants included Don Shula, Howard Schnellenberger, Chuck Knox, and Bill Arnsparger.

Before settling into the Giants' personnel department, Rutledge served as the defensive coordinator and then a special teams coach during Arnsparger's two-plus years as the team's head coach.

After seeing Simms play, Rutledge needed to probe his mental makeup. The former G-man met Simms off campus for a question-and-answer session.

"I met him at a hotel right outside the town. We talked. I took one of those tests," Simms said.

Rutledge wanted to gauge if Simms could handle being a quarterback in New York. After meeting him, Rutledge believed he could. Rutledge filed his report on Simms, which brought Jerry Shay, the Giants' chief scout, to Morehead State.

Shay had no idea what he walked into when he headed to the football office on a Monday morning late in Simms's senior season. The team had lost Saturday. Wayne Chapman, the head coach, was on his way out.

"I didn't get too warm of a welcome," Shay said.

He stood there with his own projector under his arm, hoping someone would give him some film. An assistant coach eventually set him up with a viewing area in the back of the gym.

That afternoon, Shay watched something, but it wasn't practice. It was punishment. The entire team ran more than a dozen 220-yard sprints. Simms led the pack.

"The thing that impressed me more was he stood out like a sore thumb among those guys over there—you know, bigger, faster, stronger," Shay said.

Perkins reviewed the reports from Shay and Rutledge, but because it was Morehead State, he still didn't have big expectations when he visited the quarterback.

First, he and Simms spoke. The coach wanted to get a feel for Simms's football intellect. Perkins, as he likes to say with his Southern accent, "got him on the board"—meaning he had Simms draw up some plays on a chalkboard. Perkins liked what he could glean about Simms's mind.

"I would say that you might be surprised at how little a lot of them do as far as getting on the board and drawing up stuff. But I do remember, very clearly, that he was very impressive," Perkins said.

The quarterback doesn't remember it as all that big of a deal. "We had so few plays, of course I'd know them well. So I drew them up for him."

After talking and Xs and Os, it was time to throw. For every other NFL workout, Simms only needed two receivers. Perkins told him to bring as many players as he could. Simms had more than a half dozen teammates, some of them offensive linemen, lined up to catch passes.

Simms asked Perkins what type of throws the coach wanted to see.

"I want you to throw the ball as hard as you can throw it. Every throw."

Simms went ahead of Perkins to the stadium. The Giants' coach entered by walking up a set of stadium steps. He stood at the top, looking down at Simms throw.

"I remember the first thing that came to my mind was, 'Oh, my goodness.' And the 'oh, my goodness' came from how smooth and what strength he had in his arm," Perkins said.

Perkins still had other quarterbacks to visit. He met with Alabama's Jeff Rutledge (no relation to the Giants' scout). He took a look at Chuck Fusina from Penn State. He had his eye on Steve Fuller of Clemson. His first stop after Morehead State, though, was in Pullman, Washington. He went there to visit the country's hottest quarterback prospect, "The Throwin' Samoan" Jack Thompson of Washington State. At the time, Thompson's 7,818 passing yards made him the all-time leader on the collegiate level. While some of the Giants' personnel people ranked Thompson ahead of Simms, Perkins wanted the Kentucky product. After making the rounds with the signal callers, Perkins called general manager George Young.

"George, you're not going to believe who I like."

"Yeah, I think I will. I bet I can guess who you like," Young said in that high-pitched voice that belied the general manager's size.

"Who's that?" Perkins asked.

"Phil Simms," Young said, knowing Perkins would like the Kentuckian's arm strength.

"Yup, that's our guy."

That conversation didn't make it a done deal. The Giants had Tom Cousineau and Dan Hampton high on their draft board. But the decision makers couldn't get away from the need to address the quarterback position.

"We couldn't introduce Joe Pisarcik one more time in Giants Stadium after that Miracle of the Meadowlands thing. We're liable to have gotten him killed," Shay said.

The question was which quarterback. Thompson sat above Simms on the organization's draft board. Shay said the differentiation stemmed from Thompson playing better competition and in a stronger conference than Simms.

To make his case with Young, Perkins copied the full scouting reports on Simms and Thompson, but he left the names off each packet and asked Young whom he would go with. There wasn't all that much difference.

On draft day, Simms set up headquarters with his parents at the Holiday Inn in Morehead. The NFL used the Waldorf Astoria Hotel on Park Avenue in New York City to announce the picks.

Cousineau went first to the Buffalo Bills.

With the third pick, some draft prognosticators thought the Bengals would take Louisiana State running back Charles Alexander. Cincinnati already had a Pro Bowl–caliber quarterback in Ken Anderson, but the Bengals took Thompson.

"I don't know what George would've done if Thompson was still sitting there [when the Giants picked]," Shay said.

Another player high on the Giants' draft board, Dan Hampton, a future Hall of Famer, went fourth to the Chicago Bears.

Three picks later, it was time for the Giants to grab their quarterback. Fans in attendance at the draft shouted for Missouri tight end Kellen Winslow and Alexander of LSU. At the Waldorf, Tom Power, the team's director of promotions, took the phone call that came from the organization's war room across the Hudson River at Giants Stadium. Power wrote down the pick, initially misspelling the college as "Moorehead."

When commissioner Pete Rozelle stepped to the podium, he could barely hold back a grin.

"New York Giants first-round selection, quarterback, Phil Simms, Morehead State," Rozelle announced with a toothy smile and laugh as the jeers and boos stole the scene.

The story goes that the footage of Rozelle announcing the pick was a second take to draw out and capture the ire of "long-suffering" Giants fans who had no idea who Phil Simms was nor any idea that Morehead State existed. Nobody knows with certainty if this is true, but it was common during that era to repeat picks to get a second take for the cameras, so if it did happen, Simms's selection didn't get special treatment.

More than six hundred miles away, Simms heard Ray Perkins's voice on the other end of a telephone telling him he was the Giants' first pick.

Simms never heard the boos, but he heard about them. He was "Phil Who?" to Giants fans until he arrived at Giants Stadium the next day. He caught a glimpse of the headlines. The quarterback who had never played in front of more than twenty-five thousand spectators toured an empty stadium that sat seventy-six thousand.

The Giants' top brass defended the pick of the little-known passer. "Names, that's just feeding Pablum to fans," George Young said, offering a quote that made sure to display a superior vocabulary.[3]

Simms had a more simplistic take.

"I didn't care."

7

A BRONCOS SEASON TICKET HOLDER

In the early part of 1979, Bill Parcells left behind his first head coaching job. In Denver, he boarded a New Jersey–bound plane. The Air Force coach left to become the linebackers coach of the New York Giants.

Parcells ended up on the same flight as Bill Belichick, the Broncos' special teams assistant and defensive aide who moved up the coaching ladder when Perkins named him the Giants' special teams coach.[1]

Both men checked into the Sheraton on Terrace Avenue in Hasbrouck Heights. Perkins and the other assistants lodged there during the first few months of their turnaround efforts.

The new job was a homecoming for the thirty-seven-year-old Parcells. He had lived in Hasbrouck Heights. His family's old home on Columbus Avenue split the difference between the hotel and Giants Stadium. The first pro game he saw, the one that hooked him on football, was on a Boy Scouts trip to the Polo Grounds, where he saw a Charlie Conerly–led Giants team drub the Pittsburgh Steelers 24–3 in 1954. He watched Conerly and other Giants greats Arnie Weinmeister and Emlen Tunnell on his favorite TV show, *Marty Glickman's Quarterback Huddle,* on channel 5.[2]

With the Giants, Parcells had finally reached NFL. However, his wife and their three daughters were back in Denver, and they weren't begging to move.

Parcells met Judy Goss when he was a college football player at Wichita State. She was a secretary in the sports information office. They married in 1962, and Judy followed along with the transient lifestyle that is *making it* as a football coach. Bill started at Hastings College in Nebraska, then back to Wichita State, east to the United States Military Academy, and then south to Florida State and Vanderbilt. From there, they moved a little west to Texas Tech before Bill became head coach at Air Force, a position he held for one year. The move in early 1979 to become the Giants' linebackers coach was the eighth address change in fifteen years.

Parcells had interviewed for the Giants position in New Jersey. He called home to tell Judy he had a new job about 1,800 miles away. Caught up in making it to the NFL, he failed to recognize her lack of enthusiasm. "Shit, I was a Giant," he said.[3]

Planted in the Sheraton in Hasbrouck Heights, Parcells called home each night. Finally, the signals Judy sent became clear. Their house wasn't selling, and she grew colder to the idea of moving. Part of her feelings stemmed from infidelity she suspected on Bill's part.[4]

"Most of those problems at home were my fault; I take the blame for that," Parcells said.[5]

Parcells had to make a choice: his career or his family.

A couple of months into this dream opportunity, Parcells walked into Ray Perkins's office and told the head coach he had to leave.

"Something was wrong within his family back in Colorado, and he had to take care of that," Perkins said of the meeting.

Perkins asked Parcells if he could stay through minicamp. Parcells did. Then he was gone, and the players knew very little about it.

"When I first met Bill, I liked him, and then he disappeared. I didn't know what was going on. I just knew he wasn't there," said Harry Carson.

Carson didn't ask any questions. He heard Parcells left to sell insurance.

Parcells had boarded a Continental flight in Newark "and cried all the way back to Colorado."[6]

He didn't sell insurance. He went to work for Gates Land. The company was developing five thousand acres. Parcells helped sell the land, and he set up athletic programs at the Country Club of Colorado.

"I can't describe how much I hated it," he said.[7]

He bought a pair of Denver Broncos season tickets. He sat in the end zone, a fan watching the game he had spent a decade and a half chasing.

Bill Belichick's transition hit a snag. The sale of his home in Denver fell through. In 1979, interest rates skyrocketed, and by the end of the calendar year, the Federal Reserve struck a rate at nearly 16 percent. Belichick needed a home in New Jersey, and he needed help.

Giants team president Wellington Mara stepped in. Mara cosigned a loan for Belichick so the twenty-seven-year-old assistant coach could make a down payment.

"I will always be indebted to Wellington Mara for the faith and support he showed me. I was a young nobody coaching special teams," Belichick said.

Phil Simms's pro teammates immediately took to calling him Prince Valiant. Initially, he didn't look like a hero.

He missed his graduation ceremony at Morehead State in order to participate in a Giants minicamp of rookies, free agents, and invited veterans.

"There was a little bit of intimidation. I remember seeing the other quarterbacks and going, 'Wow, these guys are pretty good.' Where do I fit into this?" he said.

He threw nervous, and it showed.

"He threw like he was a little rattled," said tight end Gary Shirk, the only other player from Morehead State in the NFL.[8]

It didn't get better at training camp.

"It's like, holy shit, I never played," Simms said.

This only fueled more questions about the unknown draft pick from out of nowhere. Simms said the outside scrutiny didn't affect him, but his focus on himself did.

One day at training camp, it changed. The only factor Simms pointed to was that he relaxed and that led him to start passing well.

"I was throwing the ball and 'Oh.'" He paused to take a breath of relief. "'This is how I throw the ball,'" he said as his belief in his ability returned after a nice pass. "It put me at ease."

His confidence shot up, and he said everybody's attitude on the team shifted in how they interacted with him.

Perkins knew Simms would have to be eased into the lineup. Being an opening-day starter wouldn't happen, and it wasn't the way the NFL worked during that time. Quarterbacks were given time to develop.

Joe Pisarcik started the first three games of the season, all losses. In week 3, Pisarcik threw two interceptions in a 27–0 loss to the Redskins as he went 7 of 24 for 112 yards. Randy Dean started the next game and quickly blew his chance of being a permanent starter. He threw two costly interceptions, one in the end zone, in a 17–13 home loss to Philadelphia. The next week, Perkins announced Pisarcik and Simms would split time in practice and Pisarcik would start.

With eight minutes to play in the first half, Simms entered his first regular season NFL game down 7–0 to the New Orleans Saints in the Superdome. His first pass was dropped. His fourth was intercepted. He threw another interception at the Saints' 2-yard line, an underthrown ball that, if thrown accurately, could've led to a score. Down 17–0, Big Blue fought back. Aided by two New Orleans turnovers, Simms and the Giants cut the lead to 17–14 before losing 24–14. Simms finished the day 8 of 19 for 115 yards with one touchdown pass to go with the two picks.

The following week, the 0–5 Giants faced 5–0 Tampa Bay. Simms made his first start, and the Giants, powered by a changed defensive front and Billy Taylor's 148 yards rushing and two touchdowns, upset the Buccaneers 17–14.

Simms only threw 12 passes. He completed 6 for a scant 37 yards, but he showed more than the stat line. On the first series, he stayed in the game after taking a shot to the face from future Hall of Fame defensive lineman Lee Roy Selmon. "I was a little woozy for a while," Simms said.[9]

When Bucs linebacker Dave Lewis started trash-talking Simms, the rookie quarterback snapped back at him. "Phil was ready to fight him," said Giants guard Doug Van Horn.[10]

Simms maintained his poise. He didn't turn the ball over. At the end of the game, with no doubt about the outcome, Simms fell on the ball. The Giants let time run out, a move that drew cheers from rain-soaked Giants Stadium fans, happy The Fumble wasn't replayed. In the locker room after the game, Simms sought out a reporter. Earlier in the week, Simms said Selmon wouldn't sack him. He didn't. Simms bet the reporter Tampa Bay wouldn't sack him more than twice, and the rookie had won the bet.[11]

The week after upsetting the undefeated Bucs, Simms faced the San Francisco 49ers and that cool coach Bill Walsh, who had visited Simms twice at Morehead State. Walsh and the 49ers never had a shot at taking Simms since he went seventh in the draft. San Francisco's first pick came twenty-two spots later. The 49ers drafted UCLA running back James Owens. Walsh did draft a quarterback with the team's second pick. It was a third-round choice. They selected Joe Montana from the University of Notre Dame. When San Francisco played the Giants, Montana sat behind Steve DeBerg on the depth chart. The 49ers rookie had thrown only one pass so far that season, an eight-yard completion in week 3 against the Rams.

Completing 17 of 32 passes, Simms threw for 300 yards and two touchdowns against San Francisco. He also ran for another score in the 32–16 win.

On Friday nights, back in Denver, Bill Parcells provided the radio analysis for the high school game of the week. On Saturdays, he and Judy went to Air Force games in the afternoon. After those games, Bill would go to dinner with pro coaches in town to play the Broncos. The next day, he and Judy tailgated before games and took their seats in the end zone section of Mile High Stadium.

Parcells wanted back in coaching. This life wasn't for him.

"Even my wife saw through the smiles and the stiff upper lip and the rest of that bullshit," Parcells said.[12]

On many mornings, Parcells lifted the phone and started dialing

Perkins. He envisioned begging for his job back, but he'd hang up before he ever finished dialing.

One night in the days following the Giants' win over San Francisco, Bill and Judy were doing what typical suburban couples do on a weeknight: watching TV.

"You're driving me nuts," Judy said. "I think it's time you thought about getting back into football."[13]

Parcells called Perkins before the TV show was over. He told the head coach he wanted back in. Perkins had a feeling this call would come. He told Parcells to meet him in Kansas City that Sunday. They had breakfast before the Giants played the Chiefs. Perkins didn't have a job, and Parcells didn't ask him for one. Perkins told Parcells to keep in touch.

Shortly after returning from Kansas City, the Parcellses put their house up for sale again. This time, they found a buyer. Bill didn't have a job, but he was committed to getting back into football, and after an extension on their closing, they had to be out of the house by mid-February.

Perkins called. He told Parcells to call Ron Erhardt, the head coach of the New England Patriots. Erhardt had an opening on his defensive staff. After flying to Boston for the interview, Erhardt offered Parcells the job to coach the Patriots' linebackers. He took it. After a brief departure, he was back in the NFL.

The day after Ray Perkins knew he was the Giants' new head coach, he called Bruce Rodgers, a friend and Perkins's football teammate from Petal High School. He told Rodgers, "If I can have them three years, they will be winners. If people stick with me."[14]

In his quest to redirect the franchise, Perkins would not be outworked. As a receivers coach with the Patriots, Perkins told his players "when he died, he hoped it would be on a football field."[15] With the Giants, Perkins's days started at 6:30 A.M. and ended at 1:00 the next morning. In his first six months on the job, he lost twenty pounds, making his frame even more rigid and befitting his stern personality.

Perkins had been through the grueling workouts of Paul "Bear" Bryant at Alabama, but he had built up his endurance to pain and struggle in high school. After practice, he worked at the Sinclair gas station in Petal, a town of eight thousand people. Some shifts, he'd work through the night, giving himself just enough time to go home, bathe, and head out to school. Growing up wasn't easy, but he didn't talk about that. *The New York Times* visited his hometown after he got the Giants job. The newspaper found out his mother was sick a lot, but it found little else about his family life.

Twice he was told to stop playing football—once after a back injury in high school resulted in the disclosure of a missing vertebrae in his back, and again in college when a head-on collision forced him to sit out a year. He became an all-American running back in high school and an all-American wide receiver in college. He knew pain, and he worked through it. The same would be expected of his players, even if they didn't have his makeup.

His first training camp was five weeks instead of four. The first week wasn't exactly mandatory; it was one of those things where the boss asks you to volunteer to come in on your day off and you get the message and show up.

Regular season practices lasted forty-five minutes longer than Giants practices under the previous coaching staff. Meetings with position coaches started at 8:30 A.M. By then, Perkins had already started drinking his second pot of coffee.[16] At 10:00 A.M., the entire team met for ninety minutes. They had thirty minutes for lunch, followed by another ninety-minute meeting. After that, they practiced, and throughout the day, Perkins fit in smoking three packs of cigarettes.

"We would meet just for the sake of meeting, and I didn't really like that," said Pro Bowl middle linebacker Harry Carson.

Players questioned Perkins's methods, and the coach questioned their desire to win. After taking a 14–0 lead in the first five minutes of the second game of the season, the Giants lost 27–14 to the St. Louis Cardinals, a game in which they lost 52 yards on sacks. Perkins closed the locker room doors and spoke to the players for twenty-one minutes after the game, keeping the media waiting eleven minutes longer than the NFL mandate.

When Perkins addressed the press, he said he wanted players willing to stay up thirty hours if that was what it took to win. "My most important responsibility to those players who want to win," he said, "is to weed out those who don't."[17]

A day later, Perkins backed away from his statement, saying it wasn't that players didn't want to win, but what had to be rooted out was the "here-we-go-again" losing attitude.[18] The coach was right, and it would take years to remove this mind-set.

Two weeks later, Perkins put Carson, the team captain, on the bench for the majority of a 17–13 loss to the Eagles. Carson registered three plays in the game. He had been sick during the week and missed practice. Perkins had told players if you don't practice, you don't play. With Carson's sickness and missed practice time, he made an example of the message he had already been sending. "In this game you have to play hurt," Perkins said, "and I think you have to practice hurt. I'm not talking about being injured. I'm talking about playing with pain. By midseason, everybody in this league should be hurting if they're playing the game the way it should be played."[19]

Perkins did his part. He served as a discomforting cultural change agent.

Belichick saw Perkins's work to alter the environment. "He made some hard decisions and was demanding—many of the people in the organization were not willing to sacrifice or work to Ray's standard."

Perkins's intensity could even be conveyed with those deep-set pale blue eyes.

"He had these eyes that were like piercing eyes," Carson said.

Instead of using that Mississippi drawl to get his point across, sometimes Perkins dropped a stare on his players.

"You feel like a little kid who's done something wrong," Carson said, "and he's your daddy giving you that stern parental glare."[20]

Perkins would walk into a room filled with players talking to each other. He stood in the middle of it. He didn't say a word. Just stood, staring at the scene until the chatter around him died down into silence.

The coach's interactions with the media could become awkward. The Wednesday before he notched his first win when the Giants upset Tampa Bay, a writer asked him if he had ruled out changing the defensive front from a 4–3 to a 3–4. Perkins gave a one-word answer. "Yes," meaning he had ruled out the change.

"Why?" the reporter followed up.

"I beg your pardon?"
"Why?"
"Why what?"
"Why don't you like the 3–4?" Pause.
"I just don't, based on the question," Perkins says.[21]

When it came time to practice that afternoon, three writers watched the Giants line up and work on the 3–4. Perkins didn't want to give away game plan details to the media, especially when a Buccaneers public relations staffer sat in on the press conference. The writers called him on the lie. "I answered within the context of the question," Perkins said.[22]

After the Giants went on a two-game winning streak, beating the undefeated Buccaneers and Bill Walsh's 49ers, Perkins cut veteran offensive tackle Gordon Gravelle. The two-time Super Bowl winner with the Steelers had started all sixteen games for the Giants the previous season. Perkins also put quarterback Joe Pisarcik on injured reserve, which wasn't strictly regulated in that era. In effect, the roster move was cutting Pisarcik but waiting until the end of the season to officially let him go.

That whole *if* people stuck with him that Perkins had spoken about with his high school teammate began to come into question.

"This is a heartless business," a veteran who had been practicing hurt told *The New York Times*. "And we have a heartless leader."[23]

George Martin knew the culture had to change. He had firsthand experience seeing his teammates circling a pile of cocaine the night before a game, but, to him, Perkins wasn't the solution.

"They went to the extreme. They went from absolutely having no adherence to rules and regulations to bringing in Ray Perkins, who was like an idiot, just an absolute friggin' idiot, who had such rigidness about him that it kind of fractured the team."

The Giants had started Perkins's first season 0–5. Beginning with Simms's first start, they won six of the next eight games before dropping the last three to finish the season 6–10. Perkins thought players quit during the late-season losing streak.

In the off-season, Perkins tried to loosen up a bit. He stopped smoking. He regained the weight he had lost. He played racquetball with some of the Giants' players who stuck around the facility to work out.

In May 1980, the Giants drafted Scott Brunner, a six-foot-five-inch quarterback whose Delaware teams had gone 20–1 in the last twenty-one games he appeared in. Brunner's training camp progress impressed the Giants enough to trade backup quarterback Randy Dean to the Packers. This left the Giants with a second-year quarterback, Simms, as the most experienced passer on the team and punter Dave Jennings as the second-most experienced.

After a 28–7 home loss to the Los Angeles Rams, the Giants were 1–3 to start the '80 season. The fans called Carson a bum. He questioned their loyalty and considered retiring. It took a couple of conversations with Perkins for Carson, who was in his second season as a captain, to stay with the team.

A few weeks after that, fellow Pro Bowl linebacker Brad Van Pelt asked to be traded to the Detroit Lions to be close to home. This was one of several trade requests Van Pelt made public.

Simms's development stalled that season. He sat out the final three games of the season with a sprain in his right shoulder. In his place, Brunner went 1–2 as the starter, producing a slightly lower passer rating—53.1—than Simms had posted in thirteen games—58.9.

Wrought with injuries, the Giants lost the season finale to the Oakland Raiders 33–17. The game included four lost Giants fumbles, an interception, and a dud of an incomplete pass that slipped out of Brunner's hand and traveled a yard. The follies also included the punter running on the field so the punt return team would have eleven men in on the play.

"We had some players on the field today that probably didn't belong in the league, realistically," Perkins said after the game.[24]

With the loss, the Giants finished with a 4–12 record, and because their schedule was weaker than the New York Jets' and the Seattle Seahawks', the Giants positioned themselves with the number-two overall pick in the 1981 draft.

The first big off-season move for the G-Men came in January. Perkins had fired defensive coordinator Ralph Hawkins after the season. He replaced Hawkins with Bill Parcells, the Patriots' linebackers coach. Parcells wanted $2,000 more to stay in New England.[25] The Pats wouldn't come up with the money, so he returned to New Jersey, less than two years after he had left his original chance to coach for his boyhood team.

8

"GOT MY LATHER GOING"

The 1981 NFL draft was a midweek thing, twelve rounds of selections over a Tuesday and Wednesday at the Sheraton in New York City.

On the weekend before the draft, staffers in the Giants' personnel department hit the phones. They dialed prospects to confirm the draft day locations and telephone numbers of the pro hopefuls. When they called Lawrence Taylor, he wasn't there. North Carolina's all-American defensive standout was in New Orleans. He was at the Saints' facility.

"Oh, shit. They're definitely going to take him," Jerry Shay, the Giants' chief scout said, recalling the collective reaction at the Meadowlands.

The Saints held the number-one pick, one slot ahead of the Giants.

Bum Phillips, the former Houston Oilers head coach, had become the Saints' coach in the off-season. He made it clear he wanted to take George Rogers, the Heisman Trophy–winning running back from the University of South Carolina. In Houston, Phillips had made the play-offs in his final three seasons, including two conference championship game appearances, and he built his success with the Oilers behind the powerful, bruising running of Earl Campbell. With the top collegiate running back available for the Saints, it was obvious Phillips would pick Rogers in an attempt to replicate the model of success the coach had with Campbell in Houston. The Giants' routine call to connect with Taylor cast doubt on that presumption.

"We thought we were going to have to take Rogers, which we would've been okay with, but we really wanted Lawrence. That scared the hell out of us," Shay said.

Once the draft order had been settled and the Giants had completed their scouting, the team figured it would get Rogers or Taylor. At that point, Shay put together highlight reels on each player.

"Lawrence Taylor's highlight reel was a whole spool of a 16mm thing, and shoot, we had less than half a reel on George Rogers," Shay said.

Taylor wasn't the most decorated linebacker coming out of college. That was Hugh Green from Pittsburgh. Green finished second to Rogers in the Heisman balloting, the highest finish ever for a purely defensive player at that point. Green won the Maxwell Award as college football's most outstanding player, the United Press International Player of the Year honors, and the Lombardi Award as the top college lineman.

On the field, Taylor had an obscure first two years at North Carolina. Away from football, he made noise honing his wild side. He frequented local pool halls playing nine-ball and looking for fights. One night, out with some Carolina football teammates and Tar Heel basketball players, one guy finished his beer and slammed down the glass, shattering it. Taylor upped the ante. He broke another glass against the bar and started eating it.

Another night, walking back to his dorm with a group of guys, a drunk Taylor decided to scale the brick building to get to his sixth-floor room. Thereafter, he made it one of his routine ways to enter the building.

"They learned your name pretty fast when they saw you go six stories up the face of a building in the middle of the night, blind drunk," he said.[1]

In his junior season, North Carolina changed how they utilized him. Taylor had been playing as a down lineman. They let him stand up. Rather than read and react to the play, Taylor went on the attack. He started to make plays, and he relished it.

"There is nothing better in life than a violent head-on collision. Look, football is supposed to be a rough game and not everybody is supposed to be able to play. So if I knock a guy silly, he'll be wondering where I am and what I'm going to do to him the next time he runs my way," he said.[2]

He became a force, and NFL scouts noticed.

"That's when his stock started going up," Shay said.

Midway through his senior season, opposing offenses constructed their game plans to avoid him. Oklahoma's head coach Barry Switzer called Taylor "Godzilla." Georgia Tech head coach Bill Curry said he "destroyed" the Yellow Jackets' offense.[3]

North Carolina finished Taylor's senior season with an 11–1 record and ranked tenth in the Associated Press poll, the school's highest end-of-season ranking in more than three decades. Taylor was named the Atlantic Coast Conference Player of the Year.

Green had received more media attention, but pro football insiders had seen enough of Taylor to put him above the Pittsburgh linebacker.

"Lawrence Taylor was the only guy I knew at that size that could take a three hundred–pound guy and walk him back to the quarterback. Not only could he outrun him, he could outmuscle him, too," Shay said.

On the college level, Taylor played stand-up defensive end. In the pros, this translated to being an outside linebacker. The transition would prove to be more than ideal for the six-foot-three, 237-pounder with an unusual combination of speed and power.

"A blue chip, a No. 1 all the way," Giants' director of player personnel Tom Boisture said in the lead-up to the draft.[4]

Meanwhile, in the background, the Dallas Cowboys had been trying to work out a trade with the Saints for the number-one pick. Dallas wanted Taylor, and Taylor wanted to play for the Cowboys. Dallas running back Ron Springs was a few years ahead of Taylor at Lafayette High School in Williamsburg, Virginia, where Taylor grew up. Springs and Taylor had played in the same youth football program. Plus, Taylor was a fan of outspoken former Cowboys linebacker Thomas "Hollywood" Henderson. Taylor would eventually shift from his collegiate No. 98 to No. 56 in the pros because of Henderson, who, a few months before Taylor was drafted, admitted to having a $1,000-a-day cocaine habit.

With Dallas maneuvering for a trade to draft Taylor and the prized pick being at the Saints' facility in the weekend before the draft, the Giants already had two strikes against them. Then came a third.

New York's strongest position unit was the linebackers with Harry Carson, Brian Kelley, and Brad Van Pelt. Why draft another one? Plus,

Taylor had retained Mike Trope as his agent. Trope had handled the rookie contracts for Heisman Trophy winners Earl Campbell and Tony Dorsett. Trope believed that high first-round picks should get three-year contracts worth $750,000.

The previous season, Trope negotiated a six-year, $1 million contract with the Los Angeles Rams for defensive back Johnnie Johnson, the seventeenth overall pick. At the Rams' training camp, this led to a monthlong walkout from veterans, including star defensive end Jack Youngblood.

Now, Giants players threatened to walk out if Taylor came in and surpassed them in salary before playing a snap of pro ball.

"There's no way a rookie deserves to make more than some of us," one unnamed Giant told the Associated Press.

Taylor heard about the comments and told the Giants' front office to back off.

"I didn't want people to be mad at me. So I sent the Giants a telegram Monday saying I would rather not be drafted by them."[5]

That night, Giants players and coaches on the offensive and defensive sides of the ball called Taylor, assuring him there would be no issues.

Less than twenty-four hours later on April 28, 1981, the NFL draft commenced. Thirty-two seconds into the event, the New Orleans Saints picked Rogers.

Phillips believed Rogers could do more than Taylor simply because you can give the ball to a running back.

"He's a great linebacker, but if you put him on one side, they'd just run the other way the whole game. I couldn't get him in a position 30 times a game to make the big play," Phillips said.[6]

Less than a minute after the Rogers pick, the Giants picked Taylor.

Making fast picks was a calculated move by Giants general manager George Young. He believed it sent the message to other teams that the Giants knew what they were doing. Plus, if you had the guy you wanted, there wasn't any reason to wait to hear trade offers.

Across the Hudson River, in the draft room at Giants Stadium, Shay said there was a feeling of elation when they grabbed Taylor. But no hoot-ing, hollering, and high-fiving. "That kind of stuff isn't allowed."

Taylor celebrated in his own way. He spent the previous night drinking twenty-five-cent beers at He's Not Here in Chapel Hill. He and five friends sat at outside tables, drank their beers, and threw their empty glasses against a nearby wall. The owner came out. The college crew thought they would be scolded. Instead, the owner sat down with them and joined the drinking and glass throwing. The final tab came to seventy-five dollars.[7] It averaged out to fifty beers a man, though; almost thirty years later, Taylor told SI.com he drank forty-one Coors Lights on draft day.

The woman who cleaned the Ards' Watchung, New Jersey, home made the sign. She used a three-by-four-foot piece of cardboard, and Bill Ard Sr. and Mary Elizabeth Ard brought it with them when they trekked to the Sheraton in New York City. Waiting for their son to be drafted, the Ards unveiled the sign among the fans in the gallery. "Let Ard Be Our Guard" it declared.

Their son Billy was a six-foot-two, 250-pound guard out of Wake For-est. A few days before the draft, Billy took a call from the Detroit Lions. They were going to take him in the third round.

The third round came. The Lions picked Don Greco, a guard from Western Illinois. The fourth, fifth, and sixth rounds came and went, and the first day of the draft ended without Ard being drafted. His mom and dad returned to the Sheraton the next day. The seventh round came and went, and Billy was still available.

"It was terrible," his father said.

After the Giants picked Taylor as the number-two overall choice, the team's next nine draft choices yielded little long-term impact for the team. Those players combined to appear in a total of 160 NFL games, averaging just a touch more than a season for each player. Only one of those picks played in the NFL beyond 1984. That was wide receiver Melvin Hoover. He was out of the league in 1985 and '86 but came back to play two games as a replacement player during the 1987 players' strike. The Giants' first pick in the eighth round was a quarterback from a Simms-sounding school: Mark Reed from Moorhead State in Minnesota. He spent time buried on the Giants' bench and eventually concluded his career after appearing in eight games for the Colts in 1983.

Fourteen picks after Reed, the Giants took Ard with the 221st pick in the draft.

"I thought I should've been a second or third worst case," Billy said.

Ard's draft stock may have dropped because NFL scouts didn't believe he could beef up his 250-pound frame.

"Information was lacking back then," Billy said.

Ard grew up a thirty- to forty-minute drive away from the Meadowlands. Ard's father had Giants season tickets since the early 1960s when the team played at Yankee Stadium and seats cost seven dollars apiece.

When Bill was about seven or eight, he went to watch a game with his dad at Yankee Stadium.

"After the game ended, I saw a friend of mine fifteen feet in one direction, and Bill walked up to the tunnel watching the guys go out [off the field]," his father said. "I finished my talking and went back to where we were sitting, and there was no Bill."

Eventually, the stadium public address system alerted Mr. Ard to his son's whereabouts. Billy had brought himself to stadium security. Before his father showed up, Billy told the authorities they should get him a cab and pay for his ride back to New Jersey.

Ard said it was "fantastic" to be drafted by his hometown team, but he wasn't taking that attitude into training camp. The draft day slight put him in the mind-set to prove his worth.

"I did not come to camp to make that team. I came to camp to start, and I did."

Ard remained focused on that goal. He didn't socialize with anybody on the team. He lived with his parents during the season. His mom made him breakfast and dinner. He paid rent to his dad.

"But I couldn't bring any girls there," Ard said. "I'm paying rent, and I can't get laid."

He did solidify a starting spot for himself that season, one he didn't surrender for the rest of his career with the G-Men.

Three picks after Ard, the Giants selected Byron Hunt in the ninth round. At six foot five and 238 pounds, Hunt was another big linebacker to add to the Giants' corps.

When the draft wrapped up, the personnel department went out for a nice dinner. The two days of talent selection is the annual culmination of their work. It is time to break bread together and relax. Except Jerry Shay didn't make the meal in '81.

As the draft ended, general manager George Young handed Shay a piece of paper with a name on it.

"Wellington wants this guy," Young told Shay as he handed him the note.

The name on the paper was University of Miami nose tackle Jim Burt. Shay knew who he was. Shay had been down to Miami to work out all the pro talent, but not Burt.

While Shay put other players through drills, Burt kept going over to him, saying, "Aren't you going to work me out? Aren't you going to work me out?"

"No," Shay told him.

Miami had a good long snapper, and Shay needed someone to catch the snaps. Shay asked Burt if he would do it.

"Well, I ended up doing a little bit of workout with him," Shay said.

Instead of heading to dinner after the draft, Shay headed to a phone booth to call Burt. With the mandate from the owner Shay revered, the scout had to deliver.

"I sat in a phone booth talking to Jim Burt that whole evening."

Burt grew up in Buffalo, New York. The middle child of Don and Jean Burt's five children started his schooling at St. Gerard's Catholic school. He stopped going there after fifth grade. "The sisters there slapped me with so many rulers, I got twitches. I'd be daydreaming at my desk and they'd sneak up behind me and whack me as hard as they could either behind the neck or across the knuckles."[8]

At home, Burt caught beatings from brother John. They had a tabletop hockey rivalry going. John, four years Jim's senior, had the edge until Jim started practicing until his fingers blistered. Pretty soon, Jim took the lead in one game and then added some more goals. In a fine hockey response, John left his side of the table.

"He stalked over and started beating me with both fists," Jim said.[9]

Their father had to come downstairs and break it up.

Don Burt had a Pepsi-Cola distributorship, and the Burt boys competed there, too. They accompanied their dad on deliveries to stores in South Buffalo and Lackawanna. They kept a tally of who unloaded the most cases of soda. For Jim, it was the most formal strength training he had until his freshman year at Miami.

Riding his bicycle to and from football provided another path for fights. In the summer of 1967, Buffalo nearly shut down because of race riots. The tension remained and "even kids like myself were swept into the war," Burt said.[10]

Burt could either ride his bike around the black neighborhood, adding about a mile of extra travel, or he could ride through it. He chose the shorter route.

"I was getting into fights every day," he said. "I got in my shots, but sometimes it wasn't enough. There were just too many other shots coming my way."[11]

The Burts moved out of the city to Orchard Park, the suburb where the Buffalo Bills' stadium sits. Jim thought the kids in his new neighborhood were soft. He rebelled against his freshman football coach. The coach wanted him off the team. Jim made a case for a team vote on the issue. He received one vote, and it came from a kid that nobody else liked. Burt started to play hockey. Naturally, he got into fights on the ice. Sometimes there were fights in the parking lot, too. He also broke his hockey coach's rule about dating his sixteen-year-old daughter. After a few years, Jim married Colleen Kempf.

Burt made it back onto the Orchard Park High School football team, playing alongside future Steelers offensive lineman Craig Wolfley and Larry Pfohl, a.k.a. professional wrestling star Lex Luger. Yet a grilled cheese sandwich almost kept Burt away from Miami. With a high school disciplinary record that included setting a classmate's pants on fire with a soldering iron in metal shop, Burt had to make the sandwich or he would fail a cooking class elective and not graduate. He refused. His sister made it for him at home, and Burt turned it in on the last possible day.

When Burt arrived in Coral Gables, the Miami football program was so bad school administrators had thought about getting rid of it. Even though it wasn't a winner, Burt, a pudgy Irish linebacker, looked around at his teammates and questioned whether he could compete.

"Oh my God," he said. "We were in shorts and shirts, and we're going over these drills. I didn't know the drills. People were like five, six inches taller than me."

The star of the team was Ottis "O. J." Anderson, a running back with NFL-caliber size and speed. The first drill when the players were in full pads was blitz pickup. It pitted Anderson, a running back who has to spot and block a blitzing defender, against Burt.

Anderson didn't buckle his chin strap. The beige mouthpiece with the outer lip protection dangled from his face mask. There would be no need for these precautions against the unknown freshman.

Burt exploded from the outside on his blitz. "I'm coming. I mean, I'm in football flow. I'm pretty wired," he said.

He hit Anderson so hard, the running back's helmet flew off. That's when the hooting and hollering started. The whole team had eyes on this. Some freshman from Buffalo just knocked O. J. around.

Anderson asked for a rematch. This time, he buckled his chin strap and loaded in the mouthpiece.

Burt came full blast again. He hit Anderson under his chin and kept running through him. He grabbed the running back, drove him back into the coaches, shoved him to the ground, and walked over him.

From that point on, Burt was no longer an unknown in the program.

The reps against Anderson fueled his frenzy at practice. "I'm hitting everything I can possibly hit. I've got my lather going." Eventually, coaches had to pull him out of the live action.

Leaving the field that day, Anderson jogged over to Burt and put his arm around him.

"We need to take care of each other."

"What do you mean?" Burt asked.

"We need to take care of each other. Let's take it easy on each other."

Burt listened to the message. As soon as he could get to a telephone, he called his father. He told him what happened at practice. "Dad, I've got 'em. I've got 'em."

Burt eventually moved from linebacker to nose tackle, and he excelled under new coach Howard Schnellenberger.

Burt, along with future Buffalo Bills Hall of Fame quarterback Jim Kelly, were the cornerstones upon which Schnellenberger built a program that became a college football dynasty in the 1980s.

"He could whip any two people that tried to block him," Schnellenberger said.

Burt kept up his crazed off-field behavior, too. He drove a car on an intramural football field, spinning doughnuts into the turf. He held a student out a twelfth-floor dorm window after the student had pitched a shopping cart out of the same window and nearly hit Burt as he happened to be walking by. "Your average drugged-out Miami undergrad," Burt said.[12]

"He was a typical upstate New Yorker. He had a little Mafia in him," Schnellenberger said before elaborating on what exactly that meant.

"He's the hit man. You got a little Mafia in you and no one is going to screw around with you."

As Burt's seniority grew on the football team, he became an enforcer. If a teammate came back to the dorm too late at night or was drunk, Burt took him to a field to run sprints. No coaches asked him to do it. Burt set his own rules.

"I had everything covered because I wanted to win."

In the draft, teams passed on him because of his size. The Miami media guide listed him at 242 pounds, which was too light, and at six foot one, he wasn't tall enough. No nose tackle who stood six foot one or shorter had been drafted since the third round six years earlier.

Yet this combination of Luca Brasi and John Blutarsky in shoulder pads kept Jerry Shay in a phone booth all night. Burt had other free agent opportunities, but Shay needed to close the deal for Wellington Mara. Finally, Shay made an offer to get Burt to New Jersey.

"I will pick you up at the airport tomorrow, personally. I will come and get you and bring you to the stadium. If you don't like what you see right off the bat, I will take you right back," the scout said.

When Burt arrived at Giants Stadium, he didn't know what to make of the first scene. Wide receiver J. T. Turner smoked a cigarette while sitting on a bench next to head coach Ray Perkins. *Is this allowed?* Burt wondered. He walked out of the room.

"I've got to smell this shit. We're athletes. This is not going to help us become better. All I wanted to do is get better and win."

He stayed with the Giants because Perkins made him a promise. If Burt outplayed his competition, he'd earn a roster spot, no matter where the other guy had been drafted.

Within a couple of months, it became clear Burt would be the lone undrafted free agent to make the team. He knew making the team didn't make him all that valuable to the Giants. He played as if he could be cut at any moment, referring to himself as a "dirtbag free agent."

Lawrence Taylor became the highest-paid Giant when he signed his contract about a month after the draft. According to newspaper accounts, he would make over $200,000 a year. The day he signed the deal, he drove away from Giants Stadium lamenting the idea of being strapped to the North Jersey landscape. "I couldn't believe how ugly everything looked and smelled."[13]

After all the bluster about walking out, it turned out to be just talk from the veterans. Taylor said his teammates made him feel welcome. Harry Carson took him to dinner at Beefsteak Charlie's on his first day.

After the meal, they went back to a hotel where a woman entertained Taylor, Carson, and a small group of players.

Being a rookie at practice, Taylor had to put in time on special teams. He ran down the field on the kickoff team. On his first play, he blew up the wedge—flattening a group of blockers meant to create a moving wall for the kick returner.

Veterans watching from the sideline could barely get out one syllable. "Man."

"Dude."

"Ah."

He did it on the next play and the next one after that.

"Bona fide. He was the man. He earned respect from everybody on the first day. Forever. And he never stopped," said veteran defensive end George Martin.

Thirty-five years later, Bill Belichick remembered a training camp scrimmage at the high school behind Pace University. "LT had several plays that clearly showed he was easily the best player on the field. He was a man amongst boys that day."

Belichick had come from the Broncos. He had an up-close view of All-Pro linebackers Tom Jackson, Randy Gradishar, and Bob Swenson. "None of these players could compare to the strength, explosiveness, and speed of Taylor."

Taylor ran stride for stride with wide receivers in pass coverage. He ran down running backs on sweeps that were run to the opposite side of the field, exactly what Saints coach Bum Phillips said a linebacker couldn't do.

On that first day, when it came time for the blitz pickup drill, Carson, the captain and middle linebacker, sat on his helmet and watched. Taylor demolished the veteran running backs standing in his way.

"You could see that the stuff that he was doing, it wasn't stuff that he had thought about ahead of time. He was going through it in real time. The moves that he made, he was just that quick and elusive," Carson said.

Chris Mara, a scout at the time, remembered hearing Perkins call him over as the scout headed off the practice field. *Oh, shit. What does he want to say to me now? Who did we fuck up on in this draft?* Mara thought.

Perkins walked over to Mara. The head coach put his arm around him and spoke in that Southern drawl. "That No. 56, he's the greatest athlete I've ever seen on a football field."

While this quick conversation happened, Taylor blitzed off the edge and jumped over veteran running back Rob Carpenter en route to the quarterback.

Parcells, the defensive coordinator, saw something beyond the showcase of speed, strength, and athleticism.

"He had a kind of relentless way he went about things."

That didn't stop Parcells from harping on the rookie. During one practice, Parcells kept dropping Taylor into pass coverage and having him fake blitzes. It frustrated Taylor because he knew he could get to the quarterback for a sack. With the pass rushing taken away, Parcells told him he looked lost.[14]

Another time, when Parcells yelled across the field at Taylor, the linebacker shot back. "You can trade me, you can cut me, you can sit me down, but just get the fuck off my back," Taylor snapped.[15]

The field went silent. No one said a word back to the rookie.

Parcells actually dug the response. He went over to some veterans and told them he liked Taylor. "Motherfucker's got a mean streak."[16]

Parcells thought Taylor might benefit from not starting. He thought about putting him in at the end of the first quarter in the preseason.

Perkins had a different plan. "We didn't draft him there to ease him into action. Put his ass in there and let him play," the head coach told Parcells, cracking a rare smile.

Taylor made a ton of mental errors in his rookie season, but he had the same impact in games as he did during the first days of practice with the Giants. Less than a full season into his pro career, he was already called the best pass rusher in the NFL. When the Giants played the 49ers in the regular season that year, Bill Walsh tried his best to avoid No. 56, only running three plays in his direction. The Saints never once ran toward Taylor.

Ten games into the '81 season, the Giants had to bring back Jim Clack, a veteran center who had worn No. 56 for the three previous seasons. The equipment staff asked general manager George Young about taking the jersey number away from Taylor, who, because of his rookie status, was technically lower in the pecking order than Clack.

"Jim Clack," said Young, "will have to wear another number because Lawrence Taylor is going to take 56 to the Hall of Fame."[17]

What Taylor did—rush the passer from the weakside linebacker position—hadn't been done before.

"Look at it on paper, you wouldn't believe a weakside linebacker could affect a defense so much," said Brian Kelley, who played the position for five seasons before moving to an inside linebacker spot because of Taylor.[18]

Parcells had to change the Giants' use of the 3–4 defense. He believed it was important to put Taylor on the defensive right side. This meant Taylor lined up outside the offense's left tackle. The linebacker on the opposite side lined up on top of or outside the tight end, making the tight end's side the strong side.

"Nobody ever asked me why we put him there. They just assumed because [five-time Pro Bowler Brad] Van Pelt was on the left side, that's where we would put him. But one of the main reasons was that the right side is the quarterback's blind side since most quarterbacks are right-handed," Parcells said.[19]

To set Taylor loose on quarterbacks, Parcells started to cultivate schemes the Giants normally wouldn't use as lead coverages.

Soon this would become the simple, routine way in the NFL, but the way Taylor played, he created the outside rush linebacker position. Opponents had to adjust to him: lining up a tight end on his side; leaving a running back in the backfield in an attempt to slow Taylor's rush on the quarterback.

In the first quarter of the fifteenth game of the season, Taylor ran over Cardinals tight end Greg LaFleur, sending him to the turf before blindsiding quarterback Neil Lomax and forcing a fumble. George Martin grabbed the ball and returned it 20 yards for the touchdown. The score put the Giants up 7–3, giving them a lead they would never surrender in the 20–10 victory.

John Madden, the former Oakland Raiders coach and CBS analyst, kept rerunning the film of the scene as he prepped to call the Giants' must-win regular season finale against the Cowboys.

"I still don't believe that play," he said and then pointed to Taylor walking off the field, while his teammates celebrated in the end zone. "Not even the waterboy congratulated him."[20]

The Giants beat the Cowboys 13–10 in overtime on the final Saturday of the regular season. The next day, the New York Jets eliminated Green Bay, defeating the Packers 28–3. The win put both New York teams in the postseason for the first time.

Taylor became the first rookie to be named Defensive Player of the Year. He picked up Defensive Rookie of the Year and All-Pro honors as well.

With Parcells in his first year as the defensive coordinator, the Giants' defense went from giving up 26.6 points per game in 1980—second to last in the NFL—to 16.1 points per game, which ranked third in the league.

During the final five games, Parcells's defense gave up 10.8 points per contest. The defense even scored a couple of sorely needed touchdowns because the offense didn't produce much. For the season, the Giants could only muster a league-low 270.4 yards per game. On the scoring front, including those defensive touchdowns, the team averaged 18.4 points per game.

The Giants won four of their final five games to squeak into the play-offs—the first postseason berth since 1963. Phil Simms watched the stretch run from the sidelines. A sack from Dexter Manley in week 11 left Simms with a separated right shoulder that kept him out for the rest of the year. Backup Scott Brunner took the reins of the offense.

In the wild card game, the Giants went to Philadelphia as seven-point underdogs, and they beat the defending NFC champs. The Giants received the opening kickoff and failed to get a first down. Giants punter Dave Jennings sent the ball into the gray, drizzling sky. As Philadelphia's Wally Henry tried to tuck the kick away at the Eagles' 25-yard line, Taylor leveled him, causing a fumble, which the Giants recovered. A few plays later, Big Blue scored the first of its three first-quarter touchdowns en route to a 20–0 lead. In the second half, the Giants ran 20 plays—one pass, two kneel downs, and 17 runs, mostly behind the left side of line and guard Billy Ard. They held on to win 27–21.

In the divisional round, the Giants went to San Francisco to face the 49ers in the rain and muddied field at Candlestick Park. On the opening drive, the Giants forced San Francisco into a fourth and 23, but Mark Haynes got caught holding on the punt, and the penalty gave the 49ers an automatic first down. Six plays later, the Giants were down 7–0. Forty-Niners quarterback Joe Montana racked up 276 of his 304 passing yards in the first half. The 49ers had a 24–10 lead at the break, but New York cut it to seven points in the fourth quarter. Down 24–17, early in the last stanza, San Francisco was about to face a third and 18. As the players headed back to their huddles, Giants defensive end Gary Jeter and 49ers tackle Dan Audick started shoving each other. Jeter took a swing at Audick and drew a 15-yard personal foul penalty. This gave the 49ers an automatic first down. Four plays later, San Francisco scored. It was 31–17, and the Giants wouldn't come back. A Ronnie Lott interception return for a touchdown made it 38–17 before the Giants added a touchdown to make the final score 38–24.

"If they had legalized murder for a day, I'm telling you all of his teammates would've killed him," George Martin said of Jeter. "He had the nerve to be unapologetic and say, 'I'm not going to let anybody punk me.' It's not about you, you dumb-ass. You idiot. You just knocked us out of the play-offs."

The good part is that the Giants won a play-off game. They clawed back into a game with the 49ers, the team with the best regular season record in the NFL and the eventual Super Bowl champions. The number-two overall draft pick turned out to have all-world talent.

The reality, though, was that they barely made the play-offs, needing another team to falter before they clinched a spot. The offense struggled. And while the culture had been altered, it wasn't fixed.

Perkins's hard-assed approach had its limits in effectiveness. Six games into the 1981 season, the coach walked out in the middle of the locker room and stared at George Martin, a defensive captain.

"George Martin, you're not getting the job done. You're not starting anymore. You got any questions?" he snapped and then walked away.

Martin was a seven-year veteran who had started the last fifty-four games. He was the team chapel leader, the married father, the guy who had walked away from a pile of cocaine. The interaction left him humiliated.

"Needless to say, that kind of ended our relationship from that point on. I don't care who you are. If you're a janitor, pull the guy aside. You can be a man of your conviction, but tell the guy privately."

They were no longer *The Fumble* Giants. They ceased being a bumbling operation, but the ingredients for a losing mentality hadn't been eradicated. Veteran players dogged it in practice, and some of them were a bad influence on younger guys. The personal foul on Jeter exemplified putting yourself ahead of the team.

From his spot as the defensive coordinator, Parcells saw that the run to play-offs didn't equal a return to glory for the franchise. "I thought we still had some issues, and I'm pretty sure I wasn't alone."

9

EUPHORIA

It's hard to pinpoint exactly when Lawrence Taylor started using cocaine.

At one point, he said it was during his rookie year. He, Byron Hunt, and fellow rookie tight end Dave Young rented a house together in Passaic, New Jersey. They kept two items in the fridge: beer and a strawberry-flavored penicillin shake to ward off any sexually transmitted diseases they might acquire.

They'd throw parties, and people had sex all over the place.

"One night, I remember that there was either a guy or girl in every room and every closet in the house, either sleeping or having sex," Hunt said. "I forgot the shower—there were two or three people in there, too."[1]

At one of these parties midway through the '81 season, somebody had cocaine and told Taylor to try it. He did.

"What I remember is instant euphoria," LT said.[2]

Taylor had met his future wife Linda during his junior year at North Carolina. They married in 1981. That same year, LT's rookie season, Linda found white powder in his jacket. LT admitted it was coke, but he told Linda it belonged to someone else.

Taylor has also said 1982, his second year in the league, was the first time he used drugs.[3]

What is known is that by the summer of 1982, seventeen active NFL players had admitted to being addicted to cocaine. They enrolled themselves in the league's confidential treatment program.

Charles R. Jackson, the NFL's assistant director of security, thought there could be as many as fifty cocaine addicts in the league and hundreds of the 1,500 other players using cocaine regularly.[4]

Jackson, a former Yonkers, New York, police officer with a record of successful narcotics investigations, based his numbers on reports from team officials, players admitting their use, and his general discussions throughout the league.

George Rogers, the player taken ahead of Lawrence Taylor in the 1981 draft, became swept up in the drug revelations. Rogers led the NFL in rushing as a rookie, and in the following spring, the U.S. Department of Justice reported that he also bought more than $10,000 of cocaine during that year.

According to a report in *The New York Times,* Rogers and quarterback David Wilson, another Saints rookie, told a grand jury they purchased the drug from Mike "The Hound" Strachan, a former Saints running back who was one season removed from the league. Rogers and Wilson, along with other Saints players, received immunity for their testimony against Strachan.

The *New York Times* article came out less than two weeks after a *Sports Illustrated* cover story by Don Reese, a former Dolphins, Saints, and Chargers defensive end. Reese started using cocaine as a rookie first-round draft pick in 1974. The weekly magazine scrapped its usual stunning sports photography cover shot and instead used the black-and-white type that opened Reese's story.

"Players snorted coke in the locker room before games and again at halftime and stayed up all hours of the night roaming the streets to get more stuff. I know. I was one of them," Reese wrote.[5]

In American society, cocaine had transitioned into a new realm. "No longer is it a sinful secret of the moneyed elite, nor merely an elusive glitter of decadence in raffish society circles," Michael Demarest wrote for *Time* in the summer of '81. "No longer is it primarily an exotic and ballyhooed indulgence of high-gloss entrepreneurs, Hollywood types and high rollers."[6]

Almost anywhere in the country, lawyers, students, government workers, waitresses, dishwashers, politicians, bankers could all get their hands on the white powder.

"A lot of people you would consider normal, successful people had an issue back then," said Gerry McAleer, a twenty-six-year U.S. Drug Enforcement Agency veteran, who was on the job at the time, tracking the influx of cocaine from South America into the greater New York City area.

Carl Eller, a former cocaine addict and future Hall of Fame defensive lineman with the Minnesota Vikings, knew this feeling. He had been hired as a substance abuse consultant for the NFL. "Now a player can get the same thrill from cocaine that he got running 90 yards for a touchdown or making an incredible quarterback sack that saves the game. And they don't actually have to do it anymore, they can get the same feeling, even a bigger feeling, from the end of a pipe," he said.[7]

This wouldn't happen to Taylor. LT wouldn't succumb to any addiction. He's bigger than drugs. At least that's what he told people around him. "Taylor controls the drug. The drugs don't control Taylor."[8]

It is during this period, the early '80s, that the NFL began to transition away from being a ruffian sport and move toward being a profession. The *North Dallas Forty* brand of pro football—the pill-popping, boozing, painkiller-injecting, recreational-drug-using, ravenous-sexual-appetite-having image—was on the way out. The league spent a good part of the '80s transforming into what it would become—the most dominant sport in the country.

Internally, the NFL was ahead of the news about players' cocaine use. Law enforcement officials and NFL security officials—who were mostly former law enforcement officials—met with teams annually. They warned players against drug use and the drug scene. In some cases, they even pointed players away from teammates who were known users.

"Every year, some guy from the league would come in and kind of give the scare tactic, you know—'You're the grass. We're the lawn mower, and we're going to cut you down if you're not careful' type of thing," said Giants quarterback Scott Brunner.

The greatest concern for the league was a player becoming hooked on cocaine and then being beholden to a dealer with an entrepreneurial criminal mind. This hypothetical scenario claimed the addiction would lead to debt. Instead of paying the debt, the player would fix the outcome of a game.

In December 1982, an FBI agent in Miami wrote a memo claiming two men from the Dallas area had given cocaine to Cowboys players in exchange for shaving points in games.[9] The report never led to any criminal charges. It never moved beyond the memo. The agent who filed it ended up convicted of accepting $850,000 in bribes and pocketing forty-two kilos of cocaine, which he should have confiscated.

"The league wasn't as much concerned about the effect of drugs on the player as much as it was the effect of drugs to the image of the league," Brunner said.

The quarterback controversy rumblings started in June of '82. After separating his right shoulder against the Washington Redskins, Phil Simms watched as Scott Brunner took over the quarterbacking duties for the Giants' final five regular season games and two play-off games of 1981.

Who would be the Giants' starting quarterback moving forward? Simms, the number-seven overall pick from the '79 draft, the first choice made by the general manager and head coaching combo of George Young and Ray Perkins? Or Brunner, the sixth-round pick from 1980?

Publicly, Perkins tabbed Simms as the number-one quarterback, saying he couldn't lose the starting spot because of injury. The two quarterbacks had their lockers next to each other. They weren't pals. They sat in meetings together, handled the competition professionally, and went their separate ways when they left work. But the questions kept coming during the summer. At training camp at Pace University, Simms said it was all people asked him about.

"But what more can be brought up? It comes to a point where it's hard to be courteous," Simms said. "How much can you milk a situation?"[10]

In a preseason game against the Pittsburgh Steelers, Brunner started and played the first half with the first-string offensive line to protect him.

He was 13 of 21 for 205 yards and a touchdown. Playing the second half, behind a second-string offensive line, Simms was sacked three times and threw three interceptions while completing 7 of 18 passes for 37 yards.

Simms watched the game film. He saw rookie running back Joe Morris open 20 yards down the middle of the field. He saw it in real time, too. Seeing the replay of the scene irritated him.

"I could have thrown it left-handed for a touchdown."[11] But he didn't. The Steelers blitzed. The Giants didn't pick it up, and the big-play opportunity vanished.

"I could have had a great game," Simms said. "But I didn't have an opportunity to make a play, not one."[12]

The following Saturday, Simms started the preseason game against the New York Jets. Late in the first quarter, he dropped back to pass. Jets defensive lineman Joe Klecko smashed into Simms's left side. The quarterback spun around after the initial hit and released the ball. As he did, the Jets' Abdul Salaam dived at Simms's right leg as the quarterback fell backward. Simms felt the pain immediately. It was his right knee.

Less than forty-eight hours later, on Monday morning, Simms underwent surgery on his knee at University Hospital in Newark, New Jersey. Less than an hour after the procedure to repair torn ligaments, the Giants placed him on injured reserve. He was done for the season. For the third year in a row, an injury ended Simms's season. A sprained shoulder cost him three games in 1980; the separated shoulder put an early end to '81, and now a season-long knee injury.

The Giants opened the '82 season with Brunner as the starting quarterback. The team traded for Jeff Rutledge, the Alabama product Perkins scouted when he first arrived at the Giants. Big Blue sent a fourth-round draft pick to the Los Angeles Rams in exchange for Rutledge, who became the number-two quarterback.

The Giants started the season 0–2. After their Monday night home loss to the Green Bay Packers, the games stopped. The NFL players began a strike. It lasted fifty-seven days and cut the sixteen-game schedule to nine. During the break, Giants head coach Ray Perkins visited Tuscaloosa,

Alabama, twice. There he met with his college coach, Paul "Bear" Bryant, and discussed the possibility of replacing the legend.[13] At the time, the meetings received no media coverage, but it wasn't a covert act by Perkins to bail on the Giants.

"You have to understand my love for Alabama. My love for Coach Bryant, I don't know if there's any parallel there. I had often wanted and thought about, mentally, being the guy that followed him. That would be just a total dream," Perkins said.

Before Perkins left for his first training camp as head coach of the Giants, he invited a group of reporters to his home for a little dinner and some cocktails. Standing on his back porch in the early evening, Dave Klein of *The Star-Ledger* cornered Perkins and asked the new coach if he would take the Alabama job if Bryant stepped down in a few years.

"I can't believe he thought of it, and I can't believe he'd ask it at that time, but he did."

Perkins answered swiftly, definitively, and honestly. "Yes."

On Thursday, December 9, 1982, the president of Alabama, Dr. Joab Thomas, called Perkins, letting the coach know Bryant planned to end his football tenure. Within hours, Perkins had permission from the Giants to interview for the job. That evening, Bill Parcells was the last coach working in the facility. George Young called him into the general manager's office. The two men spoke for an hour, an informal interview. Parcells believed he had the job, but until a formal deal was made, there was always the you-never-know factor. The Giants beat the Eagles on Saturday. Perkins flew to Alabama on Sunday to interview. He received the official offer on Monday. That night, George Young called Parcells's home to tell the defensive coordinator he wanted to speak to him after work on Tuesday. "I want the job," Parcells told Young on the phone.[14]

The next evening, they spoke for three hours. Young offered some terms, an annual salary of $125,000 a year. They shook on the deal because Parcells didn't want to sign a new contract until the end of February when his current contract ended.[15]

Parcells drove home to Upper Saddle River, New Jersey, and told his wife, Judy. He called his oldest daughter, Suzy, who was at school at Idaho State University. He called his father, Charles Parcells. Parcells spoke to his friend Bob Knight, the head basketball coach at the University of Indiana. They had met when both men coached at Army. Parcells wanted some guidance from Knight on the finances of being a head coach.

The day after Parcells's handshake deal with Young, Alabama announced Bryant's resignation. The Giants then held a press conference announcing Perkins's departure, followed by the announcement that Parcells was the next head coach.

The Giants had seen Perkins's move coming. Young focused on Parcells, and no other names were floated as possible replacements.

"George saw something in him. But really, the tipping point was the fact that he had some head coaching experience as opposed to anyone else that we had on our roster," said John Mara, the son of Wellington Mara and the eventual team president. "He [George] felt that Perkins had started to build something here, and he didn't want to blow the whole thing up and bring in a whole new staff."

In the locker room, the players cheered when they found out Parcells was the new coach.[16] Brian Kelley, one of Parcells's linebackers, strolled through the introductory press conference and offered up, "All right. Way to move in, Tuna. I mean, Sir Tuna."[17]

Kelley invoked Parcells's nickname, which started with Parcells's days as a Patriots assistant. A lasting image for players in the New England locker room was Parcells leaving the team's steam room, lighting a cigarette, and standing over a freezer of ice cream bars about to make his selection. The quip from Kelley exemplified the casual nature with which players felt they could interact with the coach. This was the early knock on Parcells: too nice; too friendly with his players.

The Giants went 4–5 as Perkins finished out the '82 season, going 1–2 after his Alabama plans were announced. George Young's move to have Perkins coach the last three games left Parcells a clean slate. The new coach wouldn't be judged by the tail end of a strike-shortened season.

Even though becoming head coach of the Giants fulfilled a dream, Parcells said he didn't pause to take in the moment. "You know, once you get one of these jobs, the turmoil starts very quickly. It gets going pretty quickly."

10

FIRE PARCELLS, PLAY FOR TRUMP

On his first day of practice as the head coach of the Giants, Bill Parcells had his father by his side.

Charles Parcells lived about twenty-five minutes from the stadium in Oradell, New Jersey. It was the town where Bill lived after the family expanded and moved out of the gray-and-white single-story house on Columbus Avenue in Hasbrouck Heights.

Charles Parcells, an Irishman, was a three-sport star at nearby Hackensack High School. He played football and basketball, and he ran track at Georgetown University. He also earned a law degree at the elite Washington, D.C., school before becoming an FBI agent and eventually settling into a career at Marine Midland Bank.

Charles married Ida Naclerio from Wood-Ridge, New Jersey. She was a fiery Italian with a predilection for superstitions, something she passed on to her son.

The couple's oldest child, Duane Charles Parcells, took to the name *Bill* after the family moved to Oradell. At the local junior high school, another boy named Bill looked like Duane. People started calling Duane "Bill," and Duane went with it. His parents found out about the name change through a local newspaper article about a youth baseball league. Charles and Ida didn't force their son to stick to Duane, but they didn't call him Bill either.

That first Giants practice was a gathering of rookies and free agents at the end of April. The forty-one-year-old Parcells, the twelfth head coach in Giants history, spoke to the players about the need to act professional. He told them they weren't on scholarship anymore, and they could forget about being coddled.

"The things I told my players, it comes from my father," Parcells said. "He'd grab me by the shirt collar and say, 'Here's what you've got to do.'"[1]

Months before that first practice, Parcells had mapped out a day-by-day schedule for front office executives and his assistant coaches. The calendar included things like when players reported for off-season programs, but it also drilled down to more minute details, such as the date the playbooks had to be delivered to the printer.

For Parcells's first draft as head coach, the Giants held the tenth overall pick. They used twelve of their allotted fifteen minutes before selecting Terry Kinard, a six-foot-one, 190-pound, two-time all-American free safety out of Clemson.

General manager George Young denied that the Giants debated the pick or took phone calls offering trades. "We just sat and had a cup of coffee," he said of the un-George-Young-like wait to make the selection.[2]

In the second round, the Giants grabbed Louisiana State's six-foot-three, 285-pound defensive end Leonard Marshall. The only problem was that when Marshall showed up at the Giants facility a few days later, he weighed 295 pounds, 20 pounds heavier than anyone else on the roster. Parcells immediately levied fines on the rookie: twenty-five dollars per pound per day for every pound above 285. The morning after Marshall's first weigh-in, he had dropped six pounds. By the fourth day after his initial weigh-in, Marshall was back at 285. Days later, Parcells proclaimed him the best defensive end coming out of college. Raiders owner Al Davis went further, saying Marshall was the steal of the draft.

The Giants had fifteen picks spread across the draft's twelve rounds. They targeted a need at tight end and selected Nebraska's Jamie Williams in the third round and LSU's Malcolm Scott in the fifth. They tried to address offensive line needs, picking Iowa State tackle Karl Nelson in the third round and Texas–El Paso center Kevin Belcher in the sixth. In the seventh round, the Giants picked cornerback Perry Williams, who played under defensive coordinator Pete Carroll at North Carolina State. The eighth round brought Clemson's Andy Headen. Recruited to play quarterback in college, Headen lost the position battle there and moved to defensive back before settling in as a linebacker. In the ninth round, they landed Michigan kicker Ali Haji-Sheikh. The team also had the very last pick in the draft, a.k.a. Mr. Irrelevant. They used it on California running back John Tuggle.

When the draft picks and the veterans settled into the familiar training camp grounds at Pace University in Pleasantville, New York, one player was missing.

Lawrence Taylor was holding out. Two years into a six-year deal, Taylor wanted his contract renegotiated. He had received a $550,000 bonus when he signed as a rookie, and after back-to-back Defensive Player of the Year awards in his first two seasons, he was scheduled to make $120,000 in base pay in '83. He wanted the deal extended and more guaranteed money.

It bothered Taylor that fellow linebacker Tom Cousineau inked a $500,000-a-year deal with the Cleveland Browns. Taylor didn't believe Cousineau was the best linebacker on the Browns, let alone somebody who deserved to be the highest-paid linebacker in the NFL.

Along with touting Taylor's superb play, Jim Paliafito, who represented LT, pointed to the emergence of the United States Football League, a fledgling spring league, as one of the reasons the Giants should renegotiate. When Taylor signed his original deal, the USFL didn't exist. Now, it meant there was another league willing to pay top dollar for pro football players.

As a policy, the Giants didn't renegotiate contracts. So Parcells opened his first training camp with his best player more than five hundred miles away in Chapel Hill, North Carolina. In answering questions about Taylor's absence, Parcells said the player would be fined as much as $1,000 a day.

Two weeks into his holdout, LT made it to Giants practice. He stood on a hillside when the team practiced at a high school in Briarcliff Manor, New York. Seeing LT overlooking the scene, Harry Carson, the Giants' captain, got down on his hands and knees and pretended to snort the white lines on the practice field. Karl Nelson, the rookie offensive tackle, said Taylor laughed off the gesture.[3]

That afternoon, Carson and a group of defensive players came out wearing Taylor's No. 56 as their practice jersey.

A few days after LT stalked practice, he sat in section 104 of Giants Stadium, watching his team play the Jets in preseason. After an early Jets touchdown, fans chanted, "LT! LT!" Spectators kept peering over at the linebacker, looking at his reaction to plays. Taylor refused to sign autographs during the first half, but once halftime came, fans smothered the area looking for his signature and asking him when he would be back on the field.

Meanwhile, Marshall, the rookie second-round pick, received first-round-pick scrutiny. Marshall came into the league as a married man. He missed his wife and eight-year-old stepson. His weight kept fluctuating. He became a late-night regular at the local McDonald's near Pace. He was put on a diet of high-protein, low-calorie shakes for breakfast and lunch and then a low-fat dinner with reduced portion sizes and grapefruit juice to drink. In practice, he wasn't getting pressure on the quarterback, and his coaches kept yelling at him.

"It's like I have a 24-hour loudspeaker in my ear. I expect to wake up in my sleep and hear them yelling."[4]

The tight ends from the draft weren't working out either. Though he'd go on to play twelve years in the NFL, third-round pick, Jamie Williams, would be cut before the season started. Malcolm Scott would make the team, but both of the draftees were outplayed by an undrafted free agent. Teams skipped over Florida State's Zeke Mowatt because he mainly blocked in the Seminoles' offense. Mowatt caught only 24 passes in his final year at Florida State, and he didn't run long passing routes.

In drills, Mowatt did two reps for every one that the drafted tight ends completed. He was used to hard work. It started for him in childhood. As a boy growing up along the Peace River in Wauchula, Florida, Mowatt picked the oranges he could reach. He placed them in his father's bucket. He was one of five children, and he had to help the family make money.

His father assigned him a certain number of oranges he had to pick each day before calling it quits. As he grew up, Mowatt graduated to climbing a ladder and placing the citrus in his own over-the-shoulder sack. During his senior year of high school and for parts of his freshman year at Florida State, Mowatt ran the water run during the midnight-to-8:00 A.M. shift at the phosphate mine.

Parcells never bothered him. If the coach barked at him, Mowatt didn't hear it that way. "I didn't need him to stay on my back for me to go out there and play hard," he said.

On Thursday, August 11, the Giants arrived in Pittsburgh for a pre-season game with the Steelers. In the Steel City, Parcells received a phone call from Taylor. He wanted to end his twenty-day holdout. He didn't receive a new contract. He made his own call to come back to the team. Taylor rejoined the Giants three days later. The few hundred fans watching practice at Pace that Sunday cheered when No. 56 stepped on the field. Speaking to reporters after the workout, Taylor joked that he came back because the team had soul food on the menu for dinner that week. With regard to the contract, he said little except that everything would be worked out.

The Giants were three weeks away from the season opener, and Parcells had yet to finalize the other biggest story at training camp. Who would start at quarterback?

Phil Simms, the first pick of the George Young era, suffered injuries that had brought premature ends to his last three seasons. Scott Brunner filled in for him, winning a road play-off game, the franchise's first postseason win in more than twenty years. After Simms's preseason knee injury in '82, Brunner quarterbacked the team to a 4–5 mark during the strike-shortened season.

As the '83 preseason progressed, Parcells added Jeff Rutledge, the quarterback the Giants had traded for in '82, to the mix as a possible starter.

This was the second year in a row that Simms dealt with the constant stream of questions about who the starting quarterback would be. This predated twenty-four-hour New York sports talk radio, but speculation and hype had a home in the newspapers. Two local papers ran polls on the quarterback decision. Brunner became the people's pick.

"I'm just sick of the whole thing," Simms said after the team's penultimate preseason game. "And you can quote me on that."

All three quarterbacks would get time in the final exhibition game. Simms started. On the first play, the Miami Dolphins sacked him. He completed 10 of 17 passes for 76 yards and threw an interception. By the time he left the game, the 58,732 fans in attendance chanted, "We want Brunner!"

Brunner was sacked on his first play, too. He went 5 for 11 for 46 yards. His best play came when he stopped a touchdown by tackling a defender who had recovered his fumble.

Rutledge didn't fare any better, throwing for 84 yards after completing 8 of 16 passes. The crowd booed him, too.

Part of Simms's frustration stemmed from the phoniness of the situation.

At night, during the preseason, the coaches met to discuss position battles and the depth chart. The following mornings, assistant coaches wanting to see Simms start reported the reality to him. Parcells had Brunner pegged as the number-one quarterback.

"All quarterback battles are predetermined. That's the biggest fallacy and biggest crock that's ever hit the NFL. 'We're going to have a quarterback battle.' Everybody knows who the starter's going to be," Simms said.

A week before the season opener, Parcells spoke with Brunner in private. He told the University of Delaware product he had won the starting job.

Two mornings later, Parcells met with Simms at the team facility. Parcells told the onetime quarterback of the future that he was now a backup. When Parcells broke the news to Simms, he asked the former first-round pick if he had any questions. Simms responded by telling the head coach he disagreed with the decision.

"Do you want to be here?" Parcells asked.

"No. I'd prefer to be anywhere else but here."

Parcells told Simms he'd make that happen.

"I'm sure he wanted to get rid of me, too, just because I was a pain in the ass," Simms said.

Later that morning, reporters entered the locker room with questions for both quarterbacks.

Brunner said he was happy and added, "I don't know if it was ever a clear-cut choice."[5]

Simms, red faced with tear-filled eyes, avoided the media. After practice that afternoon, he spoke to reporters, expressing his disappointment and joking about being an overpaid backup. He said it was nice to read that a rumored deal to send him to Atlanta was nixed because the Giants wanted high value in return.

No quarterback's performance during the preseason had put him ahead of the others. During his two seasons as the Giants' defensive coordinator, Parcells hadn't seen much of Simms in game action.

"Hey, listen, I had only seen Brunner. Simms had been hurt two years in a row [that Parcells was on the Giants' staff]. Brunner had gotten us to the play-offs in '81. I had seen it. And you know, nobody had a strong conviction about this in our whole organization, but it was a mistake. I made the wrong decision."

Almost immediately after Parcells tapped Brunner as the starter, Simms saw the vibes shift. "They weren't going to wait very long to play me. I always had that feeling."

The Giants opened the season as four-point favorites against the Los Angeles Rams. They failed to meet those expectations, posting a disheartening 16–6 home loss. Parcells said he was embarrassed. After the game, he told his players to "keep your mouth shut" and "try to improve."[6]

The G-Men turned the ball over five times. The Rams sacked Brunner five times. The quarterback completed 16 of 35 passes for 183 yards. He tossed three interceptions and joked that the boos from the home crowd were actually cheers coming in the form of "Bru."

After the game, reporters gathered around Simms's new locker location. When he was named a backup, he moved his locker from next to

Brunner's to next to the showers. On his way out, Simms told reporters he'd only be talking football when he played, and he didn't know if that was going to happen again.

Lawrence Taylor, who picked up two personal foul penalties in the loss and at one point threw his helmet coming off the field, left the locker room without speaking to the media.

The next week, Parcells notched his first pro win when the Giants upset the Falcons 16–13 in Atlanta in overtime. In week 3, the Giants played at Dallas. Down 14–13 with 6:17 to play, Brunner threw an interception, which was returned 68 yards for a touchdown. The Giants fumbled the ensuing kickoff, which Dallas returned for another score. The Cowboys won 28–13, and the Giants also lost middle linebacker Harry Carson to a left knee injury. He would miss six games. This shifted LT into Carson's spot, and Big Blue started Byron Hunt in Taylor's outside linebacker role. Four games into Parcells's first season, the Giants evened their record at 2–2 with a 27–3 home win over the Packers. This was the best it would get.

As the Giants prepped for their week 6 matchup with the Philadelphia Eagles, Simms publicly asked to be dealt to another team. That Friday, Bob Ledbetter, the team's running backs coach, died. The forty-nine-year-old was in his first season with the team after spending the previous six years in the same role with the Jets. He suffered a stroke on September 24, his birthday, and remained in a hospital until his death. When the Giants played the Eagles that Sunday, the team held a moment of silence for Ledbetter before the national anthem.

Down 14–6 in the third quarter, Brunner threw an interception, and Simms replaced him. Simms completed his first four passes and set up a touchdown, pulling the Giants within one point of the Eagles. In the fourth quarter, Simms dropped back for his fifth attempt. The pass was intended for wide receiver John Mistler. As Simms followed through with his throwing motion, his right hand hit the helmet and face mask of six-foot-eight, 275-pound defensive end Dennis Harrison. The impact of the blow mangled Simms's thumb.

"I looked at the thumb once, and I didn't want to look again. As soon as it happened, I said, 'Damn it, there goes another season.'"

The next day, Simms was in a cast. He had suffered a dislocated compound fracture. For the fourth year in a row, injury brought an untimely end to Simms's season. By the time the 1984 season rolled around, Simms would have thrown just 13 passes since November of 1981. He became the punch line to jokes. Kids playing two-hand-touch street football in New Jersey mocked the oft-injured quarterback on bad throws. "Oops, I hit somebody's helmet," they'd say.

The Giants went winless in October. In the eighth game of the season, a Monday night showcase at the St. Louis Cardinals, the Giants started Jeff Rutledge at quarterback. The teams played a scoreless overtime period and ended the game knotted at 20. Taylor wanted out. "Bill [Parcells] had to talk me out of quitting after we could only tie the dog-ass Cardinals."[7]

LT started showing up late for practice. One day he was so late, Parcells called his home. "I don't want to waste my time with a bunch of losers," LT gave as his explanation.[8]

In a players-only meeting later in the season, Taylor expressed his frustration to his teammates, ripping into them for their lazy effort.

Parcells saw the swirling mess, the impact of the losses. The injuries mounted, and division grew within the team and the organization.

"Once you get losing, it's back to the same thing that existed back in the late '70s. It doesn't take long to go back," he said. "Public opinion isn't good and rightfully so. And quite frankly, your confidence level is shaken."

Charles Parcells, the coach's father, underwent double-bypass surgery during that winless October. Soon after the surgery, Ida Parcells, Bill's mother, began feeling a sharp pain in her back. It became so intense she couldn't get out of bed one morning. The first doctor to evaluate her sent Ida to the hospital for testing. The results showed malignant bone cancer. Ida was given a few weeks to live.

In early December, two days after the Giants' tenth loss, Lawrence Taylor sat down to lunch with Donald Trump. The real estate magnate had recently purchased the USFL's New Jersey Generals. He wanted to gauge Taylor's interest in signing with the upstart league.

While LT flirted with Trump, Giants general manager George Young contemplated a coaching change. He called Howard Schnellenberger, the head coach at the University of Miami. Young had served as Schnellenberger's offensive line coach with the Baltimore Colts in 1973 and for part of the '74 season.

After the conversation ended with Young, Schnellenberger called his agent, Robert Fraley, a former Alabama quarterback who died in a plane crash with his client, golfer Payne Stewart, in 1999. When Schnellenberger spoke to him, Fraley was already in the New York City area, attempting to strike a deal with Trump for Schnellenberger to coach the Generals. Once Fraley heard about the Giants' interest in Schnellenberger, the agent knew he had to let one of his clients know. That client was Bill Parcells.

Parcells resented Young's covert maneuvering. The Giants coach called one of his mentors, the Raiders' Al Davis, the NFL's renegade owner. Davis and Parcells met when Parcells played for Davis in a college all-star game in 1964.

Parcells said Davis gave him ownership's perspective. "You have to be able to put yourself in the position of the owners and what they're looking at. And what they're seeing and why things are the way they are—that's why you're in jeopardy," Parcells said, recalling what Davis told him in the conversation.

Before the phone call ended, Davis closed the conversation, telling Parcells he'd handle the situation. Davis gave the scoop to Jimmy "the Greek" Snyder, a lead analyst on CBS's *The NFL Today*. Years before ten hours of Sunday pregame coverage spread itself across four TV networks, *The NFL Today* was the leading program for football information. Snyder took to the airwaves outing the Giants' talks with Schnellenberger, who was getting Miami ready to play Nebraska for the national championship. Snyder also backed the idea of giving Parcells another year on the job.

The Giants lost 17–12 to Seattle that Sunday. A potential game-winning touchdown pass was called back on a holding penalty. Young refused to talk to the media about Snyder's on-air comments. That week, Parcells and Young met to discuss his status. Parcells asked if he would be back in 1984. Young said that discussion would have to wait until after the season.

On Wednesday of that week, LT accepted a $1 million interest-free loan from Donald Trump. The money was part of a deal that put Taylor in a personal services agreement with Trump and called for the linebacker to play for the New Jersey Generals in 1988, after his Giants contract expired. Excluding the $1 million loan, the deal was worth $2.7 million over four years. The personal services aspect called for Taylor to immediately start performing promotional tasks for Trump's real estate operations.

"There was no way that my father was going to allow him to walk out the door and go play for somebody else," said John Mara, who at the time was a twenty-nine-year-old attorney at Shea & Gould, the New York City law firm representing Trump.

The Giants renegotiated LT's deal within a month. The organization more than tripled his base salary for the next season, increasing it from $190,000 to $650,000. The Giants added years to the contract and escalating base pay, which would reach $1 million in 1988. The franchise also added its own $1 million interest-free loan. In order to buy out his contract with Trump, LT gave back the original $1 million loan, and Trump was paid $750,000 over the next five years.

While LT was agreeing to a deal with Trump to leave the Giants, Parcells had to get ready for the Washington Redskins and make funeral arrangements for his mother. Ida Parcells died in mid-December. Charles Parcells, Bill's father, could not attend the funeral. He stayed in the hospital, still recovering from the bypass surgery.

The day after Bill attended services for his mother, the Giants lost the season finale in Washington. Parcells's first season as an NFL head coach had come to an end. His team posted a dismal 3–12–1 record.

Big Blue finished the year with a league-high twenty-five players on injured reserve. Brunner, Parcells's pick as the number-one quarterback, finished the season at number two on the depth chart. He threw 22 interceptions and nine touchdowns in 13 games. Overall, the team tallied 58 turnovers. The Giants handed the ball over to their opponents more than three and a half times a game. They racked up 113 penalties, which accounted for 1,020 lost yards. The defense tailed off, too, giving up 21.7 points per game, dropping the G-Men from eighth in the league in '82 to sixteenth.

Young had gone back to speak to Schnellenberger again. Schnellenberger's deal with Trump and Generals never materialized, but Young couldn't get Schnellenberger to commit to coaching the Giants in '84.

"I remember George talking to him and then coming back to us," John Mara said.

"I can't get him this year, but I can get him next year. So let's give Parcells one more year," Young told ownership.

"Had Schnellenberger said yes, Parcells would've been fired at the end of the '83 season, something I know Bill was bitter about for years to come," Mara said.

A few weeks after the season, Parcells knew he would at least be the head coach at the start of the next season. The overtures to Schnellenberger irritated him. At the same time, he knew he did a miserable job that first year. He knew he had to change.

When Parcells evaluated his own performance, he saw he wasn't the head coach he wanted to be. He was friendly with players. As a coordinator, a cozy relationship with players didn't hurt him. As a head coach, it did. He saw poor habits and let them slide. Veterans players, who by virtue of their experience were role models, weren't held accountable.

"I just don't think I was assertive enough, demanding enough."

In January, linebackers coach Bill Belichick was offered a position with the Minnesota Vikings. Belichick visited Minnesota, where Les Steckel had become the head coach and Floyd Reese was set to serve as the defensive coordinator. Belichick discussed the opportunity with Parcells. The looming backdrop to a conversation like this one was the lack of security with the Giants. Sure, Parcells and his staff would start 1984, but that was the only guarantee. There were no reassurances that they would be with the Giants for the long term.

"Bill did not discourage me from taking the job," Belichick said. "I decided to stay and finish what I came to New York for with Coach Perkins—to produce a winner in New York. The deck appeared to be stacked against us, but I was committed to Bill, Ernie [Adams], and the organization to help put a good team together."

In February of '84, Charles Parcells, who had been at Bill's side during that first practice with the Giants, died. He never did leave the hospital, dying six weeks after his wife. Charles had dealt with complications after the bypass surgery. Bill believes an infection his father suffered stemmed from a blood transfusion during the bypass.[9]

No doubt, it was painful for Parcells to lose both parents. Asked years later about the impact of the losses amid an awful football season, Parcells offered four words: "That's a separate issue."

Asked if the deaths added more stress to a life that already had plenty of it coming from the football side, Parcells backed away from that idea, too.

"It's just what it was at the time. You have to either go forward and do what you can about it, or give in to it and develop that poor-me syndrome and 'why did this happen to me?' and allow it to invade your professional life as well. I tried not to do that."

Today, Parcells understands George Young's rationale in looking to make a change at head coach. Going 3–12–1 looked like a mistake, and a fix was needed. It turned out Parcells was the fix. The experiences of '83 forever defined Parcells as a head coach. It kick-started a transformation that began even before Parcells knew he would be retained.

A few days into the off-season, Parcells spotted Phil Simms working out in the weight room. The coach stopped what he was doing to speak to the quarterback.

"You know, Simms, I don't know if I'm going to survive this, but if I survive it, we're going to do things my way now."

PART

Identity

THREE

11

GANGSTER

The three letters, printed on official New York Giants stationery, sat on the desk of a state superior court judge in Passaic County, New Jersey.

Vincent Ravo, an associate of the Genovese crime family, had pleaded guilty to weapons charges, and three-fourths of the Giants' starting linebackers had reached out to the judge as character references for the mobster. Brad Van Pelt, Brian Kelley, and Lawrence Taylor asked the judge to show leniency at sentencing.

Ravo managed The Bench, a go-go bar on Paterson Plank Road in Carlstadt, New Jersey, about a mile from Giants Stadium.

The Bench had it all. It was a typical mid-1980s den of debauchery; great burgers, great chicken wings, legal nudity, pay-for sex, and any other vice of the era. Its closeness to the stadium made it an easy stop for Giants players.

"Listen, certain players were drawn to certain things. If you went to the Bench to hang out, watch, and eat, that's what you did. If there was a seedier side to it, the guys who were attracted to that went to that," said Carl Banks, a rookie outside linebacker in '84.

Brian Kelley had become close to Ravo—close enough that Ravo was godfather to one of Kelley's daughters. By the time Kelley's letter made it to the judge in April 1984, the Giants had already traded him to the San Diego Chargers. He would never play another down of pro football. After Kelley's retirement, Ravo helped Kelley arrange a deal to buy an ownership interest in the Lodi Charcoal Pit on Route 17, about six miles from the

Giants' facility. Kelley renovated the place and reopened it as Satin Dolls, the place viewers of the HBO series *The Sopranos* know as the Bada Bing! strip club. Each week in real life, Kelley slid $500 cash into an envelope. He placed it under the bar for Ravo. It was the mobster's consulting fee.

Giants general manager George Young told authorities the organization had nothing to do with the letters to the judge. The communications from the linebackers were not approved by the team.

Giants officials and NFL security personnel had already told these players to stay away from Ravo. Beyond the weapons charge, Ravo had also been arrested for drug offenses, larceny, stolen property, assault, kidnapping, rape, and homicide, according to the New Jersey State Commission of Investigation.

LT said Ravo's girlfriend, Nicolena Santoro, wrote the letter for him. After the existence of the letter became public, Bill Parcells asked Taylor to stay out of The Bench. Furthermore, Young and Parcells told Taylor to cut ties with Ravo because of Ravo's connection to organized crime. The director of NFL security, Warren R. Welsh, spoke to Taylor and echoed the Giants' message.

Taylor admitted Giants and NFL officials spoke to him about spending too much time at The Bench. He said the team didn't like the fact that it was a go-go bar, but LT denied that Parcells, or anyone else, ever told him to specifically stay away from Ravo.

"He thinks he's Dick Tracy," LT said of Parcells. "He thinks he knows everything about everything and simply that he felt that The Bench was a place where undesirables hung out, okay," he continued while testifying before the New Jersey State Commission of Investigation in 1992.

The linebacker considered Ravo a friend, and he wasn't going to back away from the friendship. In between Taylor signing with Donald Trump and renegotiating with the Giants, he and Ravo went to the Bahamas together. "We just went there to fool around," said Ravo, who was sentenced to three years in prison but only served ten months.[1]

At Ravo's request, the NFL star would do appearances for gangsters. LT showed up at a child's birthday party at the home of Alan "Little Al"

Grecco, a member of the Genovese family and the son-in-law of Genovese capo Louis "Streaky" Gatto. LT also made an appearance at a furniture store owned by Angelo "the Horn" Prisco, another capo in the Genovese
family and Ravo's boss in the criminal outfit.

While Taylor admitted hearing the warnings to stay away from The
Bench, he acted as far in the opposite direction as he could. When the name
changed to 1st and 10, Taylor bought an ownership interest in the place.

Being seen with mobsters and using drugs weren't the only acts in LT's
sideshow. During the Giants' 1983 swoon, Taylor faced a paternity and
child support lawsuit.

Kathy Louise Davis gave birth to Whitney Taylor Davis on March 28,
1980. LT was the father—something he denied at first. Then he admitted
to it during legal proceedings that would take four years to settle.

The Giants had already taken out a $2 million life insurance policy on
Taylor. In March after his rookie year, Taylor, driving with a buddy and a
six-pack of beer in the car, hit a patch of ice after leaving a banquet in North
Carolina. The car spun off the road and hit a tree. No reports of this showed
up in the news, but LT's reckless off-field behavior kept Giants owner Wellington Mara up at night.

"You never knew what was going to happen with him," said John Mara.
"The thing about Lawrence was he had such an endearing personality, too.
My father loved him. He was funny. He played so hard and he practiced
hard that you kind of overlooked a lot of the other things. We tried to help
him on any number of occasions."

The Giants had a drug problem. It was part of the unraveling of a team that
went 3–12–1. Bill Parcells knew this. He knew something had to be done
about it. Exactly what he could do? He'd have to figure that out. "The rules
were not the way they are now. There was not a standard protocol. You
were kind of left on your own."

This heightened use of cocaine was new territory for everyone in the
league. NFL teams had dealt with players drinking alcohol and smoking
marijuana. Cocaine, that was different. As the drug became more readily

available throughout the country, its price dropped, and as a natural out-come, the abuse of it rose. What the Giants faced wasn't all that different from other NFL teams during the early to mid-1980s.

"I'll make a blanket statement without specificity: they all had their issues," defensive end George Martin said about league-wide drug prob-lems.

Parcells attacked the issue by educating himself. During the off-season owners' meeting in Palm Springs, California, he visited the Betty Ford Center. When he returned to New Jersey, he registered as an outpatient in the drug addiction treatment center at Fair Oaks Hospital in Summit.[2] He befriended the center's clinical director at Fair Oaks, Dr. Jane Jones. "She was the best," Parcells said.

She advised Parcells on how to approach players he suspected were abusing drugs. Her counsel left the coach with some tools to address the situation.

"The first thing you don't want to do is be an enabler. You don't want to be sympathetic, too. In the respect that 'Hey, I'm going to try to do what's good for you.' That doesn't work with addicted people. You have to kind of bust their chops. You have to do things to get their attention. Threatening their livelihood can be one of those."

Parcells utilized other options besides cutting a player loose. He devised a multistep plan. If he suspected a player of abusing drugs, that player would be tested. If the test came back positive, the team, with the backing of ownership and the front office, would provide the player with the rehabilitation needed to fight addiction.

The problem with this plan was that neither Parcells nor the Giants had any right to test players. The policy on drug testing had not been ironed out in the collective bargaining agreement between the players' union and the league.

To implement this, Parcells needed buy-in from his team. He met with Martin, the Giants' rep for the players' union.

Martin agreed with Parcells that a solution was needed. Even though what Parcells proposed was outside the collective bargaining agreement,

Martin knew something had to be done. He believed the NFL as a whole moved too slowly on the drug issue.

"We were all pretty unsophisticated as to what was going on," Martin said.

Parcells shared the entire outline of the plan with Martin. The coach knew if Martin supported the approach, it put the veteran defensive end in a tough spot. It could leave the union members Martin was responsible for representing with the impression that the guy who was supposed to be looking out for them had sided with management's interests. "I wasn't there to appease the union. You're there for a higher calling."

Martin had built a reserve of leadership equity. He was the team chapel leader. He spearheaded the creation of a program for his teammates to complete their college degrees at Fairleigh Dickinson University. He saw drugs as an impediment to winning. He viewed Parcells's plan as an opportunity to help players if they had a problem.

"George is a good person. He wanted to do the right thing," Parcells said.

If a player had a drug problem, it was kept confidential. Those players that could be helped received it, and there were cases in which the help that was offered couldn't make a difference.

Malcolm Scott had served as a second-string tight end in his rookie year in '83. In May of '84, the fifth-round pick from LSU was arrested in a New Orleans hotel room with Jerry Reese, a teammate from high school, not the current Giants general manager. Reese called the police because he thought someone was trying to break in the room. When police arrived, they found a small amount of cocaine and marijuana. The case against Scott fell apart because of insufficient evidence. No police report ever made it to the district attorney. A little more than two months after the incident, the Giants cut Scott for "inability to adhere to team and club policies," said general manager George Young.[3]

In August 2014, the Web site for *The New Orleans Advocate* posted a video, which is no longer available online. In it, Scott claimed to be homeless, living under the Pontchartrain Expressway in New Orleans. He spoke about getting into drugs in college at LSU. In February 2015, Scott was arrested for allegedly punching, kicking, and hitting a man in the face with a cinder block in a dispute over a found wallet.

When the Giants tested LT for drugs, the urine came back clean. He found teammates to provide it. Running back Butch Woolfolk didn't drink, smoke, or do drugs. LT asked Woolfolk to meet him in the bathroom, where the running back would provide the clean urine sample. LT put the urine in a pill bottle. When it came time for this test, LT shoved it in his jockstrap. He went in the bathroom stall and poured the clean urine into the test cup.

"People would write that we looked the other way. We never looked the other way. He managed to deceive us back then as he freely admitted later on, but they were always trying to get him straightened out," Mara said. "There was only so much that could be done."

Soon enough, LT wouldn't even be able to deceive himself.

12

THE BIRTH OF "PARCELLS GUYS"

The Giants listed a league-high twenty-five players on injured reserve by the time Bill Parcells's dismal first season came to an end. That was more than half an NFL roster back then.

He needed to hire a strength-and-conditioning coach. The Giants didn't have one. Offensive line coach Tom Bresnahan and defensive line coach Lamar Leachman sort of did the job. These coaches oversaw the workouts, but they didn't have or develop weight lifting programs. They lifted weights or rode the stationary bike while players worked out.

Parcells had interviewed three candidates for the position when Indiana University basketball coach Bob Knight recommended Mississippi's Johnny Parker. Parker had become the first strength-and-conditioning coach in the Big Ten Conference when he started with the Hoosiers in 1979. Along the way, Parker had also worked with Steve Sloan, with whom Parcells served as an assistant coach at Vanderbilt and Texas Tech.

During the interview, Parcells opened up to Parker about where he lost the team during his first season.

"Last year, when I got this job, I thought that I could depend on guys that I coached. And I was wrong. Those guys screwed me. I thought I could trust them, and they screwed me. I'm getting rid of those guys."

Parcells offered a similar message to the one he gave Phil Simms when the off-season had just started.

"Now if they get me this year, it won't be because I didn't do it my way.

Last year, I tried to be *the head coach*. This year, I'm going to be Bill Parcells. That ain't good enough, then it's just not good enough."

Parker took a look at his new facility. It was about 750 square feet of shared space under Giants Stadium. Covered in Astroturf, it was called the Turf Room. It was the team's version of an elementary school's multipurpose room. The Giants stored equipment in there and served lunch there. Sometimes the room hosted light practices.

"There were pizza boxes and just stuff scattered all over," Parker said.

Offensive coordinator Ron Erhardt had a net set up for himself. During lunch, he practiced his golf swing, hitting balls into it.

After seeing the conditions, Parker weighed the weights the players used. Turns out the forty-five-pound plates weighed anywhere from thirty-five to fifty-four pounds. The rickety squat rack shook when anyone touched it, making it a gamble to rerack the barbell after completing a set.

"I mean, it was bad. It was as bad as you can get, let's just put it that way."

Parker had some hesitation in going to work for a coach on the hot seat. He checked with football people he trusted. They told him Parcells would make it and that was good enough for Parker.

His first call after accepting the post was to Leonard Marshall. Parker was Marshall's strength-and-conditioning coach during Parker's brief stint at LSU. Parker planned to be rigorous with these players, but to be effective, he needed their commitment and willingness to go through the pain it takes to become stronger.

"Leonard, you know I only know one way to do things, and that's hard," Parker said to him over the phone. "These guys might run me back to Mississippi the first day. But if I've got one guy that'll do what I ask him to do, then maybe I can get some more."

"I'll do anything you want me to do," Marshall said, pledging his commitment to Parker's program.

On Parker's second day, Simms showed up ready to lift. "Hey, I want to start training with you."

Parker didn't have a program for quarterbacks. He told Simms to come back the next day. He'd have one then. Simms balked. The quarterback began lifting with the same program as his offensive linemen, doing the same exercises but using less weight than the big guys.

After four straight years of season-ending injuries, Simms would get another chance to lead the Giants in '84. During the off-season, the G-Men traded Scott Brunner to the Denver Broncos for a fourth-round pick in the upcoming draft.

When he looks back at the thumb injury from '83, Simms thinks getting hurt might have saved his Giants career. "If I'd stayed the starting quarterback and we'd have flip-flopped back and forth . . . who knows what would've happened? They might have shipped my butt out, too."

The Giants organization still believed in him. They saw the toughness he displayed. They watched him work out with the linemen. But one question remained.

"Physically, mentally, the way he'd practice, we knew he had what it took," said Chris Mara. "The whole thing was going to be the injury thing. Could he overcome those? Is he a china doll?"

In Bill Parcells's first game as the Giants' defensive coordinator, the team trailed the Eagles 24–3 late in the fourth quarter. Parcells stood on the sidelines eyeing the field. He turned toward the bench and called over to Carl Barisich, a Princeton-educated defensive lineman who was on his fourth team in nine seasons. Parcells told him to get in the game. With the outcome determined, this was a meaningless late-game substitution, but Barisich had something to say before taking the field.

"Coach, do you want me to win the game or just tie it up?"

Parcells turned his attention away from the field. He locked his eyes on Barisich and cracked up laughing.

Parcells came to the Giants with a reservoir of Jersey sarcasm. He was serious about his work, but he could joke around, too.

"Life is too short to walk around with your teeth gritted," he said at his first press conference as the team's head coach. "Most of you know I like to crack a joke now and then."

In '83, the players enjoyed a relaxed training camp atmosphere. Parcells delegated responsibilities to assistant coaches. He figured he could rely on the men he had coached on defense to lead the team during the season. The approach backfired. The team stunk, and he'd almost lost his job.

"Everything was falling apart for the team, and he had to make a lot of changes," said nose tackle Jim Burt. "It was bad. It was a cesspool of people."

By the nature of their behavior, some veterans had a bad influence on younger players. The partying, the carousing, the boozing, the drugs, that couldn't be tolerated, especially when it was coupled with lazy practice habits and a revival of the Giants' losing mentality. These players no longer fit.

"Some of those had to go," Parcells said. "But they weren't bad guys. They enjoyed themselves and had certain things they did."

Parcells was close with veteran linebackers Brian Kelley and Brad Van Pelt. He had been their coordinator, but they were viewed as having introduced Taylor to the after-hours life of the NFL, drinking and partying past team curfew. "Brad and Brian put me through their program their way," Taylor said.[1]

Van Pelt had all-star looks to match his play. The ladies loved him, and he loved them back. In practice though, he was not a worker. Like Kelley, he was traded away before the start of the '84 season. These two had been Giants mainstays. Paired with Taylor and Harry Carson, the foursome posed with a John Deere bulldozer for a poster that dubbed the quartet "The Crunch Bunch."

Was it hard for Parcells to jettison players who had been seen as stalwarts?

"No."

The amiable Bill Parcells had been buried with the 3–12–1 season.

"His demeanor became a lot more serious, a lot more unfriendly, even toward me and everybody else that was around back then. I'd always considered him, prior to that, to be an affable, personable guy. That was not the case starting in '84," John Mara said. "That's when things started to take off for us."

On the first day of training camp in '84, Parcells gathered the team after practice. He had delivered similar messages to Phil Simms and Johnny

Parker in the off-season. Now, he had his players and coaches encircling him on the field under the July sun.

"They're going to fire my ass if we don't win," he told them. "I'm going to be honest with you, I'm going to make some decisions, but I need to know that the guys that are going to be on this roster are going to be my guys. Whoever's going to make this team, they're going to be willing to fight for me as hard as I'm going to fight for you. Whoever's going to make this team. And I don't know who it is. You know, you're going to be my guys. And I need you to be my guys no matter what happens."

It wasn't rah-rah motivation. It wasn't intended to be that. It was a larger pronouncement of who Parcells was going to be as a head coach. It was an admission that he wasn't himself as a head coach in '83. Without speaking specifically to all the rumors about his job security, he let the players know what they had heard was true. Wrapped in words about fighting, Parcells let his vulnerability show, and he made a promise to the men around him. If it was possible to point to one moment in time as the birth of "Parcells guys," this was it. The men who were willing to fight the fight, anytime, anywhere, they would make the team. He'd give all he could give to those guys.

"It was the pact you made so you never disappoint each other," said outside linebacker Carl Banks, who was a rookie at the time. "He never took a day off. Parcells didn't. He never took anything for granted because from that moment on he meant what he said. Other guys knew that."

The decisions Parcells spoke about transformed the roster. The Giants who took the field to open the '84 season weren't the same Giants. That's not a cliché. Parcells, in conjunction with George Young, got rid of twenty-one players from the '83 team, turning over 43 percent of the roster in one off-season.

"We're going to try to get the losing players and the players with losing attitudes out of here and try to integrate younger and hungrier players in here," Parcells said.

13

GATORADE AND AN EXORCISM

Jim Burt and Brad Benson bought into Johnny Parker's off-season strength-and-conditioning program.

One afternoon, after a workout, the early adopters walked into the locker room and spotted some poor sap in the training room being looked at by medical staffers. The two veterans passed by on the way to their lockers. Burt looked over at Benson and said, "This guy isn't going to last."

Benson, the offensive lineman plucked out of a middle school teaching gig in Altoona, Pennsylvania, and Burt, the undrafted nose tackle from Miami, knew what a free agent looked like. They saw it on the six-foot-four frame sprawled across a training room table.

"He looked beat up. He *was* beat up," Burt said.

Benson and Burt ate dinner at the facility and walked out to their cars that evening. In the parking lot, they spotted the guy from the training room. He stood next to a car, a new car, a Jaguar.

"Who is that guy?" they asked each other.

It was Carl Banks, the Giants' number-one draft pick and the number-three overall pick in 1984. Banks had tweaked something with his groin when Burt and Benson first saw him. The rookie had been invited to a minicamp of fellow first-year players and a spattering of nonstarting veterans.

In practices, Parcells and special teams coach Romeo Crennel played good cop, bad cop with Banks as they overworked the rookie.

"If it was a five-minute drill, I had to go all five minutes running bags, or whatever, until the whistle blew," Banks said.

Everybody else caught a break by getting back in line and waiting for their turns. Not Banks. He kept working as the soundtrack of Parcells barking at him played in his ear.

"Romeo would try to be the soothsayer. He [Parcells] wouldn't let up. I don't know if he wanted to try to break me or not. My body broke down a little bit. But I never broke down. It just kind of increased my determination."

Banks responded by fighting. A lot. He'd snap and shove his teammates. The shoves became punches, and fists flew between him and offensive tackle Karl Nelson. If the plan had been to push Banks over the edge, it wouldn't work. Banks was "the Killer."

That was his nickname. He got it from digging ditches at Gracelawn Cemetery on Saginaw Street in Flint, Michigan, where he grew up the middle of three sons. His father was a corrections officer, and his mother worked in the post office. Starting in his junior year of high school, Banks worked for Pete Buterakos at the cemetery.

"I dug graves. I worked the backhoe. I cut grass. I did all that."

Buterakos put Banks to work alongside ex-convicts who were trying to rehabilitate their lives. As he became a star at Michigan State, Banks continued to labor at the cemetery. He felt pride earning his way up to a $5.25-per-hour wage.

"That work ethic shaped the way I would approach sports," he said.

With the Giants, Banks was the new guy, an outsider, the team's number-one pick who broke up the "Crunch Bunch." By the time he was drafted, Brian Kelley had been traded. The same day Banks signed his contract, the Giants dealt Brad Van Pelt to the Minnesota Vikings for running back Tony Galbreath.

When Banks introduced himself to Lawrence Taylor and Harry Carson, the veterans had little time for the newbie.

"What the hell are you going to do to get on the field?" Carson asked.

Frustrated—as he was during various patches of his career—Carson walked out of training camp for a few days. Parcells told reporters Carson should head to a library and look up the definition of *leadership*.

LT shot back at his coach, defending Carson and, without saying it directly, questioning Banks's ability.

"Harry Carson has more leadership and respect by more players than anybody in the league. While he's looking up the word leadership, maybe management should look up the word honesty.

"You can't get rid of a Brad Van Pelt, a Brian Kelley . . . and have a great defense."[1]

Banks didn't mind the comments. "I was a little different. I was a different type of guy. I was a different type of player. But I fit what they wanted."

Carson wasn't the only veteran to leave camp in '84. Wide receiver Earnest Gray left for a stint. During that abysmal '83 season, Gray had 78 receptions for 1,139 yards. Cornerback Mark Haynes left and came back less than a week later. He was coming off his second consecutive Pro Bowl year. Both Gray and Haynes wanted more money, but the Giants didn't budge.

If veterans had gripes with management, it wouldn't be the only spot where they had to battle. Training camp went from a relaxed atmosphere in '83 to a battery of physical and mental tests.

"It seemed like it went on for five years. And it was beating the hell out of each other every day. But you could tell Parcells—there was a sense of desperation. Parcells was looking for his guys, as he always used to call them. And he was testing everybody," said rookie offensive lineman Conrad Goode.

Goode grew up in the Midwest. He played college ball at Missouri. He played for coaches who coached him up. They built and reinforced his confidence, and in return, Goode would do anything for those men. But he wasn't in the Midwest anymore. This was Jersey.

"Hey, Goode, what are you gonna do today?" he'd hear Parcells jabbing at him. "You know, are you gonna do anything? Are you gonna—are you gonna make any blocks? I got someone else on the bus coming in next week, if you don't make any blocks today."

Goode didn't know what to make of it. *Is he kidding?* he wondered. The fourth-round draft pick never felt safe. He never felt like he secured a spot on the roster. This was the atmosphere of competition Parcells cultivated.

"He coached from a perspective of it was almost, I don't want to say a bully, but he challenged you as a man, almost on a day-to-day basis."

Banks and Goode were part of a draft class that included offensive lineman William Roberts, whom the Giants traded up to select at the end of the first round. Big Blue picked West Virginia quarterback Jeff Hostetler in the third round and Northwestern State (Louisiana) inside linebacker Gary Reasons in the fourth round. Hostetler and Reasons tallied the highest scores on that year's Wonderlic aptitude test.

Giants scouts counted on Reasons's smarts. They figured what he lacked in athletic ability, he would make up for with his brain. "He was so smart he could anticipate what the offense was doing," said Chris Mara. "I don't care if it was thirty years ago or it's now. You need those type of guys to win."

Big Blue added Pacific wide receiver Lionel Manuel in the seventh round. They brought in free agent offensive lineman Chris Godfrey. He played his college ball at the University of Michigan. In 1980, the Washington Redskins cut Godfrey, who had been playing on the defensive line. Godfrey had brief stints with the Jets and Packers but was out of the NFL before the 1981 season. Back home in Michigan, Godfrey couldn't find work. The country was in the midst of a recession, one that saw the unemployment rate rise to a startling 9.7 percent. Godfrey joined other jobless men and women standing in a Detroit unemployment line. He didn't stay there too long because the USFL's Michigan Panthers reached out to him. He switched from the defensive side of the ball and became a guard. He came to the Giants fresh off a nineteen-game USFL season that had ended in a triple-overtime play-off game a few weeks before training camp started at Pace University.

At wide receiver, the Giants picked up Kansas's Bobby Johnson as a free agent as well as Phil McConkey, who was back again for another try at making it in the NFL.

The Giants generously listed McConkey at five foot ten and 170 pounds. The height placed him tied for second shortest on the team, and if the 170 pounds was accurate, that made him as light as Ali Haji-Sheikh, the place-kicker.

McConkey grew up in Buffalo, New York, with fantasies of playing pro football. He dived into snowbanks, he leaped across the family couch, pre-tending to be Bills quarterback Jack Kemp lofting a pass to Elbert "Golden Wheels" Dubenion. He played street football, putting spin moves on parked cars and dreaming of catching a touchdown pass in the Super Bowl.

His father, a vice cop in the city, and his mother, who worked with in-mates at a juvenile detention center, put money aside so their altar boy son could attend the local Catholic grammar school. At eighty-two pounds, playing for the West Side Bills in the youth league Tyro Football Confer-ence, McConkey heard the conversations about how he was too small.

He arrived at Canisius High School, a private Jesuit institution, weigh-ing 125 pounds. Coaches again thought he was too small to play. He beefed up to 145 pounds by his senior year and garnered all-state honors. But college football powerhouses didn't salivate over puny players like him. He chose to go to the U.S. Naval Academy. The transition from western New York to Annapolis, Maryland, proved challenging for McConkey. He cried every night.

"I hated it so much. I hated the regimentation, the loneliness, the dif-ficulty of the classwork. I missed Buffalo, my friends, the neighborhood."[2]

But he did make the adjustment in football. He starred for the program, returning kicks and playing receiver. He became a team captain in 1978. Overall, he caught 67 passes for 1,278 yards to go with 13 touchdown recep-tions. He capped off his career in the first Holiday Bowl. Down 16–3 in the third quarter versus Brigham Young University and quarterback Jim McMahon, the Midshipmen mounted a comeback, sealing the game on a 65-yard McConkey touchdown catch with 11:38 to play in the fourth. McConkey took home the game's offensive MVP award.

After graduation, he didn't consider the NFL. He owed the navy five years. He planned to serve the country for twenty. He became a commissioned officer. He went to flight school in Pensacola, Florida. He flew the CH-46 Sea Knight, a helicopter that transported supplies and could carry up to twenty troops. During one winter, he headed to Maine for prisoner of war training. While on tour in the Mediterranean, McConkey kept getting seasick aboard the USS *Concord*. The sickness had started when he was an underclassman at the academy. McConkey and everybody around him thought over time his body would adjust. That never happened. It became troublesome enough that the navy sent McConkey home from the Mediterranean. He underwent a battery of medical tests that showed nothing conclusive. One thing was clear: not being able to be at sea put a ceiling on a sailor's career.

McConkey started putting together his résumé. At home during Christmas leave, staring down the limits of his future in the navy, McConkey's father suggested he give football a try. He had been removed from the game for four years. McConkey thought his father was nuts, but McConkey's mother and his good friend, former Navy quarterback Kit McCulley, helped convince him to give it a try.

While stationed in Norfolk, Virginia, in the winter of 1983, McConkey began to train for football. He focused on his speed. During his lunch hour, he ran 40-yard sprints. He'd run one, rest for fifteen seconds, and run another until he completed four sprints. Then he rested for five minutes and started another set of four. He completed four sets of four sprints each day.

Two of the assistant coaches he had at Navy, Tom Bresnahan and Len Fontes, had become assistant coaches for Parcells with the Giants. Plus, longtime Navy assistant coach and scout Steve Belichick was the father of Giants assistant Bill Belichick. McConkey asked these men to help get him a tryout with the team. He also wrote personal letters to the Giants and his hometown Bills asking for a shot.

In February of '83, McConkey took a trip to visit McCulley, his former teammate, who was stationed in Pensacola, Florida. He wanted McCulley to time his 40-yard dash. They used a four-foot-long fold-out ruler and black spray paint to create a track in the street. They marked each yard with a dash of paint.

McConkey stretched out and moved to the starting line. He stood behind the line for a moment and took off. McCulley started the digital stopwatch with a tap of his forefinger. He tapped it again as McConkey blew past the finish line. McConkey stopped himself and walked back toward the finish. McCulley turned the stopwatch toward McConkey to show him the time: 4.48 seconds. McConkey rejoiced. That's NFL speed. He ran two more sprints to make sure the original time wasn't an anomaly. He clocked a 4.53 and 4.49. Now, he knew if a team gave him the opportunity, he had a real chance to make it.

After the draft in '83, twenty-six-year-old McConkey received his invite to the rookie minicamp for the Giants. Before he arrived in New Jersey, he found inspiration in a movie theater, watching *Flashdance,* the classic '80s film about a woman who works a day job as a welder in a Pittsburgh steel mill and dances in a go-go bar at night, all in an effort to live her dream of breaking into a ballet company. "She burned to make it as a dancer, and I knew exactly how she felt."[3]

McConkey grabbed attention early on in '83. *The Star-Ledger* wrote about him making spectacular catches in practice. A runt free agent had to find ways to get attention. He hustled everywhere. During breaks, he sprinted to the water, and coaches noticed.

"I had that free-agent mentality, that feeling that no matter how hot I was or how tired or sore, I had to keep pushing myself," he said.[4]

McConkey hung on throughout the preseason. A few days before the Giants' final exhibition game, the navy informed McConkey he would not be discharged early. He owed the service five years after graduation, and he was going to have to finish that final year. The Giants cut him and put him on a rarely used military-reserve list. McConkey's final naval assignment sent him back to Pensacola to teach servicemen how to maintain their aircraft. He continued to train, catching passes from McCulley and even former Jets quarterback Richard Todd, who lived in the area after being traded to the New Orleans Saints.

In '84, McConkey came back to Giants training camp, a twenty-seven-year-old rookie free agent trying to make the team again. The G-Men brought seven receivers to the summer workouts at Pace University: three rookies—McConkey, Bobby Johnson, and Lionel Manuel—and four veterans—Earnest Gray, Mike Miller, Byron Williams, and John Mistler, McConkey's training camp roommate. Only four of these men would make the final roster. McConkey snagged a touchdown pass in the first preseason game, and he distinguished himself catching punts. Some teams treated special teams like an afterthought, a distant third behind the importance of offense and defense. That was not the case with the Giants under Bill Belichick and Romeo Crennel, who had been elevated to special teams coach as Belichick moved to the defense.

In practice, McConkey stood back awaiting a punter's booted ball. He drifted under it and made the grab. Then another ball came propelling in his direction. He caught that one while still holding the first. A third ball came dropping out of the sky, and McConkey caught it between the other two.

"I'd stick them under my armpit, between my elbow and body, one in each hand, one stuffed down my pants," he said.

He'd juggle to make another grab, tossing a couple of balls in the air in order to make room to catch another punt and retrieve the balls he had just released.

He could get up to seven balls on his body and make an attempt on the eighth, a feat verified by Crennel.

"Anywhere he could stuff them, he would stuff them. He would catch them and put them in his shirt under his jersey, under his arm, in between his legs. Usually you could get as many as you could in your jersey, under your arms, and then when all of that got filled, okay, then you could put one between your legs."

In '84, McConkey put together another solid training camp and preseason. Before the last exhibition game, McConkey arrived early at the stadium. He had made it this far the previous season. The final cuts would come two days later. McConkey sat on a stool in a mostly empty locker room when Parcells walked up to him.

"You've made this team. I want you to go out tonight and relax and just play your ass off," the coach said.[5]

McConkey caught three passes and registered a 48-yard punt return that night. The following evening, he ate dinner at Mistler's home. It was quality time with his twenty-five-year-old training camp roommate along with Mistler's wife, children, and parents. Before the group sat down to eat dinner, the telephone rang. It was a Giants assistant coach looking for Mistler. Parcells wanted to see him the next day. That only meant one thing: Mistler was cut.

That next morning, across the country, Tom Flores, head coach of the Super Bowl–defending Los Angeles Raiders, called safety Kenny Hill into his office. Hill had been trying to crack the Raiders' starting lineup. He was in his fourth year in the league and had yet to make a start. The majority of his game action came on special teams.

"You're finally going to get your opportunity to play," Flores told him from across the coach's desk.

Hill felt excited. His opportunity had arrived. Flores told Hill he deserved to play. The coach reached out and handed Hill the telephone. It was Parcells on the other end of the line. Hill had been traded to the Giants.

Hill, a Yale graduate with a degree in molecular biophysics and biochemistry, quickly recovered from his initial thoughts of starting for the silver and black.

"We're going to win. I want you to know that, Coach. We're going to win," he said, making a promise to Parcells.

The conversation went on for a few minutes. By now, it was the early afternoon in New Jersey. Hill told Parcells he had to handle some things with his home and some business endeavors before he left Los Angeles and flew across the country.

"Okay. Do whatever you have to do. Practice starts tomorrow morning at nine. See you there."

In the off-season, Phil Simms had spent more time than ever before at Giants Stadium. When he wasn't lifting weights with his offensive linemen, he pulled up a chair next to offensive coordinator Ron Erhardt and watched film. It was the most time Simms had ever spent watching film. For him, it wasn't an exercise in learning football. Instead, watching film together with Erhardt ensured that the quarterback and coordinator saw the same options and opportunities for the offense. "We were working to get to the point where I would know what he was thinking, and he would know what I was thinking, where we could communicate almost without saying a word," Simms said.[6]

Before the Giants headed to training camp, the team offered the oft-injured quarterback a new deal. Even though he had played in only two of the team's last thirty-two games, the Giants were willing to pay him more than $1 million over three years. Simms was in an option year of his contract. If he didn't sign the new offer, he'd make $275,000 in '84. After that, the unproven quarterback would have to rely on his play in the upcoming season to negotiate the next contract. It was security versus risk. Simms's agent, David Fishof, advised his client to decline the offer, and Simms chose to gamble on himself.

"Pretty cocky, huh, for a guy who hadn't started a game in three years?" Simms said.[7]

Parcells named him the starter in the middle of August. This put an official end to what wasn't that much of a quarterback competition with backup Jeff Rutledge.

The Giants' offensive philosophy shifted in '84. Instead of a conservative approach of running often and throwing short passes, Parcells wanted the ball thrown downfield. He wanted Simms to take chances if it could result in a big play. In the final preseason game, though, a Giants drive ended because Simms avoided throwing into tight coverage over the middle of the field. He chose caution over the new philosophy. Parcells jawed at him as he came off the field.

"Oh. My God. No, Simms," Parcells said, almost whining. "Take a chance. Throw it in there."

In that moment, Simms got the message. His attitude about taking chances and making risky throws changed.

"The biggest thing about it, we validated everything day one of the season."

Simms completed 23 of 30 passes for 409 yards. He threw four touchdown passes, two to rookie Bobby Johnson and one to Zeke Mowatt and a 65-yarder to Byron Williams. The 409 yards in the air ranked as the second-highest single-game total in Giants history and the most since Y. A. Tittle threw for 505 yards in 1962. The Giants beat the Philadelphia Eagles 28–27.

In week 2, Big Blue hammered the Dallas Cowboys 28–7, sacking quarterback Gary Hogeboom five times. On one sack, Lawrence Taylor separated Hogeboom from the ball. Linebacker Andy Headen scooped it up and ran 81 yards for the touchdown. Simms threw three more touchdown passes in the win. Through the first two games, he had a 146.2 passer rating.

The Giants headed to Robert F. Kennedy Stadium to face the 0–2 Washington Redskins. New York entered the game as six-point underdogs. They took a 14–13 lead into the fourth quarter. After the Redskins took the lead 16–14 on a 21-yard Mark Moseley field goal, Simms threw a pick six to Vernon Dean, and Lionel Manuel added a fumble that Curtis Jordan returned for a touchdown. Powered by the two defensive scores, the Redskins won 30–14. The Giants gave up five sacks and turned the ball over five times, three on Simms's interceptions.

Led by a four-sack performance from Taylor, New York recovered, beating Tampa Bay 17–14 to go 3–1. They headed to Los Angeles to face the 2–2 Rams. The Giants scored on the game's first play. After Big Blue kicked off, Phil McConkey recovered the mishandled ball in the Rams' end zone. The Giants then missed the extra point to start the brutal part of the performance. Los Angeles sacked Simms five times. New York receivers dropped six passes. The offense ran for a total of eight yards on 13 carries.

They converted only 1 of 14 third-down attempts. The special teams unit let up an 83-yard punt return for a touchdown and allowed two blocked punts. The blocked punts and one of the sacks resulted in three safeties, all in the third quarter. A goalpost even fell down at one point, causing a ten-minute laughter-inducing delay to repair it.

The offensive line picked up four holding penalties. The flags, twelve in all, became so prevalent, that at one point Parcells told the team the next player called for a penalty would be cut. Soon after, rookie Carl Banks ran down on punt coverage. He got into a shoving match with a Rams player. The officials tagged Banks with a 15-yard unsportsmanlike conduct penalty. He walked off the field straight toward Parcells.

"You're cut. Go sit on the fucking bench," Parcells said.

Banks tried to explain himself to no avail. Parcells had no time for and no interest in the reasons. Frustrated by his inability to get his message across to Parcells, Banks snapped, "Fuck you."

"What'd you say, son?"

"Fuck you," Banks reiterated before walking to the bench and taking a seat.

"I didn't even know if I was going to be on the plane back home," Banks thought while sitting on the sidelines.

The Giants lost 33–12. The team arrived back in New Jersey at 2:45 A.M. Banks did have a seat on the flight, and he remained on the team. Parcells slept in his office, waking up at 6:15 A.M. to start watching film of the undefeated San Francisco 49ers. The Giants faced Joe Montana and the buzz saw that was the '84 49ers at home on Monday night. Midway through the first quarter, San Francisco led 21–0. By the start of the fourth, it was 31–3. Half the fans had left, and most of the ones who stayed booed the home team.

Fans hazed Simms, who completed 24 of 43 passes for 290 yards and threw two interceptions. During one game in '84, one fan caught Simms's ear as the quarterback came to the sidelines after a failed offensive possession. About fifteen feet separated the first row of fans and the players' bench. Banks couldn't help but turn his head when he heard his quarterback giving it right back to the heckler.

"'Fuck you, you motherfucker. You don't know me.' He's going on and on," Banks said before Simms had to be pulled away.

After the 49ers game, the Giants fell to 3–3. After two blundering 21-point losses, Parcells's job security came into question, again. In the media, Parcells played it cool. He spoke about the team getting back to the form that helped them open the season with impressive wins. Privately, the pressure mounted. His staying for a second season wasn't a vote of confidence from George Young. It was a short-leash, wait-and-see approach, and nobody liked what they saw in the last two games.

The Giants had a trip to Atlanta to play the Falcons next. Parcells opened up to some of *his guys*. He pulled them aside individually during the week. He told them if they lost, he'd be fired.

"Hey, listen, I could've got fired anytime," Parcells said. "It was still nip and tuck right there. We had demonstrated we could play better early in the year. Then we slipped up here and there, took a couple bad beatings. Had we not bounced back from that and started to win some games, that very, very easily could've happened."

Quietly, the message spread through the locker room: "Shit, he's going to get fired if we don't win this game."

The five-point underdog Giants started two rookie linebackers at Atlanta. Banks stepped in for an injured Andy Headen, while Gary Reasons got the nod in place of an ineffective Joe McLaughlin.

In the first quarter, the Falcons drove to the Giants' 1-yard line. On first down, Lawrence Taylor stuffed the running back Lynn Cain at the line of scrimmage. On second down, defensive lineman Jerome Sally stopped Cain a foot short of the end zone. On third down, the Giants pressured Atlanta quarterback Steve Bartkowski into throwing an incompletion out of the end zone. On fourth down, Bartkowski rolled right, looking for the tight end, who was covered. The quarterback had a blocker in front of him to lead the path to a touchdown. Bartkowski made a run for it, but Banks slipped away from the blocker and sacked the quarterback for a one-yard loss. It was the closest the Falcons would come to having a lead in the game.

In the fourth quarter, Reasons thwarted an Atlanta comeback attempt, breaking up a fourth-down pass and tallying an interception. Banks finished with a game-high nine unassisted tackles and two sacks. The Giants won 19–7.

Harry Carson and Lawrence Taylor changed their opinion about the young guys. Carson told reporters they played great. Taylor said he was proud of them and punctuated it with: "This is the defense we can be."[8]

Jim Burt helped stall the Atlanta running game. It was the first time in three weeks that the Giants didn't allow a 100-yard rusher. Burt also added a sack of Bartkowski to his defensive output. "That game, right there was the difference between Bill Parcells' being a high school coach or an NFL Hall of Famer. 'Cause if we lose that game, and he gets fired, he never gets another chance again."

By now, Burt had ingratiated himself to Parcells, but the relationship had soured early. In the first game in '81, Burt's rookie year and Parcells's first as the coordinator, the Eagles outplayed the Giants, which cleared the way for Burt to get in the game. He played well enough that the coaching staff decided he would alternate series with starting nose tackle Bill Neill in week 2 against Washington. All week in practice, Burt and Neill prepped for the game by alternating.

"I'm all fired up," Burt said. He called all his family in Buffalo and told them to make sure to watch the game. He'd be playing a lot.

After the first series of the game, defensive line coach Lamar Leachman told Burt, "We're going to stick with what we got."

This confused Burt. "What do you mean, stick with what we got? It's my turn to go in."

Helmet on, chin strap buckled, Burt stared at Leachman.

"Hey, it isn't my decision. He makes the decision," Leachman said, nodding toward Parcells, who was standing flush with the sideline.

Burt turned away from Leachman. He marched toward Parcells. He was ready to confront his defensive coordinator, but when he reached Parcells, instead of using words, he forearmed the coach in the back. Parcells's headset flew off as he stumbled a couple of steps onto the field. Parcells steadied his footing, turned around, and realized what happened.

"Get him the fuck out of here."

A couple of players grabbed Burt and pulled him back toward the Gatorade. As Burt's temper cooled and his thoughts turned to the likelihood of him being cut from the team, Parcells had walked back to him.

"You little motherfucker," Parcells said. "You get your fucking ass in there. If you fuck up, you're going to fucking get cut. I'm cutting your ass."

Parcells played Burt in games that year, but they didn't speak until the season ended. In the locker room, after the Giants lost in the play-offs to the 49ers, Parcells went down the line of defensive players, shaking their hands and congratulating them on a great season. He had a different message for Burt.

"Let me tell you something," Parcells said. "Next minicamp, I'm going to have four guys in your position. I'm going to get four guys in there. They're going to take your position next year. You wait and see next year. Watch and see."

Burt stared at him. "I wouldn't expect any different. I'm looking forward to it."

Burt survived. His dogged approach and desire to win won Parcells over. That is why in '84, after the Giants beat Atlanta but then followed that with a loss to Philly, Parcells applied direct pressure on Burt.

The Giants faced the Redskins at home. Washington had won five of its last six games. Anchored by an offensive line nicknamed "the Hogs," Washington averaged nearly 37 rushes per game. The Redskins mostly handed the ball to John Riggins, whom Giants defenders recall as a headache to tackle. Jeff Bostic, the starting center, suffered a knee injury the previous week, so Rick Donnalley would square off against Burt.

In 1982, Donnalley had won the NFL's "Strongest Man in Pro Football" competition. Donnalley lifted forty-two thousand pounds in an evening competition that included four hundred–pound bench presses, seven hundred–pound squats, and six hundred–pound dead lifts.

On every snap, Burt's job was to engage the center and another player—a lineman, a tight end, a fullback. This way, if Burt could take on two blockers, it freed up the middle linebackers—Harry Carson and Gary Reasons—behind him to have an open path to make a play.

"You're getting pissed on from everybody. You're the fire hydrant at a dog show," Burt said.

Parcells talked up Donnalley's strength. At practice, when the defense completed its regular work, Parcells had three linemen, alternating two at a time, fire off the snap at Burt. Parcells left and worked with the offense while Burt took on two men with no rest for fifty reps. After one practice, back in the locker room, Parcells had Burt hold twenty-pound dumbbells in each hand and punch a padded wall for forty-five minutes. Parcells made sure everyone saw it. He used Burt to get the rest of the team's attention. If he treated Burt this way, then everybody had better be keyed into the game.

"I took my medicine," Burt said. "I knew what it was. I didn't talk back."

While he remained quiet, Burt did become incensed reading a story in one of the New York tabloids. Parcells told the newspaper how the game came down to Burt being able to neutralize Donnalley. If that happened, then the Giants could stop Riggins.

"He's making our life freakin' difficult. I mean, I don't mind the other shit, but he's going to alert the other guy?"

Burt waited until after practice on Friday to say something. Even then, it was a short, private conversation with Parcells.

"Okay, we done now? Just remember, I've taken it. You dish it out; can you take it the same way?"

Parcells assured Burt he could take whatever the player sent his way.

The Giants crushed the Redskins. Chris Godfrey made his first start at guard and helped the running game bust loose. Big Blue had been averaging 83 rushing yards per game and an NFL-low 2.8 yards per carry coming into the game. Joe Morris led the way running for three touchdowns and 68 of the team's 130 yards on the ground. Burt had little trouble with Donnalley. Turns out the center was strong but lacked agility. The Giants held Washington to 79 yards rushing, limiting Riggins to 51 yards. In the closing minutes of the 37–13 win, players on the Giants' sidelines waved to the fans to cheer louder.

Burt was on the sidelines. He made the spontaneous move. He grabbed the Gatorade bucket, which was filled with water. He walked up behind Parcells and dumped the whole thing on him. It was the first "Gatorade bath" for a coach. With that, the game-ending victory tradition had been created. Parcells turned around and was soaked with a body shot of water from another bucket.

When the water washed away, Parcells emerged with a wide smile. Burt had walked back behind the bench, where he had grabbed the Gatorade jug. Parcells walked over to him. "See, I told you I would take it."

Starting with the Washington game, the Giants won five of six games. They lost to the St. Louis Cardinals in week 15, giving them a 9–6 record and putting their play-off hopes in the hands of other teams. Even though the outcome didn't matter, they posted a miserable 10–3 home loss to the New Orleans Saints to close the regular season. The Saints sacked Simms seven times. The offense only gained 189 yards, and 43 of those came from the leading rusher, Simms.

The Redskins defeated the Cardinals, and the Dolphins beat the Cowboys on Monday night to put the Giants in the play-offs. New York headed to Los Angeles for a wild card round game with the Rams, the same team that gave them that 33–12 whooping twelve weeks earlier. On Wednesday before the play-off game, Parcells walked into a defensive meeting with an announcement.

"You know what? I've got $1,000 for the first guy who puts Eric Dickerson on his ass. Guys, we've got to send him a message."

Dickerson had rushed for an NFL single-season record 2,105 yards. He averaged 5.6 yards per carry. The Giants' defensive game plan focused on him.

On the Rams' first play of scrimmage, they pitched to Dickerson on the right side, and Banks leveled him.

"Literally put him on his ass," said Banks, who collected the prize money.

In the last six weeks leading up to the play-offs, the Giants felt the temperature rise above sixty degrees just twice. Now, the mercury reached nearly seventy degrees in Anaheim Stadium. Sweat-drenched Giants breathed heavily, and that old sense of losing crept into the defensive huddle early in the game.

"But to be a Giant is to always feel sad underneath, always a little bit unsteady," Carson, the team captain, had said at the onset of the season.[9]

Running back Tony Galbreath was new to the team in '84, and he witnessed the quitter's attitude on the sidelines when the Giants fell behind in games. "I heard a few guys whining, 'Here we go again. We ain't gonna win.'"

The Giants did know how to lose, and early in the game, the Parcells guys sensed the resignation. They started chattering at the doubters. Not a conversation, more like the output of phrases. "Get your fucking ass going." "You're not tired. You're not the only one out here."

After a Giants field goal opened the scoring, Lawrence Taylor forced a Dickerson fumble, which led to New York's lone touchdown on the day, a one-yard Rob Carpenter run.

The Giants took a 13–3 lead in the third-quarter. The defense had held Dickerson to 37 yards on 12 carries in the first half. In the second half, though, the six-foot-three future Hall of Famer picked up 70 yards on 11 carries and scored a touchdown to make the score 13–10. Big Blue answered back with the third Ali Haji-Sheikh field goal of the day. Down 16–10, the Rams had the ball at their own 42-yard line when Dickerson busted loose on what looked like a touchdown run if not for safety Terry Kinard tackling him from behind after a 24-yard gain. A seven-yard pass followed by three Dickerson runs gave the Rams first and goal from the 7-yard line midway through the fourth quarter.

With twenty-one feet between the defense and losing the lead, Big Blue had to beat back an all-world running back as well as the vestiges of a losing era. Belichick had created the mantra of "We need that stop on first down." Some players repeated that before breaking the huddle.

On first down, Rams quarterback Jeff Kemp pitched the ball to

Dickerson, who picked up three yards. On second down, defensive end Leonard Marshall slid between two offensive linemen and tackled Dwayne Crutchfield for a three-yard loss. On third down, Kemp could only get two yards on a pass to Henry Ellard. The Rams settled for a field goal with 7:02 to play, making the score 16–13.

Los Angeles wouldn't get a shot at scoring again for the rest of the game. On fourth down and six from their own 30 with about two minutes to play, Kemp dropped back to pass. He fell victim to an LT hit, which jarred the ball loose and gave possession back to the Giants. Big Blue held on for the win.

After advancing to the divisional round, the Giants lost 21–10 to the San Francisco 49ers, the eventual Super Bowl champs. But the win against the Rams forever exorcised the loser demons. The coach who had nearly been fired a year ago now had the confidence he could lead this team further.

"That win did a lot for our organization. It certainly did a lot for me personally. That was the point—'Hey, Parcells, if you can get going, you can do this.'"

14

"HEY, PARCELLS, YOU GOT TO FIND A WAY TO BEAT THOSE GUYS"

During one off-season when Giants general manager George Young needed to negotiate a deal with David Fishof, Young didn't open the talks with financial figures and stats. Instead, Young, a Catholic, asked the agent religious questions. He mentioned to Fishof that Passover was coming and he had never attended a Seder. Fishof hosted the traditional Jewish feast and invited Young to his home.

"He came to my house, and—poor guy—he had to sit through a three-hour Seder," said Fishof, who represented more than 10 percent of the Giants' roster during the '80s.

It was a genuine move by Young, and it was also one of the unique tactics he employed to build relationships that would help ease contract negotiations.

Typically, after the NFL draft, Young flew to the agent representing the Giants' number-one pick. Teams usually brought top draft choices to their facility, and the agent came along to negotiate the rookie's deal. Young made the trip to endear himself to the agent and, at the same time, keep the local media away from the contract talks.

Agents who met with Young over lunch hoped to talk football and a new deal for their clients, but Young, a former high school teacher, conversed about history and politics. Finally, toward the end of the meal, Young would slip the agent a piece of paper with the note "I can offer you," followed by some figures.

Even though he operated in a time before the NFL salary cap, Young had his own valuations on players and positions, and he didn't budge from his structures.

Fishof represented athletes and entertainers. His clients included the Turtles, the Association, and the Village People. His stable of athletes included New York Yankees outfielder Lou Piniella, 49ers linebacker Jack "Hacksaw" Reynolds, and Phil Simms.

Everywhere Fishof went he'd hear comments about the Giants' quarterback. He'd walk into his synagogue and the fans in the congregation freely criticized Simms or questioned whether he'd ever establish himself as a serviceable NFL signal caller.

When Fishof walked the streets of Manhattan with Simms, hecklers held little back. Strangers passed by Simms, warning the injury-prone quarterback not to trip over a crack in the sidewalk.

Nothing Simms heard at the stadium bothered him. Those insults didn't stay with him, but he grew tired of the comments made elsewhere. He went to pick up shirts at his dry cleaner, but before the man handed Simms his clothes, he decided to give the pro quarterback some tips on how to play football. Simms played the part of a polite Kentuckian. He stood and listened, but his mind drifted.

"Well, I want to go, 'What if I come back there and kick the crap out of you? What would you think of that?' God, I was like, '*Give me my clothes.*'"

In '84, fans remained ready to boo him, but the quarterback who had been demoted, injured, and ridiculed threw for 4,044 yards. It set a single-season Giants record, blowing 800 yards past the previous mark set by Y. A. Tittle more than twenty years earlier. It was only the tenth time in NFL history that a quarterback had eclipsed 4,000 yards in a season. Simms also added 22 touchdown passes, which ranked fifth in team history.

Simms had bet on himself in '84. He played out the final year of his contract rather than signing a new one. In the off-season leading up to the '85 campaign, it was time to collect on that bet. The numbers Simms racked up gave Fishof leverage when he sat down with Young to work out a new deal.

The negotiations lasted two days into training camp, but Simms took the field at Pace University on the third day after signing a five-year, $3.8 million deal. He'd make an average of $760,000 per year, nearly tripling his salary from the previous season.

When Simms's play improved, Fishof received more requests for the quarterback to make appearances and speak at events. More endorsement offers came in. Simms declined the vast majority of the non-football propositions. He wouldn't allow anything to interfere with his daily workout schedule.

"That part frustrated me," Fishof said.

It endeared Simms to his teammates, though, especially to his linemen, the guys he worked out with nearly every day.

"He lifted first, before he played golf, unlike most quarterbacks. And we respected that," said guard Chris Godfrey.

Tight end Zeke Mowatt saw Simms break his thumb in '83, and he heard the jeers from fans after the injury. Then he witnessed Simms come back and have the best year of his career.

"You don't find quarterbacks that tough," Mowatt said. "This guy is in all this pain, and y'all booing him. And then—the way he handled that, I got a lot of respect for the guy, 'cause he could have just said, 'You know what? I'm not gonna come back. I'm gonna call it a day.'"

Nineteen eighty-four was the first time Simms started a full NFL season, and that came on the heels of Johnny Parker's arrival.

"He just believed in Johnny Parker," Fishof said. "And he was just so motivated."

The success of Parker's strength-and-conditioning program led the Giants to invest in facility upgrades. Parker oversaw the construction of a new $200,000 weight room. The padded flooring alone cost $40,000. Through the locker room, past the trainers' room, behind the equipment room, and a few more steps past the washers and dryers, players—and some coaches—gathered in the brightly lit, mirrorless weight room.[1]

Parker had pushed the program by vowing to be there whenever a player could work out. 4:30 A.M.? Parker was there. 10:00 P.M.? If that's what a player needed, Parker was there. The facility served its primary purpose: the Giants got stronger. It also became a team-chemistry-building lab. In between sets of lifting, teammates could talk about anything—families, parties, politics. They joked around and laughed.

"It's a great environment for players to bond. But not just 'cause they sit around and talk but because they're doing something that's difficult together," Parker said.

As much as Parcells rode players in practice, he usually took a more relaxed approach when he visited the weight room. He'd ask about a player's family or what the player planned to do after football.

"It gave me a chance to be down there with them in the off-season, see them working. Talking about things. Not football. Just kinda get to know them better."

And sometimes, the discussion could get awkward and elicit cringes. This was nearly always the case if the conversation lasted long enough with Lamar Leachman, the defensive line coach.

Leachman played high school football in Cartersville, Georgia, in the late 1940s. He was the state's leading rusher until Hershel Walker surpassed him in 1979. During one of his college recruiting trips, someone offered Leachman a shrimp cocktail, to which he responded, "No, thank you, sir. I don't drink." Leachman played center and linebacker for the University of Tennessee before becoming Mr. Irrelevant, the last player taken in the thirtieth and final round of the 1955 NFL draft. He played one year in the Canadian Football League. He coached high school football in Georgia and in the college ranks, but he came to the Giants after a stint in the CFL. Ray Perkins hired him. Leachman impressed Perkins so much during the interview process it made the head coach wonder why Leachman had been up in Canada for a handful of years.

After his interview with the Giants, Perkins said he made dozens of phone calls to check out Leachman's background.

"It was a consensus that people thought his mouth got him into trouble," Perkins said. " 'Hey, I'm going to hire ya,' I said, 'but here's the deal: if I have to call you in my office to talk to you about your mouth, I'm not calling you in there to talk to you to start using better language; I'm calling you in there to let you go.' He said, 'Fair enough, Coach.'"

Leachman referred to his players as *boy*, pronounced *buuoy* in that deep Southern accent.

Leachman encouraged players to get in shape with such motivational quotes as: "Boy, your titties are gonna get moldy if you don't start liftin' some of those weights. Ya know what I mean, boy?"[2]

"Loud, boisterous, completely inappropriate. Would not survive in today's world. He said more politically incorrect things," said John Mara.

Leachman was about six feet tall with sides of beef for arms. A newspaper wrote a story about Leachman being able to lift 360 pounds as an assistant coach with the Toronto Argonauts.

"He always wanted to be in there trying to lift weights like he was playing," said Giants tight end Zeke Mowatt.

In the new weight room, Leachman shared his political views, talking up the value of segregation and how George Wallace, the Alabama governor known for his inflammatory quote "Segregation now, segregation tomorrow, and segregation forever," would make a fine president of the United States of America.

Yet, the players seemed to tolerate him. His commentary on Wallace was filed to the shoulder-shrugging "That's Lamar" category.

"There are still a lot of things that go on in families that never come out. Other issues on other teams that go on that don't come out, but it didn't bother me," Mowatt said.

George Martin believes his mother would smack him if she heard his take on Leachman. "At times he was a loveable racist."

Martin also said there wasn't a coach he learned more from than Leachman. He watched him hug black players and kiss them on the forehead. "A racist is not going to do that," Martin said.

If your team used a three-man defensive line, as the Giants did, Leachman was one of the best, if not the best coach, for it. Martin compartmentalized the negative. He extracted the techniques that benefited his career and tried to avoid an antagonistic or confrontational environment.

"Now, sometimes that's not possible because you know there are very many times where there was no connection between his brain and his mouth."

Special teams coach Romeo Crennel spoke to Leachman about his upbringing. Crennel found him to be a down-to-earth guy who could coach. "He couldn't help where he's from," Crennel said.

Leachman also had a motto: "If it's free, take two."

He stepped off the team charter plane clanging as he walked because of the soda cans he stuffed into his baggage. Players came back to their lockers to find pinches of dipping tobacco missing from their tins. A ring of powder in front of your locker meant Lamar had "borrowed" some protein powder. The hangers, team-issue shorts, and sneakers that went missing? That's Lamar, too. Towels in his house bore Sheraton, Marriott, or Hilton logos.

At minicamp, the coaches received new polo shirts embroidered with a team logo. After the day's practice finished, the coaches took off their shirts and threw them in a bin of dirty laundry. They'd be washed and dried and returned to the coaches' lockers the next day, but the shirts went missing. No problem. The team ordered another set. After the minicamp ended, the coaches decided to go out together for a meal and some drinks. They headed to Manny's, a bar and grill down the road from Giants Stadium. Sitting at the bar, they found their missing shirts. The staff at Manny's was wearing them. The coaches noticed, but most didn't say anything. Bill Belichick had to find out. He asked where they got them. In a matter-of-fact tone, the bartender told him Lamar gave them to the restaurant staff as a gift. It wasn't so much a kind gesture from Leachman as much as it was an exchange to build equity for free drinks and food.

Nose tackle Jim Burt had a contentious, always-on-the-edge-of-explosion relationship with Leachman. Burt played with the lights during defensive line meetings, flicking them on and off and grinding meetings to a halt. During film sessions, Leachman made sure to overemphasize any mistake Burt made.

Burt kept some food in his locker. Typically, he'd want something to eat during the day, so he stashed it there. He relied on it being there. Then he spotted Lamar taking some of it. Burt, the All-Pro ballbuster, couldn't let it go. He grabbed a garbage can and dumped it over Leachman's head.

"A big-ass garbage can, and it covered his whole body and everything," Burt said.

Leachman wrestled the thing off and grabbed one of the stools that was placed in front of every player's locker. He whipped it at Burt. It missed.

"I'll kick your ass," Leachman said.

Burt laughed at him. "You ain't kicking no one's ass."

The players in the locker room didn't know what to make of the tension. Were they really going to come to blows?

Parcells intervened. He stepped toward the situation and asked what happened.

"He's fucking stealing shit out of my locker, so I took the garbage can and threw it over the top of his head."

Parcells burst out laughing.

"Tell Erhardt. Tell Erhardt," Parcells said in between laughs, asking Burt to relay the story to the team's offensive coordinator.

The coaches knew Leachman's maneuverings, and it gave them a moment of joy knowing he had been caught.

No incident ever stopped Leachman. At training camp, he continued to take dipping tobacco from Brad Benson's locker. The offensive lineman had tins of Skoal and Copenhagen that Leachman took chunks of at his leisure.

"You've got to get him," Burt said.

The training camp grounds at Pace University had a Canadian geese problem. The geese inhabited the place, chomped the grass, and left their waste behind. When Benson took Burt up on his suggestion, both players stepped out onto the dew-covered grass. With a tissue in hand, they grabbed some goose turd. They mixed it into one of Benson's Copenhagen tins and left it in his locker.

At the start of practice, the players stretched out. Burt noticed the sour look on Leachman's face.

"Damn, Benson," Leachman said loud enough for the team to hear. "Benson, damn. This tastes like shit."

"Yeah, it's goose shit," Burt deadpanned.

A red-faced Leachman spit everything out of his mouth as the laughter of his fellow coaches interrupted the stretching.

Rookie defensive back Herb Welch entered training camp in 1985 as the 326th player taken in the draft—not exactly Mr. Irrelevant, but ten spots away from the last pick. There was no guarantee the UCLA product would make the team. Welch's lack of status only deepened when you took into account the player the Giants took before him. The eleventh-round pick, Allen Young, was listed as a defensive back, but he never played college football. He played point guard on the Virginia Tech basketball team.

At the first day of training camp, Bill Belichick walked over to the group of defensive backs. Close to twenty men were getting ready to start their drills.

"Just so you guys know, only seven of you guys are going to make the team. Go out there and shine."

At UCLA, Welch competed at the highest level of college football. In high school, he ran track. During some meets, he was the lone representative from Warren High School in Downey, California. It was in the loneliness of those meets that he began to use the mantra that all he could do was give his best. That attitude combined with the UCLA experience left him undaunted by Belichick's message. He didn't see the same fortitude when he looked around at the other defensive backs.

"A lot of guys kind of folded up at that point," Welch said.

A day of training camp came when there were no meetings that night. The players would have a chance to go out. This meant practice ended with a beer round, a one-on-one drill between a wide receiver and a defensive back. Whichever side lost the drill had to buy the winners a round of beers. The drill was skewed to favor the offense, since the quarterback dropped back and faced no pressure before zinging a pass to the receiver. As part of the drill, the defense picked the receiver, and the offense chose the defender.

"The defense always has honor with the Giants, so we picked their best guy," Welch said.

They called Lionel Manuel's name. The second-year wide receiver, skilled in making sharp, quick cuts, averaged nearly 19 yards per catch as a rookie.

The offense picked Welch. He hadn't been cut yet, and several weeks into training camp, he hadn't played any defense either. Instead, he played scout team offense against the defense.

Welch lined up across from Manuel. The quarterback's cadence put the drill in motion. When Manuel made his cut, the quarterback released the ball, and Welch made a play for it. Welch extended his arm and batted down the pass. The defense won the drill.

As the beer-winning hero trotted off the field, Belichick walked up to him.

"You know, maybe tomorrow you ought to play a little bit on defense."

"That would be a welcome relief," Welch said.

Welch had his moment in the Bill Parcells–driven prove-yourself training camp gauntlet. The '85 camp was particularly long because the Giants played in the preseason-opening Hall of Fame game, which added an extra week of preparation. Rookies, and some veterans, had to report a week before that, adding two extra weeks to the grind. As the days mounted, the team's captain, Harry Carson, noticed his teammates were reaching a breaking point in the summer heat.

Carson decided to go see Parcells about it. The Pro Bowl middle linebacker had done this before. When things weren't going well in the past, he went to Parcells to use fine money to take players to dinner at Beefsteak Charlie's on Route 4 near Giants Stadium.

Carson enjoyed keeping things together in the locker room. He believed the team would get better if players had the opportunity to build a bond away from the football environment. "When you get to know a guy, then you want to play harder for that guy," he said.

But when he met with Parcells at Pace University, he had something other than dinner in mind. Carson told Parcells the players were doing everything Parcells asked of them. Carson mentioned a break.

"What are you talking about?" Parcells shot back.

"Guys are really working their asses off."

"What do you propose?"

"Well, what if I think of something that we can do to just sort of relax and let our hair down?"

Parcells responded to the veiled language with a quizzical glare darting from his blue eyes. "What in the fuck are you talking about? Speak English."

"What if I got some entertainment and ordered some beer?"

"You do whatever you're going to do, but if anybody gets out of line, I'll have your ass," Parcells said, ending the conversation.

Carson went back to his dorm room on the Pace campus. He grabbed a copy of *New York* magazine. He flipped to the back pages, to the ads for exotic dancers. He ordered three for the next night.

Carson had forewarned his teammates: "Don't fuck up, because if you fuck up, it's on me." He knew not everyone on the team would go for this, especially the devout Christians, but even some of them snuck a peek. After the strippers changed in Carson's room, the nearly naked women put on their show as the players ate pizza and filled their cups from a keg of beer.

The next day, all the players showed up on time for practice.

Mark Bavaro played in Giants Stadium as a senior in college when his Notre Dame team faced Navy in the Meadowlands. On the Friday before the game, a New Jersey state trooper boarded one of the team's buses for a walk-through as it headed to the stadium.

"Is Bavaro on this bus?"

What the—? I didn't do anything, Bavaro thought.

Bavaro raised his hand, and the trooper headed back to his seat.

"I just want to shake your hand. We love watching you. My wife loves you. We all love you over here in Jersey."

After the walk-through, Notre Dame headed up to the press box, and the Giants took the field for practice. Bavaro saw backup linebackers Andy Headen and Byron Hunt come out of the tunnel leading to the field. They looked bigger than the starters. He watched Carl Banks come out, followed by Lawrence Taylor and then Carson. *I wouldn't want to have to deal with this linebacking crew on a regular basis,* Bavaro thought as he watched them limber up before practice.

Bavaro had made the Associated Press All-America team, but he didn't receive an invitation to the NFL Combine. He had suffered knee and shoulder injuries, and the Notre Dame program floundered under coach Gerry Faust. As a result, players' reputations suffered in the eyes of NFL talent evaluators. Bavaro conducted a predraft workout at the Bears' facility and took a physical there. After that, the Patriots, Falcons, and Seahawks invited Bavaro to their facilities, but he left each team thinking they had no interest in him. He had little idea how much interest the Giants had.

During Bavaro's senior year, Chris Mara sat next to Giants general manager George Young in the press box at Notre Dame Stadium. The six-foot-four, 245-pounder from Danvers, Massachusetts, hadn't made the Giants' scouting list yet, but Mara became impressed the more he watched him play.

"We have to keep an eye on him, because he's kind of a late bloomer—big, tough, strong kid. He's got great hands," Mara recalled telling Young that day.

The Giants' scouts, future Chicago Bears general manager Jerry Angelo in particular, fell in love with Bavaro.

Angelo visited Bavaro at Notre Dame, and the scout made up his mind. He told Parcells that Bavaro might not be the player for every coach, but Parcells would love him.

The Giants grabbed him in the fourth round, with the one hundredth pick in the '85 draft.

At training camp, Bavaro's socks soaked up the blood oozing from his feet. The team-issued cleats didn't fit him properly, but the rookie tight end wasn't going to say anything about it.

"He had these massive blisters, and they were bleeding through his socks. I'm like, 'Mark, are you crazy?'" said Don Hasselbeck, a ninth-year tight end brought to the Giants to compete with Bavaro and mentor him at the same time.

Hasselbeck told Bavaro to see a trainer and at least get some Band-Aids. Bavaro declined and said everything was all right.

The veterans had already taken to calling Bavaro "Rambo," based on the rookie's similar mullet, musculature, and look of Sylvester Stallone's Rambo character in the season's blockbuster film *Rambo: First Blood Part II*.

Bavaro spoke so little, his strength lifting weights and blocking was about the only thing his teammates knew about him. During training camp, Johnny Parker created a makeshift weight room adjacent to the practice field. Under a tent and on a floor made of plywood, Bavaro squatted 555 pounds, more than double his body weight. He power-cleaned 385 pounds.

"I don't know that Mark was a fighter or anything, but I just think his look kind of intimidated some guys," Hasselbeck said. "He had those big arms. And probably the fact that he didn't say anything kind of made him even tougher."

Parcells wasn't exactly sure what to make of him, but Bavaro craved the head coach's approval.

The first time Bavaro ran a seam route in training camp, he caught Phil Simms's pass in the end zone. It drew some cheers from the offensive side, but more importantly to Bavaro as he ran back to the huddle, Parcells slapped him on the back of the head and said, "Good play, kid. You know what? You look good doing it."

"I can't tell you how inspiring that was," Bavaro said.

Behind the mysterious, quiet persona, Bavaro was intimidated. He had to compete with Hasselbeck, a six-foot-seven veteran he had watched play for the Patriots while growing up in Massachusetts. Zeke Mowatt was the incumbent starter, and he maintained the same work ethic he started with in '83 as an undrafted free agent. Mowatt had tied for the team lead in receptions in '84, and heading into the '85 season, he had become one of the premier tight ends in the league.

"That guy never took a day off, never took a play off. If it was up to him, he would've taken all the reps," Bavaro said.

The Giants trimmed the roster down before the final preseason game. Only two tight ends remained. Hasselbeck was out.

New York traveled to Pittsburgh for its final exhibition game. Mowatt took the field for his last series. Once the offense finished this drive, he'd be done for the night and ready to start the regular season. There was still time left in the first quarter when he caught the pass from Simms for a 20-yard gain. Mowatt didn't see Steelers safety Eric Williams chasing him down. Williams hit Mowatt's left shoulder. Mowatt's body thrust in one direction, but his right foot didn't follow. It remained planted on the Astroturf. He felt his knee pop.

"I thought somebody shot me with a hot iron. My knee just started burning with fire," Mowatt said.

He looked up at running back Joe Morris and asked him to straighten out his leg. Morris did. The pain subsided. By the time Mowatt made it to the sidelines, he didn't think anything was wrong. A team doctor checked out the knee. He asked Mowatt to walk. The tight end took a few steps, and the knee gave out. He had torn his medial collateral ligament. He was done for the season.

With Mowatt out, Parcells scanned the sidelines a couple of times. Bavaro was the only other tight end on the team, but the rookie didn't think it was his place to run out on the field.

"I really believe he was looking for anyone else but me to put in, someone with experience. Someone he thought could kind of work in the position even though they weren't a tight end because there were no other tight ends. Finally, it was almost like the last resort, and he said, 'Get in there. What are you waiting for?'"

The Giants won the game 24–14. They finished the preseason 5–0. They opened the season with Bavaro as the starting tight end. "There's no way. I'm not ready for this," he said.

The Giants brought Hasselbeck back after the Mowatt injury. The team started with a 21–0 victory against the Philadelphia Eagles. In week 2, Big Blue headed to Green Bay.

Bavaro dropped some passes and missed an assignment, and Parcells sat him on the bench. It wasn't a big display. Just, "Bavaro. Get out." The rookie agreed. *Eh, figures. I wasn't ready,* he thought as he watched from the sidelines.

Hasselbeck subbed in and caught five passes for 71 yards, including a 20-yard touchdown reception. The Giants lost 23–20 with Ali Haji-Sheikh missing a 47-yard field goal that would've tied the game in the final minute.

The next time the first-string offense practiced, Bavaro didn't know what to do. Neither he nor Hasselbeck ran out with the other ten players. They both stood on the sidelines. The offense noticed there was no tight end in the huddle. Parcells looked around and barked, "Bavaro, get in there."

"That's when I knew I was still the guy for him."

After wins against Philadelphia and St. Louis and a loss against Dallas, the Giants headed to Cincinnati with a 3–2 record. Boomer Esiason carved up the Giants' defense early, giving the Bengals a 21–3 lead at halftime.

After giving up 202 yards in the first thirty minutes, Big Blue's defense reversed course in the second half, stifling Cincinnati to minus three yards of total offense. Simms, who was coming off a 432-yard, three-touchdown performance against the Cowboys, put together a record-setting day. He completed 40 of 62 pass attempts for 513 yards, still the most passing yards in a game in Giants history and second most in NFL history at the time.

Running back George Adams, the Giants' rookie first-round pick, coughed up his third fumble of the season at the Bengals' 2-yard line. He also dropped a pass in the end zone. The Giants closed the lead to 21–20 in the third quarter when Simms, who was sacked seven times, threw a pick six and followed it with a fumble on the next possession. The Bengals scored two touchdowns in sixty-nine seconds, extending their lead to

35–20. With less than ninety seconds to play, Simms connected with Adams on a 24-yard touchdown pass, but the Giants failed to recover the onside kick. They lost 35–30 and left Riverfront Stadium with a 3–3 record.

"We just gave it away. I'm kind of embarrassed the way we played. I think we're a better team than we showed today. Nobody got it done, coach or player," Parcells said.[3]

Coming into the game, Bavaro only had four catches in the first five games. Against Cincinnati, he set a Giants single-game record with 12 receptions for 176 yards. The media gathered by his locker after the game. He felt uncomfortable with the microphones in front of his face. He didn't like being the center of attention.

"I don't even know what they were asking; all I knew was that I looked over and Parcells was kind of giving me the stink eye from the other corner of the locker room."

Parcells stood with his arms folded in the distance. He didn't say anything. He stared at the scene, looking at how Bavaro would respond. Would the rookie celebrate his performance even though the team lost? Would Bavaro be smart enough not to?

Bavaro packed his belongings into his bag. He offered a cliché quote about the passing routes being the same and that he just happened to be open. He told the reporters he had to board the team bus before slipping through the scrum and leaving the locker room.

"That kind of made him respect me a little bit more," Bavaro said of Parcells. "It was like I was the kind of guy he was looking for physically, mentally, and personality-wise."

Bavaro, an Italian, Mass-attending Catholic, started to become a folk hero, especially to the large population of Italian Americans that planted their roots in the New York–New Jersey area. To them, Bavaro was a *paisan*, a buddy.

"They never treated me like a football player. They always treated me like one of them," Bavaro said.

After home games, Bavaro walked into the players' parking area and was greeted by fans drinking beers and eating sandwiches while hanging around his '79 Chevy Malibu clunker with the worn tires. They were mostly Italians, and they all spoke with that thick Jersey accent. They spoke to Bavaro using his first name. "Hey, Mark, great game today." But when Harry Carson walked to his car, it was all "Oh, Mr. Carson." They went wide-eyed with adulation when Lawrence Taylor passed by. Meanwhile, their pal Bavaro was ready to drive away.

"All right, I've got to get going," Bavaro said politely, asking them to unseat themselves from his hood and to take their beers off the roof.

The Giants rebounded from the Cincinnati game by beating Washington 17–3 at home. The Redskins came into the game leading the NFL in rushing, posting 183 yards a game. The Giants' defense limited their ground game to 69 yards. New York intercepted Washington quarterback Joe Theismann three times and sacked him seven times. Lawrence Taylor accounted for two of those sacks.

After the game, LT told reporters he focused on his preparation that week. "I got some sleep. I didn't go to bars much. I decided to go back to my old self."

In '84, he started the season with eight sacks in the first four games and played subpar for a stretch in the middle of the season. He started the '85 campaign with a string of pedestrian games, but his postgame comments hinted that the rumors about his wild, reckless off-field lifestyle held truth.

"I've had a lot of things on my mind the last couple of weeks," he said. "Maybe football wasn't as important to me as it should have been. Last year, it lasted eight games. This year, I have to catch it before it starts. I have to stop it now."

The Giants kept winning after the Washington game, peeling off victories at New Orleans and home against the Buccaneers and the Rams. The G-Men pushed their record to 7–3 and were tied with Dallas for the division lead heading into a Monday Night Football showdown on national TV at Washington.

With the game tied at 7, a minute into the second quarter, Washington had the ball at its own 45-yard line. The Redskins called a flea-flicker. Quarterback Joe Theismann handed the ball to running back John Riggins, who took two short, quick steps before turning around and pitching the ball back to Theismann. The Giants blitzed both their inside linebackers on the play. The pocket collapsed. Harry Carson's pressure up the middle forced Theismann to step up to his left. Theismann moved forward past Taylor, but No. 56 leaped in the air with outstretched arms, pouncing on the quarterback's back. Theismann's body twisted and crumbled to the ground. On the sidelines, they heard a pop. Gary Reasons and Jim Burt piled on to finish the play. LT sprang off the ground. He frantically waved to the Redskins sidelines, motioning them to send out their medical staff. He put both of his hands to his head as he stared at Theismann lying on the grass.

Theismann's leg had snapped below his knee. Before the medical staff reached the field, the referee tried to move his leg, and blood spurted up, hitting the ref in the chest.[4] The play has been viewed more than a half million times on YouTube. It is the play shown in the movie *The Blind Side* because when Michael Lewis, the author of the book on which the movie is based, started talking to NFL executives about why left tackles get paid so much money, inevitably the conversation turned to this play. The play ended Theismann's career, and Taylor felt bad. "But I've never felt guilty because there was no intent to injure. It's just one of those plays that unfortunately happens sometimes in football."[5]

The game finished with backup quarterback Jay Schroeder leading Washington to a 23–21 win.

While the season played out, LT's drug use blossomed. During a preseason minicamp, LT's urine tested positive for illicit drugs. Parcells tried to get him help. The coach resents the idea that he allowed Taylor's drug use because of the game-changing results he produced on the field.

"We would not have the relationship we have today if we hadn't gone through this whole thing. Because deep down, no matter how bad it got, he always knew I cared about what the hell happened to him. And I did care about it, genuinely care about it. Not just for selfish reasons. I cared about him long after, when I wasn't the coach and he wasn't the player," Parcells said.

He sent Taylor to see someone, but the linebacker stopped going after a short while.

The positive drug test in minicamp gave the Giants the right to test LT frequently. He either avoided the tests by not showing up at them or he acquired clean urine from someone else and used that. In the meantime, he went from using cocaine a couple of times a month to buying a gram and finishing it in one night to buying an eight ball—which is three and a half grams—and finishing it. Taylor no longer controlled the drugs as he said he would.

He smoked crack cocaine for the first time. "Oh shit, I have to lie down. Then I said, 'Damn. I need some more of this shit.'"[6] After that, he started freebasing. He'd go on binges, spending days away from his wife and children and his $400,000 Upper Saddle River, New Jersey, home. He tried to stay clean. He spent a few weeks living with a friend. The pal dropped him off at the Giants facility and stayed with Taylor every moment he wasn't with the team. It worked until it didn't. The lowest point might have been when his wife had to physically remove him from a crack house in Hackensack.

When the Giants coaches graded players after the '85 season, Taylor ranked third on defense and eighth overall.[7] Despite the drug addiction and his drop in play, he was the lone Giant to make the All-Pro team, his fifth time in as many years in the league. The Giants had five players named to the Pro Bowl. Carson was headed to the postseason all-star game for the seventh time in his career. Defensive end Leonard Marshall, who set a Giants single-season record with 15.5 sacks, was going to his first Pro Bowl. So was Phil Simms, who led the NFC in passing yards with 3,829, and Joe Morris, the five-foot-seven running back who led the NFL in touchdowns with 21 and finished with a Giants record 1,336 yards.

The Giants started the season giving prime carries to rookie George Adams. Morris headed into December averaging 66 yards per game. In the final four games, Morris more than doubled that average, rushing for 135.5 yards per contest, and he added 10 of his touchdowns during this stretch.

The Giants finished the regular season with a 10–6 record—the same as the Cowboys, but because Dallas beat New York in both regular season games, the Cowboys took the NFC East Division title. The Giants grabbed a wild card berth for the second year in a row. This time, they hosted the matchup, the first home play-off game in twenty-three years.

They hosted the defending champs, the San Francisco 49ers. Bill Walsh, the coach who'd left a lasting impression on Simms when he'd visited the quarterback at Morehead State, had built the 49ers into a winner after taking the reins as head coach in 1979. His system of short, quick passes, well executed by quarterback Joe Montana, had become a marvel.

"You get tired of hearing things after a while," Parcells said.

Walsh had been anointed a football genius. Parcells respected that by the mid-1980s San Francisco had won two Super Bowls, but he demeaned their style of play and abhorred the gushing attention it received. This feeling filtered down to the Giants players who referred to the 49ers as a finesse team, coded words for saying San Francisco was soft.

The bitter feelings weren't eased by the fact that the Giants hadn't beaten the 49ers yet that decade, going 0–5 against them in the 1980s, or that San Francisco was traveling across the country as a three-point favorite. In the days leading up to the game, Montana, Walsh's third-round pick in 1979, took a shot at Simms, the number-seven overall pick that year. Montana claimed Simms made excuses after losses in which the San Francisco defense held him in check.

"Every time [Simms] says the same thing. 'We could have beaten you. If we had a little more time, I could have thrown the ball up and down the field anytime I wanted to,'" Montana told the *San Francisco Chronicle*. "I mean, for a guy our defense has played well against, he's got confidence bordering on cockiness."

Simms, who the *Washington Post*'s Christine Brennan described as having "the temper of a street brawler," jabbed back, saying Montana wasn't as smooth as his "Joe Cool" nickname inferred.

"They hated me and rightly so," Simms said years later.

Simms simply didn't back down. If anyone said something to him on the field, he jawed back at them. It wasn't one galvanizing remark he had said, but he knew he had given the 49ers enough reason to dislike him, and that was fine with Simms. When he played, he had no intention of being liked by, or making friends with, an opponent. He wanted to win.

A bold black sign hung in the Giants' locker room. It read: "Nothing could be finer than to beat the 49ers."[8] During practice that week, Carl Banks got into a fight with Vyto Kab, a backup tight end who would be deactivated for the game. Fans even fought waiting in line to buy a few of the 3,596 tickets that had become available days before the game. Officials estimated that ten thousand people lined up overnight at the Meadowlands for the chance to pay twenty-two dollars to get a seat. Giants punter Sean Landeta tried to be enterprising in the parking lot, offering tickets for fifty dollars apiece. He even sweetened the deal by adding an autographed picture of himself. This drew a letter from the state Division of Consumer Affairs informing Landeta and his teammates that scalping was illegal. When news broke about Landeta's attempted sale, he arrived at the stadium to find his teammates turned his locker into a mock ticket booth.

On game day, 75,842 fans filed into the stadium. When Phil Simms ran onto the field, it was the most palpable atmosphere he had played in. "Wow, this is what I really do feel—the electricity," he said. "Well, hell, there's no way we're going to lose."

The Giants smacked the 49ers around. They sacked Montana four times, hit him a bunch of other times, and intercepted him once. Simms connected with Bavaro and Hasselbeck for scores. In smashmouth style, the G-Men rushed for 174 yards, 80 yards more than their guests. The crowd chanted, "We want the Bears! We want the Bears!" as Big Blue closed out the 17–3 win.

"What do you think of that West Coast offense now?" Parcells said to reporters after the game, landing the final, disparaging blow.

The Giants headed to Chicago to clash with the 15–1 Bears. It was the second consecutive year New York faced a one-loss team in the divisional round of the play-offs. Outside of a Monday night loss at the Miami Dolphins, the Bears cruised through the regular season. They averaged more than 28 points per game and held opponents to just over 12. They touted their greatness in a rap song and music video. The "Super Bowl Shuffle" broke into the Billboard Top 100 rankings and made the rotation on MTV. Nicknames and personalities marked the Bears' roster. They had the rebellious and "Punky QB" Jim McMahon; "Sweetness" Walter Payton; the "Samurai" linebacker Mike Singletary; and, William "the Refrigerator" Perry.

Days before the game, Giants guard Billy Ard walked out of his West-field, New Jersey, home to find a delivery on his front lawn: a refrigerator with Perry's No. 72 painted on it. A TV camera had been tipped off to the prank and filmed Ard's reaction. After fans started to make visits to Ard's house to take pictures with the refrigerator, the kitchen appliance found a new home outside a gate at Giants Stadium. With Ard standing in the tun-nel where the players entered the stadium, a fan driving a tractor-trailer sounded the rig's horn, put it in reverse, and slammed into the fridge. "That's what you've got to do!" the driver yelled to Ard.[9]

The freezing wind in Chicago sliced through Soldier Field, making the twelve-degree-Fahrenheit temperature feel like it was thirteen below zero. Johnny Parker tried to warm himself up on the sidelines before the game. Each sideline had heated benches. On CBS's *NFL Today* pregame show, Irv Cross reported that the seat part reached 110 degrees, the back 150 degrees, and the slots below maxed out at 200 degrees. Parker had stuck his foot into one of the slots.

"I didn't feel it warming, nothing. I didn't feel anything. Then all of a sudden."

Running back Tony Galbreath tackled Parker down to the ground.

Maybe he's gone around the bend. He's snapped, Parker thought.

Lying on the ground, Parker looked at his pants. They were burned up to his knee, the long thermal underwear, too. His sneaker had melted. It was so cold he hadn't noticed.

The Giants opened the game receiving the ball. Joe Morris picked up 19 yards on the first two plays from scrimmage. On the third play, Morris cut back, and Singletary smashed him for no gain. On the next play, Simms dumped a pass over the middle to Rob Carpenter. He darted into Bears territory only to have Chicago linebacker Wilber Marshall poke the ball out from behind. Singletary recovered the fumble, dulling the Giants' momentum.

With the game still scoreless, on third down and eight, late in the first quarter, the Bears sent only three pass rushers. Defensive end Richard Dent started on the right side and made a looping stunt up to the left side before sacking Simms for a 12-yard loss back to the Giants' 10-yard line. On the next play, Landeta lined up two yards deep in the end zone. He took the snap on the right side. Dropped the ball to boot it, but the wind moved it. He whiffed. The wayward ball bounced left, wide of the hash mark on the 5-yard line. The Bears' Shaun Gayle recovered it and took it in for the touchdown.

The Giants' offense closed the first half with an opportunity to tie the game. They drove the ball to the Bears' 2-yard line with thirty seconds to play. On first down, Simms dropped a fade pass into Bobby Johnson's hands, but the ball bounced off Johnson's fingers and was almost intercepted.

"I won't ever forget that," Johnson said. "I cried."

On second down, Simms lofted a pass intended for Don Hasselbeck. It landed out of the back of the end zone. On third down, Simms threw it over the head of Johnson on a fade pattern. Eric Schubert lined up for the 19-yard field goal. He clanged it off the left upright. Six feet away and the Giants came away with nothing. They headed to the break down 7–0.

Midway through the third quarter, the Bears had taken a 14–0 lead. At this point, Chicago had gained 261 yards on offense to the Giants' 69.

"We just had a very dominant defense," said Bears coach Mike Ditka. "We did all the right things that year. That was our year . . . It's not too complicated, you know, you can't make it harder than it is."

McMahon threw a 20-yard touchdown pass to Dennis McKinnon. It was the second time the duo hooked up for a score that quarter. The Bears led 21–0 and would win by the same score.

The defense tormented Simms all day. They sacked him six times, knocked him around, and left blood on his jersey.

"We ran a bunch of very elaborate games where we were doing a lot of three-man line stunts," said Dan Hampton, the Bears' defensive lineman who called the stunts. "Dent was coming around underneath, untouched. They never figured it out."

Typically, the Giants' offensive line didn't make those kinds of mistakes, but they did against the Bears. "We didn't know what the fuck we were doing," Ard said.

Skirmishes broke out toward the end of the game. Things had become so tense that when Lawrence Taylor smacked Carl Banks on the back after Banks made a tackle, Banks turned around looking for a fight until he realized it was Taylor. Jim Burt and Taylor found themselves on the Chicago sidelines, exchanging shoves, heated words, and pointed fingers.

"I'm out on the field being a sore loser. And all of the Bears guys, that vaunted defense, they're standing on the sidelines giving us a ration of grief," said safety Kenny Hill.

The Yale graduate and former Raider took offense to McMahon running a bootleg. Hill hit the quarterback as McMahon headed out of bounds and both players slid into the bench on the Bears' sideline. A fracas ensued and LT and Burt ended up in the mix, retrieving Hill. The next play, Chicago ran Dennis Gentry on a fly route at Hill. It was incomplete and Hill pointed over at Ditka.

When the G-Men had the ball another scuffle broke out after a 13-yard Galbreath run. George Adams and Bears safety Dave Duerson started to get physical. Phil McConkey moved toward the action and took a swing at Duerson. Bears defensive back Reggie Phillips jumped into the scene. He grabbed McConkey around the neck and tackled him to the ground before officials pulled Phillips off.

The Bears went on to become world champions. They crushed the Rams 24–0 in the NFC Championship game. They pounded New England 46–10 in the Super Bowl. Their closest play-off contest was the 21–0 drubbing of the Giants.

Hampton, not trying to take a swipe at the Giants, viewed them as a jayvee version of the Bears. "You could tell they were built the right way. They just weren't ready for their moment."

When asked about the game years later, Giants defensive coordinator Bill Belichick said the stage was too big for the team that day. "We didn't play or coach well enough on defense even though we only gave up 14 points. LT played one of his worst games. He didn't have many."

After the loss, the Giants' locker room was quiet. The medical staff treated Joe Morris for a slight concussion and bruised ribs. McConkey needed attention for hyperventilating, and Jim Burt was looked at for a concussion. A friend asked Burt how he was feeling. "It doesn't matter now," he said.[10]

Bart Oates, the twenty-seven-year-old rookie center, sat by his locker, exhausted. He finished the USFL season in mid-July and started with the Giants three weeks later. This was his thirty-ninth game in the last forty-five weeks.

"Oh, my gosh, they kicked our butts," he remembers telling Simms.

The Giants knew the Bears were good; the realization of how far apart the teams were left New York shell-shocked.

"We knew we could play with them. But Chicago dominated us, and that did not feel good at all—not with the players we had. We didn't think we could be dominated like that," Galbreath said.

Parcells cut short his time with the media. He wasn't communicative with his assistant coaches. "My attitude was very poor," he said.

On the bus to the plane, Parcells sat next to Mickey Corcoran, his high school basketball coach. Corcoran had played high school basketball for Vince Lombardi at St. Cecilia's in Englewood, New Jersey. He remained a mentor and confidant to Parcells throughout the coach's career. The two men didn't exchange a word on the way to the airport.

On the plane ride, they sat together and remained silent. Parcells kept cycling through everything it had taken to get to this point and how much work it would take to get back there.

You need to remember how you feel next year. Remember how you feel after this game right here. You're pretty close to having a chance to do something good, he told himself.

About halfway through the flight, Corcoran tapped Parcells on the leg. "Hey, Parcells, you got to find a way to beat those guys."

"That's just what he said. That's his statement. Just as cold as that. That kind of snapped me out of it. Snapped me back."

It didn't lead to a conversation. It left Parcells with one thought. *You know, he's right.*

35–20. With less than ninety seconds to play, Simms connected with Adams on a 24-yard touchdown pass, but the Giants failed to recover the onside kick. They lost 35–30 and left Riverfront Stadium with a 3–3 record.

"We just gave it away. I'm kind of embarrassed the way we played. I think we're a better team than we showed today. Nobody got it done, coach or player," Parcells said.[3]

Coming into the game, Bavaro only had four catches in the first five games. Against Cincinnati, he set a Giants single-game record with 12 receptions for 176 yards. The media gathered by his locker after the game. He felt uncomfortable with the microphones in front of his face. He didn't like being the center of attention.

"I don't even know what they were asking; all I knew was that I looked over and Parcells was kind of giving me the stink eye from the other corner of the locker room."

Parcells stood with his arms folded in the distance. He didn't say anything. He stared at the scene, looking at how Bavaro would respond. Would the rookie celebrate his performance even though the team lost? Would Bavaro be smart enough not to?

Bavaro packed his belongings into his bag. He offered a cliché quote about the passing routes being the same and that he just happened to be open. He told the reporters he had to board the team bus before slipping through the scrum and leaving the locker room.

"That kind of made him respect me a little bit more," Bavaro said of Parcells. "It was like I was the kind of guy he was looking for physically, mentally, and personality-wise."

Bavaro, an Italian, Mass-attending Catholic, started to become a folk hero, especially to the large population of Italian Americans that planted their roots in the New York–New Jersey area. To them, Bavaro was a *paisan,* a buddy.

"They never treated me like a football player. They always treated me like one of them," Bavaro said.

After home games, Bavaro walked into the players' parking area and was greeted by fans drinking beers and eating sandwiches while hanging around his '79 Chevy Malibu clunker with the worn tires. They were mostly Italians, and they all spoke with that thick Jersey accent. They spoke to Bavaro using his first name. "Hey, Mark, great game today." But when Harry Carson walked to his car, it was all "Oh, Mr. Carson." They went wide-eyed with adulation when Lawrence Taylor passed by. Meanwhile, their pal Bavaro was ready to drive away.

"All right, I've got to get going," Bavaro said politely, asking them to unseat themselves from his hood and to take their beers off the roof.

The Giants rebounded from the Cincinnati game by beating Washington 17–3 at home. The Redskins came into the game leading the NFL in rushing, posting 183 yards a game. The Giants' defense limited their ground game to 69 yards. New York intercepted Washington quarterback Joe Theismann three times and sacked him seven times. Lawrence Taylor accounted for two of those sacks.

After the game, LT told reporters he focused on his preparation that week. "I got some sleep. I didn't go to bars much. I decided to go back to my old self."

In '84, he started the season with eight sacks in the first four games and played subpar for a stretch in the middle of the season. He started the '85 campaign with a string of pedestrian games, but his postgame comments hinted that the rumors about his wild, reckless off-field lifestyle held truth.

"I've had a lot of things on my mind the last couple of weeks," he said. "Maybe football wasn't as important to me as it should have been. Last year, it lasted eight games. This year, I have to catch it before it starts. I have to stop it now."

The Giants kept winning after the Washington game, peeling off victories at New Orleans and home against the Buccaneers and the Rams. The G-Men pushed their record to 7–3 and were tied with Dallas for the division lead heading into a Monday Night Football showdown on national TV at Washington.

With the game tied at 7, a minute into the second quarter, Washington had the ball at its own 45-yard line. The Redskins called a flea-flicker. Quarterback Joe Theismann handed the ball to running back John Rig-

PART

Giant Football

FOUR

15
REHAB

Nobody said anything about it on the plane, but with ten minutes left in the team's flight home from Chicago, an engine on the left wing blew out.

The DC-10 ran on two-thirds power. Fire trucks lined the runway at the airport in Newark in case of an emergency. Luckily, the plane landed safely. Big Blue returned home, their '85 season ended.

As they deplaned, Lawrence Taylor made a point to say something to Kenny Hill.

"Hey, homeboy," LT said, getting Hill's attention.

"You know what I like about you? You'll fight and that's what we need on this team."

The next day, Parcells met with reporters. Two years earlier, it wasn't clear how much longer he'd be an NFL coach. Now, he fixated on one thing.

"I'm only interested in winning the championship. It's the only reason I'm coaching," he said.

He scoffed at the idea of being satisfied that the once floundering Giants had for the first time in franchise history won play-off games in two consecutive years.

"Wild card games and all that, I don't care about that," he said. "I just want to get in the championship game, and that's all there is to it. I'm not interested in doing the job just good enough to keep it. It's too hard on me."

During the regular season, the Giants had lost six games by a total of 20 points. Going into Chicago, they thought they could beat the Bears.

They lost by 21. A lot of players look back at the dejected postgame feeling as a rallying point for the '86 season. Phil Simms has a different take.

"That's always what everybody says. I wasn't thinking that way. I never thought about it. We're going to training camp in '86. 'Here we go and let's just work,'" Simms said.

When the players packed up their lockers, Simms was headed to the Pro Bowl. He rallied the NFC to a 28–24 victory, calling most of his own plays and winning the game's MVP. Both of his backups with the Giants wanted out. Jeff Rutledge spoke to Parcells, asking to be traded. For the first time in his career, Jeff Hostetler headed home for the off-season. Hostetler was going into the final year of his rookie contract, and he had yet to have an opportunity to compete at the position. "For two years they haven't looked in my direction," he said.[1]

Players started their off-season-conditioning program in the days after the Bears loss. When this began, Parcells sought out linebacker Carl Banks. In his first two seasons, the number-three overall pick from the '84 draft and the third-highest-paid Giant had only started nine games.

Parcells planted himself in one of the burnt-orange chairs near the stereo system in the middle of the locker room. The coach's lounging appearance wasn't random. Typically, they were timed so he could interact with a player or group of players who were scheduled to work out. He called Banks over, and Banks sat with him.

"Hey, Banksy, you know what? I don't know if you realize this, but my expectations for you are probably a little higher than you have for yourself. I know you want to be a good player and the best player you can be. And you're doing a good job for us, but I expect you to be even better. I know you think you are working hard, but I expect even more than that from you."

Banks, not one to acquiesce, told Parcells he thought the coach was wrong, but he agreed to work harder and produce more.

Parcells shook his head. "No. I'm not wrong. Just know my expectations for you are higher than any you have for yourself."

This was not Parcells trying to motivate a player. He believes the term *motivation* is overused. "You can't motivate anybody that doesn't want to be a self-starter. If a guy is not a self-starter, you can't make him a self-starter."

He believed in offering encouragement to a player who made progress. "But when you get in a situation where, 'Hey this guy isn't doing what I think he can do,' you have first got to see if you're teaching him and giving him the vehicles and the wherewithal to complete the task you're asking him to complete."

This inward look started when Parcells was a twenty-three-year-old assistant coach at Hastings College. All week, Parcells had coached Hastings' Jack Giddings to stop a bootleg play in practice. On game day, Giddings missed the assignment, and Parcells lost it on him. Hastings' head coach, Dean Pryor, backed Parcells off, saying whatever preparation Parcells had done, it wasn't enough. Giddings still missed the play.

From that point forward, Parcells was going to find ways to reach his players, even if it meant chastising them and even if it looked unorthodox to the outsider.

"Listen, I got into coaching because I thought I could affect people and try to help them. I always try to do that. It's part of me. It's the way I was brought up as a player. Coaches tried to help me personally with things. That's what I tried to do. Still do."

Parcells and Banks bonded by talking about boxing, a sport they both enjoyed. "We ended up having a great relationship," Banks said.

They played basketball together on a hoop set up in the tunnel in Giants Stadium. Parcells would tap Banks during lunch, or the coach would wait in the tunnel, ball in one hand, cigarette in the other, looking for Banks. Once he saw the linebacker, he'd drop a "Let's go," and it meant a game of one-on-one or H-O-R-S-E was about to get under way.

"He had a nice shot. He'd win his share," Banks said.

Two days after Chicago defeated New England 46–10 in the Super Bowl, *Boston Globe* reporter Ron Borges broke the story that the Patriots had a drug problem. Head coach Raymond Berry told the newspaper five players had a serious problem and five to seven others were suspected of having a problem. Berry confronted the players after they attended a drug party following a 30–27 Monday night loss at Miami. The day after the Super Bowl, Berry held a team meeting in which the players voted to accept a one-year mandatory drug-testing program. The report became national news. It opened the door for the New York media to ask questions about the Giants' policy on drug use and drug testing. The operation Parcells set up with the backing of George Martin was a rogue one.

George Young admitted that the Giants had established a drug-testing policy. "We don't talk about it publicly because anonymity is very important and rehabilitation is very important. We're not trying to be punitive, we're trying to help players help themselves. It's an ongoing process, and I don't want to air it out."[2]

Newspaper accounts reported that as many as twelve Giants had been tested and that the team had sent players for drug rehabilitation.

Within days of these reports, Lawrence Taylor called Phil Simms. He asked the quarterback to replace him at a speaking engagement that was scheduled for Wednesday, February 12, in White Plains, New York. Taylor told Simms he was going to visit his sick grandmother in North Carolina.[3]

On Valentine's Day morning, two days after Taylor missed the speaking engagement, Howard Cosell's voice came crackling through the dial on ABC Radio. He announced the bombshell: Lawrence Taylor was in a drug rehabilitation center. The NFL's revolutionary defensive player had been somewhere in Texas receiving treatment for cocaine abuse.

LT shared the front page of the *New York Post* with a headline about poisoned Tylenol pills and a picture of mob boss John Gotti being patted down as he arrived in court. No. 56 had the back page all to himself.

George Young and Parcells took questions from the press, but they said nothing of consequence. They refused to talk about Taylor's whereabouts. They didn't acknowledge if they knew where he was nor did they say anything about Taylor's alleged medical treatment for drug use.

The news about cocaine use was a curveball to his teammates. "We knew he had some problems," said defensive end Leonard Marshall. "But I'm surprised to hear about cocaine."[4]

He slept during team meetings, sometimes sprawled out on the ground, sunglasses covering his eyes and his body partly under a table. Lamar Leachman stood in front of a defensive meeting room installing that Sunday's pass rushing plan. The lights were off as Leachman showed film of the opponent's pass protection. Thirty minutes into the session, Leachman had enough of the snoozing superstar. He barked at somebody to turn on the lights.

"We're trying to install a pass rush that you're a part of, and goddamn it, wake up."

"What the hell are you talking about?" LT answered.

Taylor asked for the lights to be cut off and to roll the film. He watched one play. He asked for the lights to be turned back on. He grabbed a piece of chalk and drew up the entire pass-rushing scheme. A dumbfounded look spread across Leachman's face.

"Anything else? Or can I go back to sleep?"

Teammates knew about LT's drinking and partying. Most say Taylor shielded the hard-core drug use from them, splitting off from the teammate social scene to do his own thing.

Taylor raced his BMW 740iL against Brad Benson's Corvette in the stadium parking lot. They weaved through the steel drums, which divided parking lot sections. Benson's car was clearly better suited for the competition. LT pushed the limit, driving so fast the BMW rolled over, doing a full revolution. He stepped out of the car and motioned over to his opponent. "Take that shit, Benson."

He had won the race and ruined the car. The car didn't matter, though. He bought another one. Money wasn't all that big of a deal. Teammates found one of his uncashed checks floating through the parking lot after it had blown out of his car. He cared about other things: winning and being the guy who drank the most beers on the charter plane flying back home after road games.

Because he was the best and never acted better than anybody, his teammates viewed his wild side from a unique perspective. "That was kind of an endearing quality of taking on challenges and doing things that were daring rather than being a petulant star that would breed resentment," said guard Chris Godfrey.

As LT's specific drug rehab location remained unknown, news stories speculated as to how this could've happened. How could a guy who was by far the best at what he did in professional sports wreck it with drugs? Did it start after the Giants made him richer with a new contract after the Donald Trump fiasco? He had pretty much stopped talking to the media during that awful 3–12–1 season. Did it start then? Articles recapped the game-by-game breakdown of his play in '85, looking for some originating point. All unnamed "associates," "highly placed sources," and "insiders" were quoted in stories, adding to further speculation.

"There are guys who really have their claws into him," said one teammate, referencing LT's ties to the mob and Vincent Ravo.[5]

Taylor had checked into Houston Methodist Hospital using the alias Paul Davis, the name of a former teammate who lived with Taylor and his family. LT's time there didn't last long. His room felt like a jail cell. Using the same alias, he checked into another hospital. This time, he stayed in a $1,500-a-day suite. That place worked briefly until he became frustrated during a therapy session because a woman couldn't figure out how to fit a hammer into its place on a pegboard. He left. He decided golf would heal his cocaine addiction.

On March 20, a little more than a month after Cosell's broadcast, Taylor issued a statement through the Giants. Parcells handed a copy of the message, which was typewritten on plain paper, to Tom Power, director of promotions. He read the statement to media members via individual phone calls.[6]

In the statement, Taylor talked about understanding his responsibility as a public figure, wanting to win a championship, and portraying the proper image for the youth of America. He admitted to needing professional help for a substance abuse problem but stayed clear of detailing the substance. He never mentioned the hospital stays or the self-prescribed golf therapy. He concluded by saying he wouldn't be talking about his problem or the remedies.

While this was going on, wide receiver Bobby Johnson had a teammate and a couple of women over to his apartment in Hackensack, New Jersey.

With his father served in the air force, Johnson and his family—a brother and two sisters—moved around early in his childhood. When the family moved to East St. Louis, Illinois, Johnson's mother filed for divorce. The divorce didn't have a devastating impact on him, but the adjustment to the new area hit its bumps. Johnson and his brother would get into fights on the way home from school.

"From being in the service and not being around a whole bunch of black people, it was scary," Johnson said.

The public high schools in East St. Louis were packed with up to two thousand students and great athletes. Johnson grew up hearing stories about San Diego Chargers Hall of Fame tight end Kellen Winslow and Jackie Joyner-Kersee, the three-time Olympic track-and-field gold medalist.

Johnson wanted to play varsity football early in his high school career, so he went to Assumption, the private Catholic high school. He played college football at the University of Kansas before making the Giants as a free agent in 1984.

He had never seen cocaine before he came to New York. He'd drink a couple of beers every now and then, but he wasn't a drinker.

That day at Johnson's apartment, the foursome hung out in the living room. One of the women brought out some cocaine. She combined it with water and baking soda and boiled the mixture in a spoon. Rocks emerged from this crude chemistry process. She had made crack cocaine.

"You have to try this," she said, looking at Johnson.

She lit the pipe, and Johnson took a hit. "It was just overwhelmingly good," he said.

He thought he was mentally strong enough. He thought he'd do this a couple of times and be done with it. "But it don't work like that."

Johnson wanted the feeling from that very first high. It is the tease of addiction, because that first-time feeling never returns, but the addiction forces the addict to pursue it.

"If you have $500, you'll spend $500. If you have $5,000, you'll spend $5,000 just chasing that," he said.

That night, Johnson and the woman split off into the bedroom to have sex. He stayed up until dawn, continuing to use the drug.

A press release for a charity golf and tennis event finally disclosed Lawrence Taylor's location. He was scheduled to be at Old Oaks Country Club in Purchase, New York, for a Juvenile Diabetes Association fund-raiser in early May.

The release had been sent to New York City newspapers, and four sportswriters and a photographer showed up ready with questions. Taylor was displeased with the scene. "I ain't talking to nobody."[7]

A week later, a reporter saw him outside the stadium. The media member asked how he was doing. Taylor's one-word response: "Hi."[8]

Everybody wanted to know what was going on with the Giants' top star. Parcells met with fans for a Q&A at Manny's, the bar and grill down the road from the stadium.

"I know he's worked hard at it, but they don't sell any insurance on that kind of a thing," Parcells said in a message point Taylor would echo.[9]

On May 21, Taylor arrived in the Giants' locker room for minicamp. This would be the first routine setting for reporters to ask Taylor questions. Parcells called him into the coach's office. He walked past the media. A half hour later, Taylor walked out. Parcells had a big smile on his face.

"I'm not talking. You've done that well already," Taylor said in the midst of his brief series of "no comments" to reporters who had waited outside the office.

Parcells proceeded to unload on the media. "I don't expect him to make a statement, and, in fact, I would advise him not to," Parcells said.[10]

He referred to the gathering at the country club charity event as horseshit. Parcells didn't want Taylor's drug issue to be the focus of minicamp. "We're not here to talk about that, although I know the issue is your favorite subject . . . What's he supposed to do, spill his guts out to you guys?"[11]

As he held court, Parcells accused the media of trying to make the story a distraction, and he wasn't going to let it happen. He threatened to ban the press from the locker room, which was unregulated and open in that era.

"If you think this guy is gonna be scrutinized every week, that ain't gonna be the case. I can assure you that. You can write that on your little chalkboard."[12]

The next day, LT made it clear. He had no plans of talking to the media.

"I read what you guys wrote, picking me apart game by game when I was talking to you. Let's see what you write if I don't talk to you."[13]

The subject didn't go away, though. In the early morning of June 19, hours after the Boston Celtics had taken Len Bias with the second overall pick in the NBA draft, the all-American from Maryland suffered cardiac arrest brought on by cocaine use. The twenty-two-year-old died. Eight days later, Cleveland Browns safety Don Rogers died from a cocaine overdose hours after his bachelor party and on the day before he was supposed to get married. A coroner said Rogers had used enough cocaine to kill an elephant.

In July, at the Giants' training camp, Parcells reiterated his stance that the LT topic was off limits. This time, the head coach added more force to his words.

"The next guy who asks me about him is going to have trouble getting up."[14]

16

THE LOCKER ROOM PAY PHONE

Joe Morris didn't make the preseason trip with the Giants to Atlanta.

The starting running back wanted a new contract, and the Giants believed Morris was obligated to stick to the one already in place. He had been attending training camp practices and team meetings, but he didn't take part in any contact drills. As a result, the Giants levied daily fines on him for his lack of full participation.

"We don't negotiate with a player who is in violation of his contract. We won't reward anyone who is breaking his contract," said general manager George Young.[1]

Morris made $150,000 in base salary in '85 and was scheduled to make $195,000, according to the ball club's option clause in Morris's contract. The Giants informed Morris they would pick up the option the previous December. The Pro Bowl running back signed a receipt acknowledging he had received the letter stating they would pick up the option. Morris's agent, Tom Toner, countered, saying it was an option to allow for renegotiations and that there was a verbal agreement in place to renegotiate terms.

In early August, when the Giants left for a series of combined practices with the Falcons before a preseason game with Atlanta, Morris had been asked to stay at home. The back-and-forth between Toner and the organization had reached a stalemate. It tore at Morris. He sat at home watching his team play on TV. "It's killing me. But my whole thing was I was trying to get a contract, that's all I was trying to do. I didn't want to be a distraction. God knows, I didn't want to be a distraction."

Morris didn't always feel wanted with the Giants. As he emerged from the lower rungs of the depth chart, the G-Men drafted George Adams in the first round and Lee Rouson in the eighth round in '85. "I don't think Parcells wanted them to draft me in the first place," Morris said.

In the first round of the 1982 draft, the Giants took Butch Woolfolk, a Michigan running back who played for Westfield High School in New Jersey. They expected Woolfolk to be a 1,000-yard gainer. Morris came out of Syracuse as the school's all-time leading rusher. In his first three seasons for the Orange, all under offensive coordinator Tom Coughlin, Morris surpassed the career yardage numbers of Jim Brown, Floyd Little, Ernie Davis, and Larry Csonka. His five-foot-seven stature was a drawback to draftniks, but his 4.38 40-yard dash time made Giants scouts believe he could, at the very least, return kicks.

When it came time for the Giants to make their second-round pick, Parcells, who was the defensive coordinator, wanted Calvin Daniels, a linebacker out of North Carolina.

"Bill thought he was going to be the next Lawrence Taylor of the middle linebackers," said Jerry Shay, the Giants' director of college scouting.

Wellington Mara, head coach Ray Perkins, Young, and Parcells huddled in the hallway outside the team's war room at Giants Stadium. Shay stayed back in the room catching stares from scouts who had seen both Daniels and Morris play. Shay stepped outside and interrupted the meeting. "Hey, everybody in that room does not like that linebacker. They want running back Joe Morris."

"Frankly, I said what Wellington wanted to hear, and we end up taking Joe Morris," Shay said.

Morris had a breakout year in '85, leading the NFL in touchdowns and setting a Giants single-season rushing record with 1,336 yards. On the Friday before the play-off loss to the Bears, Morris gave eight offensive linemen and three tight ends inscribed Movado watches as thanks. He gave his lead blocker, fullback Maurice Carthon, a Rolex. At the Pro Bowl in Hawaii, Morris noticed when the Bears players were announced they were called world champions. He wanted that for himself. Even though the contract hadn't been settled, Morris attended every off-season strength-and-conditioning workout. The diminutive back weighed a shade under 200 pounds, but he could bench-press 415. He completed extra running circuits at local high school fields. He knew the Giants who held out in the past became a scourge in Parcells's eyes. Earnest Gray went from tied for the NFC lead in receptions in '83 to holding out and catching only 41 passes for the rest of his career, just 17 more games over two seasons. Two-time All-Pro cornerback Mark Haynes held out, and he wasn't even mentioned in the team's 1985 *Bound for Glory* highlight film. In the following off-season, the Giants traded Haynes to the Broncos for second- and sixth-round picks in '86 and a second-round pick in '87.

Morris's wife, Linda, was pregnant with the couple's first child. He had moved into a new house. Teammates started calling him, asking him to return to training camp. "You've got all these pressures on your mind. You've got a season you're preparing for and all this is going on," Morris said.

In the lead-up to the '86 draft, Giants brass spoke about getting a "burner," a speedy wide receiver to supercharge the offense and catch passes from Phil Simms. As the draft drew closer, it became obvious New York would use its first-round choice, the nineteenth overall pick, on Notre Dame defensive end Eric Dorsey. "I've met with the Giants six times since the Combine and all that attention strikes me as being very strange," Dorsey said days before the draft.[2]

After trading Haynes to the Broncos, the Giants dealt future Hall of Fame offensive lineman Gary Zimmerman to the Minnesota Vikings. The Giants had the rights to Zimmerman, who played in the USFL, but the lineman refused to play in New York. The deals left New York with six picks in the first three rounds, including four selections in the second round. For all the talk about grabbing some offensive firepower, the Giants, who led the NFL in sacks and ranked second in overall defense in '85, loaded up on defenders. Big Blue drafted three defensive linemen, a middle linebacker, a cornerback, and a safety with those first six picks. They picked up Ohio

State's Thomas "Pepper" Johnson with the fifty-first overall selection. They added Erik Howard and John Washington to the defensive line spoils that included Dorsey. They chose safety Greg Lasker with the fifty-third pick and cornerback Mark Collins with the forty-fourth.

The Giants had three picks spread across the fifth and sixth rounds. There they chose wide receivers Vince Warren, Ron Brown, and Solomon Miller. When the rookies took questions from the media during a post-draft lunch at Giants Stadium, a reporter asked Miller if he had met Phil Simms. "Who is Phil Simms?" asked the Utah State rookie before following it up with "Oh, wow," when he learned it was his quarterback.[3]

The first six picks the Giants made would play an average of 123.5 games in their NFL careers. The receivers were a different story. They played in a combined total of thirty-one games. Brown didn't make the Giants' '86 team. Warren played in four games that year, and Miller had the longest career, playing all season with the Giants and then appearing in eight games for Tampa Bay in '87. The Giants had not acquired that pass-catching speedster.

The team continued its efforts to gain an edge in performance. In the mid-'80s, in the midst of the Cold War between the United States and the Soviet Union, strength-and-conditioning coach Johnny Parker visited the Russian Federal Institute of Physical Education. He brought back exercises that included football movements and ones that focused on the use of free weights rather than machines. He trained players from their legs, up through their backs, and into their upper bodies because he believed football strength started in the lower body. He emphasized cardiovascular workouts because he believed players were more likely to suffer injuries when they were fatigued.[4] It was no longer lifting to add brawn; there was a sophistication to it.

Big Blue also changed up the training table offerings in '86. "They want every edge in terms of competition. I'll bet half our team has read *Eat to Win*," said head trainer Ronnie Barnes, referring to the *New York Times* bestselling sports nutrition book.[5]

They shifted away from red meat and served more fish. Phil Simms ate a new cereal, Nutri-Grain, with almonds and raisins. During training camp, the Giants went through sixty pounds of bananas per day. The team ate a total of three and a half tons of beef, 1,750 pounds of fish, 1,680 heads of lettuce, 1,050 pounds of grapes, 1,225 gallons of ice cream, and 2,940 fruit bars.[6]

The team broke training camp at Pace University and headed back to New Jersey without Joe Morris. The posturing between the player and the team became contentious. The Giants sent Morris a letter letting him know he had five days to return to the team or he could be placed on the "reserve-left camp" list. If the team made this move, it meant Morris would have to sit out the '86 season and honor his contract the following year. Plus, he'd lose his medical benefits for the year. Morris responded to the threat of losing medical benefits for his wife and unborn child by holding a press conference. He countered the Giants' argument, saying they had asked him to leave camp.

After a twenty-one-day absence, Morris returned to the team without a new contract. Both sides agreed to work toward a new deal. Over four years, Morris wanted $2.6 million. The Giants offered $2 million. On his first full-contact play, Morris took a handoff and ran off left tackle. The defensive linemen and linebackers fell down, a joke to welcome him back.[7]

The Giants placed Morris back on the active roster before the final preseason game, an August 30 home tilt with the Pittsburgh Steelers. Morris played well enough, gaining 13 yards on his first carry and picking up a total of 53 yards on 11 rushes. The season opener at Dallas was nine days away, and the rumblings were that if Morris didn't have a new contract, he wouldn't play.

On the same day the Giants closed out their preseason against Pittsburgh, John Tuggle, Mr. Irrelevant from the '83 draft, lost a two-year battle with cancer. He died at the American Biologics Hospital in Tijuana, Mexico. Tuggle started for an injured Rob Carpenter in the final five games of his rookie season. He rushed for 49 yards and scored his lone career touchdown in a 23–0 win over the Eagles. In July of '84, he found out he had a malignant tumor in his shoulder, and the cancer had also spread to his lungs. He vowed to fight the disease, buying champagne and toasting the challenge the day he was diagnosed. "He'd be in the weight room the same day he had chemotherapy and he'd be outdoing all of us. You could never tell anything was ever wrong with him," said guard Billy Ard.[8]

Tuggle made it back to minicamp in May 1985, but he had lung surgery seven months later. The Giants said they would welcome him back if he regained his health, but the team released him in February '86. The Mara family continued to pay for all of his medical expenses. Before he entered the hospital for a final time, Tuggle spent the day water-skiing. Thirteen days later, he died.[9]

To honor Tuggle during the '86 season, the Giants wore a black sticker with a white 38 on the back of their helmets. The team was already set to honor former Giants defensive back Carl "Spider" Lockhart, who had died in July at age forty-three, succumbing to cancer. Lockhart made two Pro Bowls playing for the Giants from 1965 to 1975. On the front of their left shoulders, players wore a circular patch with the fierce arachnid centered between "SPIDER" and his number, 43.

Two days after Tuggle's passing, the Giants made their final cuts, dropping center Conrad Goode, defensive end Dee Hardison, and wide receiver Phil McConkey. The youth of Warren and Miller, combined with the kick return ability shown by rookie cornerback Mark Collins, made McConkey, the U.S. Navy veteran, expendable.

McConkey's wide receiver coach, Pat Hodgson, said it was the most difficult cut he ever made. "He is what football's all about."[10]

The Packers picked up McConkey, sending him from a contender to a team that had won only one play-off game since Vince Lombardi coached them to a Super Bowl II victory at the end of the 1967 season. Depressed, McConkey packed one bag before getting on a plane for Wisconsin. By the end of the day, the nameplate on his Giants locker had been swapped out for kicker Bob Thomas.

Morris didn't have a new contract when he boarded the team's charter plane for Dallas. When the team rode two buses to Texas Stadium, Morris stayed in his hotel room. Parcells had no idea about Morris's absence until all the players took the field for the twenty-five-minute walk-through. The head coach walked past reporters, not answering any questions as the team reboarded the buses to return to the hotel.

"It was a pretty big distraction. The night of the game there, it was still uncertain," Parcells said.

Young and Tom Toner, Morris's agent, continued negotiating on game day. Morris maintained his routine of heading to the visitors' locker room early. He started to get dressed, but he wasn't sure if he was going to play. He spoke to his wife. She wanted an update on the contract status. He had nothing new to report. He hung up the phone with her and kept thinking, *Get me something, Tom. Get me something fair.* About two hours before kickoff, the pay phone in the locker room rang. It was Toner for Morris. The agent told him to get taped. The deal ended up being $2.2 million over four years. It made Morris the fourth-highest-paid Giant behind Taylor at $1.2 million, Simms at $760,000, and Carl Banks at $650,000 per year.

The Giants took the field on the Monday night season opener as the favorites to win the NFC East. The Cowboys remained a chief Giants nemesis, though. New York had only beaten the Cowboys four times since September 1974. After a scoreless first quarter, the game seesawed. The Cowboys scored on a 36-yard screen pass from Danny White to Tony Dorsett, a deft call against the Giants' blitz. On the ensuing New York possession, a series of miscues led to more Dallas points. A mishandled kickoff by Lee Rouson gave the Giants possession at their own 14-yard line. After throwing for a first down, Simms fumbled under pressure. Morris recovered at the Giants' 7-yard line, giving Big Blue a third down and 30. On the next play, Dallas's Randy White, a player the Cowboys drafted with a pick they received in a trade with the Giants, recovered a fumbled snap at the 2-yard line. Two plays later, Hershel Walker, playing in his first NFL game, took the handoff, set his two feet at the 4-yard line, and launched his body skyward, clearing the pile of offense and defense and landing softly in the end zone. The Cowboys led 14–0.

More than halfway through the second quarter, Simms had completed

4 of 12 passes for 35 yards. He rallied the G-Men on the next drive, going 4 of 5 for 62 yards and connecting with Bobby Johnson for a 13-yard score on third down and 10. The Giants took possession of the ball with 1:12 left in the half. Aided by a 36-yard pass interference penalty against Everson Walls, Simms finished a 66-yard scoring drive, hitting Stacy Robinson for a three-yard touchdown to tie the game at 14. The Cowboys had twenty-five seconds left in the second quarter and managed to get a 35-yard field goal from Rafael Septién, taking the lead back, 17–14, at the half.

The teams traded second-half touchdowns, Morris scoring on a two-yard run to put the Giants up 21–17 and White throwing a one-yard pass to Thornton Chandler to give the Cowboys a 24–21 lead.

New York had the ball with five and a half minutes to play. They lined up on second down and nine from the Dallas 44-yard line. Simms dropped back against a Cowboy blitz that sent seven defenders charging at the quarterback. He lofted the ball high down the left side of the field. The pass bounced high in the air after hitting Bobby Johnson's hands. Cornerback Ron Fellows overran the play to the sidelines, allowing the pass to float back into Johnson's arm before the receiver took it into the end zone. Simms watched from field level after being floored by a hit from Jim Jeffcoat.

The Giants led 28–24, but the defense couldn't hold the lead. With 2:10 left on the clock, Dallas drove 72 yards in less than a minute. Walker went untouched on a 10-yard run to the end zone.

In his NFL debut, Walker ran the ball 10 times and caught six passes, tallying 96 yards from scrimmage and scoring twice. Dallas moved the ball easily against the Giants' defense, gaining 392 yards and scoring on drives of 80, 74, and 72 yards.

"Bad coaching, bad playing, bad football. We didn't perform well enough defensively to win any game, let alone the Cowboys. I didn't prepare the team well enough," said defensive coordinator Bill Belichick.

The Cowboys had scored four touchdowns against the Giants' defense that night. No team would score more than two offensive touchdowns against Big Blue for an entire year after that, a streak unmatched by the heralded '85 Bears and '00 Ravens defenses.

Lamar Leachman lit into his defensive line publicly. Parcells kept his comments private.

"I just told them, 'What the hell was that about? We didn't have it in the clutch. We're not going anywhere. You guys think you're going to show up and win? You're wrong. That's a perfect example of it right there. You've got to get your ass in gear.'"

17

KICKERS IN THE BASEMENT

Joe Cooper sat in a conference room in his shirt and tie. He took notes while his boss, William Thornhill, Esq., met with a client about a myriad of issues involved in a soon-to-be divorce.

Listening to the client, Cooper realized he never wanted to practice family law. Thornhill's secretary interrupted the meeting. This was unusual. She asked to see Thornhill in the hallway. "Bill, the New York Giants are on the line for Joe. Should I take a message?"

Cooper was Thornhill's law clerk. He was taking classes toward his law degree at San Joaquin College of Law in Fresno, California. In college, at the University of California, Cooper was a placekicker for the football team. His last collegiate game included "The Play," when the Stanford band came on the field prematurely as Cal returned a squib kick for a touchdown. In 1984, Cooper made all his extra points and nailed 11 of 13 field goal attempts for the Houston Oilers. He had been out of football since then. The Giants called his mom's apartment looking for him. She forwarded them to the law office.

Thornhill's secretary didn't take a message. She put Joe on the phone. The Giants sent a scout to Fresno State to watch Cooper kick. "I was just thundering the ball, and the next day I get a call," he said. "'Hey, we want to sign ya.'"

Cooper flew to Newark, New Jersey. The Giants put him up at the Sheraton in Hasbrouck Heights. He went to the hotel bar to grab himself a beer the night he arrived. He wound up sitting next to Hossein Khosrow Ali Vaziri, better known as WWE star The Iron Sheik.

Cooper's stay at the hotel was short lived. The Giants found him housing in an Italian couple's basement in the nearby working-class town of Lodi. After practice, Joe took a walk around the neighborhood. He grabbed something to eat at the local Italian deli. The couple prepared him dinner that night. They served Italian bread and wine with bow tie pasta in a red sauce Cooper called a potpourri of meat. "They called it gravy."

During dinner, Cooper mentioned his stop at the deli. "They dropped their forks down, and they looked at me. And they all looked at each other."

They asked Cooper if he went behind the beaded curtain. He said he hadn't. They warned him to stay out of the place because some people there might want to become friendly with a young man who is responsible for scoring—*or not scoring points*—in an NFL game.

That Sunday, Cooper handled kicks for the Giants in their home opener against the San Diego Chargers. The Chargers came into the game after a 50–28 romp of the Miami Dolphins. Powered by quarterback Dan Fouts, tight end Kellen Winslow, and all-purpose running back Gary Anderson, the Chargers gained 500 yards against Miami.

On the Giants' second possession, New York drove the ball 68 yards to the Chargers' 3-yard line and settled for a short field goal from Cooper. On their next possession, Big Blue moved the ball 61 yards before lining up for Cooper's second attempt. He hit the crossbar and missed from 43 yards. The Giants led 3–0 at the end of the first quarter, and the hometown fans started to boo.

Two plays later, Lawrence Taylor took his customary spot, his left leg and shoulder almost perpendicular to the line of scrimmage as he stood over the left tackle ready to explode off the ball. He took two quick steps forward and read Fouts handing the ball to Lionel James on a sweep away from Taylor. James ran behind his blocking as LT chased him from behind. He crashed into James just beyond the line of scrimmage. Carl Banks hit James low. The impact from Taylor jarred the ball loose, and safety Terry Kinard recovered the fumble. A 29-yard pass from Simms to Mark Bavaro put the ball at the 1-yard line. Joe Morris took it to the end zone from there, giving the Giants a 10–0 lead.

The Chargers added a second-quarter touchdown to make it 10–7 at halftime, but there was little evidence to believe the Giants would lose this game. New York only sacked Fouts once, but they kept the pressure on the future Hall of Famer all game. At times, Fouts took a seven-step backpedal drop back. It was like trying to win a sprint by walking as Taylor, Leonard Marshall, and George Martin surged toward the quarterback. The defense intercepted Fouts on all five of San Diego's second-half possessions, and the Chargers only made it as deep as the Giants' 28-yard line.

Big Blue held the ball for nearly forty minutes. In the fourth quarter, Simms added a 12-yard touchdown pass to Lionel Manuel, and Cooper made another field goal, making the final score 20–7.

The Chargers mimicked some of the Bears' 46 defense, which gave the Giants trouble. Morris finished the game with 83 yards on 30 carries. San Diego held him to zero or negative yards on 13 rushing attempts. The Chargers sacked Simms four times. After one hit, Simms had trouble getting up off the turf. "I mean, I got killed," Simms said. "It crushed me."

Manuel came over to help his quarterback get up. "C'mon, man, you need to go out of the game," he told Simms.

"Lionel, I would never come out of the game. I wouldn't give the fans the fucking thrill of me coming out of the game."

The story made its way into a newspaper, furthering Simms's contentious relationship with some of the Giants' faithful.

With the game in hand, NBC game analyst Bob Trumpy turned his attention away from the field. "Watch out for that water jug over there. Whenever the Giants win, Burt seems to get his hands on that water jug."

Moments later, Burt doused Parcells with the Gatorade bucket. Simms was named the Budweiser player of the game. He threw for 300 yards for the second consecutive game.

The following week, the Giants headed across the country to face the Los Angeles Raiders. Cooper stayed in his hotel room listening to Joe Starkey call the radio broadcast for Cooper's beloved Cal Bears. After the game, he left his room, walked to the elevators, and pressed the button. When the doors opened, Parcells was there. Cooper stepped in. "Hey, Coach." To which Parcells gave a low mumble of "Hey" back.

The interaction gave Cooper a bad feeling. "He just had a way about him, and you knew he didn't like me."

On the opening drive of the game, Raiders quarterback Jim Plunkett connected with tight end Trey Junkin, who collected 19 yards before Taylor tackled him. LT caught Junkin on the sideline, wrapping him up with full momentum. Junkin's leg locked into the field, and the rest of his body swayed like a tree in a storm ready to snap to the ground. Two Raiders staffers helped Junkin off the field. The hit injured his knee. He was done for the season. Years later, in 2002, Junkin was the Giants' long snapper who botched the snap on what could've been the winning field goal in a wild card game against the 49ers, a game in which the Giants had already surrendered a 24-point lead.

Against the Raiders in '86, the Giants were down 6–0 at halftime. Kicking off the Bermuda grass in the Los Angeles Memorial Coliseum, Cooper missed a 39-yard field goal wide left. The CBS broadcast, which was handled by John Madden and Pat Summerall, noted that Cooper was the Giants' fifth kicker in the last seventeen games. "They haven't considered bringing you out, or dusting you off, and putting you out there? Have they?" Madden asked Summerall, who had kicked for the Giants from 1958 to 1961.

Simms threw two second-half touchdowns to Lionel Manuel. Aided by a 52-yard run, Joe Morris went over 100 yards for the first time that season, totaling 110 yards on 18 carries. The defense held the reigning NFL MVP, Marcus Allen, in check. Allen came into the game having rushed for 100 yards or more in eleven straight contests. Big Blue held him to 40 yards on 15 carries. The Giants left Los Angeles with a 14–9 win, the first time New York beat the Raiders franchise.

An elated Bill Parcells jogged off the field after beating his friend, Raiders owner Al Davis. Jim Burt was in front of the head coach. The nose tackle spent the day nullifying Raiders Pro Bowl center Don Mosebar, who was a half foot taller than Burt and outweighed him by at least twenty-five pounds. Burt walked off slowly, catching his breath in the seventy-eight-degree heat after the Giants' defense ended the game, stopping the Raiders' last-gasp effort. Parcells didn't notice the exhaustion. From behind, he grabbed Burt around the neck, knocking his helmet off.

"What the fuck are you doing?" Burt yelled, not knowing who had touched him.

He looked back, saw his coach, and became embarrassed. Parcells didn't quite understand the reaction, and he walked away from the awkward moment.

John Madden asked Burt about it in the locker room. "John, I have a bad back. That fat fucker jumped on my back!"

Madden started laughing. "That was the funniest thing ever. You looked at him like you wanted to kill him."

Three days after the Raiders game, the Giants cut Cooper. "I was basically used as a pawn to get Raul Allegre in line so he'd sign."

When Allegre arrived at the facility, the kickers shook hands, and Cooper wished Allegre good luck. Parcells introduced Allegre to the team at practice. "We have procured yet another kicker."

Allegre stood in front of his new teammates and waved. He had kicked for the Colts for the past three seasons, but Indianapolis had let him go in the summer. After the introduction, Burt walked over to him and told him not to buy a house in the area.

Allegre had been in New Jersey a few weeks earlier. He went through a tryout with the team. He kicked well, but things hit a snafu when it came time to sign the contract. Giants assistant general manager Harry Hulmes suggested Allegre call his agent to review the terms. At the same moment, Parcells called Allegre, Hulmes, and George Young into his office. "Parcells, in his wonderful style, said, 'What the hell is going on?' And I said, 'Well, I'm trying to find out what the contract is.'"

Parcells asked Hulmes what the offer was. It was more than Allegre made in base salary for the Colts, but the bonus structure for making field goals and extra points was different. Parcells had heard enough. "Get him the hell out of here."

The day after Allegre returned home to Indiana, he met with his best friend from the Colts, punter Rohn Stark. Allegre had dinner with Stark, Stark's wife, and the couple's young child. During the meal, Stark suggested Allegre write Parcells a letter explaining what happened.

On a couple of sheets of eight-and-a-half-by-eleven unlined tablet paper, Allegre wrote in cursive. "I don't know why you were so upset about it, I was just trying to understand the structure of the contract," he wrote before closing the note with, "Would you sign a contract that you hadn't read? Thank you, Raul Allegre."

Without a job in football, Allegre went back to work for the Indiana Department of Transportation. He started the job after being cut by the Colts. Allegre, who grew up playing soccer in Mexico, earned a civil engineering degree from the University of Texas. He didn't have a professional engineering license, so he assisted another engineer in bridge design. After Parcells booted him out of New Jersey, Allegre spent the next three weeks supervising bridge construction.

On Monday after the Raiders game, Allegre received a call from Parcells. "Would you still be interested in playing for the Giants?"

Allegre said, "Yes."

"Well, get a pen and a piece of paper, because I'm going to dictate to you the terms of your contract."

Parcells told Allegre to call his agent and go over the contract. If he was interested, he should call the coach by 10:00 the next morning on Parcells's private line. If the clock moved past 10:00 A.M., Parcells would know the kicker had lost interest in the Giants. Allegre called back the next day and agreed to the terms. Parcells told him to hurry to the airport. When he arrived back in New Jersey, Allegre took the basement apartment in Lodi, the one vacated by Cooper.

The Giants hosted the New Orleans Saints on a gray, sixty-two-degree day. Joe Morris wasn't at the stadium. He broke his nose in the Raiders game, and the team gave him a quinine-based drug when it happened. "In my dad's infinite wisdom, he never did mention to his son that he had an adverse reaction to quinine," Morris said.

The medicine thinned Morris's blood. It wouldn't clot. It led to a brief leukemia scare before Morris and the Giants realized it was a reaction to the drug. The running back would be fine, but he did have to miss the game.

The Giants opened the contest going three and out. The Saints started backup quarterback Dave Wilson in place of an injured Bobby Herbert. On New Orleans's third play from scrimmage, Wilson connected with Eric Martin for a 63-yard touchdown pass, beating Terry Kinard and putting the Saints up 7–0.

On the second play of the ensuing Giants drive, Simms hit Bavaro for 13 yards. Two plays later, on second and 11 from the New York 26, Bavaro lined up on the right side. The Giants had two receivers left. Lee Rouson, who'd started in place of Morris, left the backfield to go in motion to the left. Simms dropped back and threw a strike to Bavaro as the tight end made his cut on a five-yard out. Bavaro caught it at the 31 and turned up-field. Saints free safety Frank Wattelet bounced off him. Bavaro covered more yards as cornerback Dave Waymer grabbed his legs. Bavaro stumbled and stretched forward. "I remember just tugging him along. I probably just should've went down. I was reaching out," and strong safety Antonio Gibson came flying in with the finishing hit, his helmet battering into Bavaro's jaw. Immediately, Bavaro's white face mask turned red from the blood. His body did half a revolution, his chest rested at the 38-yard line while his feet were ahead of him facing the Saints' end zone at the 40.

"It was not a cheap shot. He was making a tackle. I don't think he targeted my chin. I don't think you can do that with any sort of accuracy. I wasn't wearing a mouth guard. I didn't wear a mouth guard usually. That was part of the problem," Bavaro said.

He rose up from the turf and strolled off the field. Middle linebacker Gary Reasons squinted at him to get a closer look at what happened. Bavaro thought he knocked a tooth loose. He sat on the bench with a towel in his mouth to stop the bleeding.

Three plays later, Simms threw an interception on a pass intended for Lionel Manuel. The Saints took the ball on an eight-play, 48-yard drive to go up 14–0. The Giants got the ball back, and Simms threw another interception. New Orleans turned that into a field goal. They had a 17–0 lead early in the second quarter on the road against a team that was supposed to be a Super Bowl contender. This was a Saints team that had never had a winning season since it had come into existence in 1967. The crowd at Giants Stadium booed the home team.

Zeke Mowatt subbed in for Bavaro and caught on two passes, collecting 37 of the Giants' 57 yards as they drove to the Saints' 12-yard line. On first and 10, Simms looked for Manuel. The ball sailed through the back of the end zone. It was past Manuel when Gibson hit Manuel's knee. Manuel was taken off on a cart. He wouldn't play another game in the regular season.

In the offensive huddle, Simms was without his Pro Bowl running back, his top wide receiver, and his starting tight end, and he never gave it a second thought. "All these years, I've never thought about it one second," he said nearly three decades later.

On the sidelines, Parcells wouldn't allow any wallowing. "My mentality is they're not canceling this game here just because we're having a little adversity. Your team is trained to respond that way. Just because something happens that you don't like, you can't throw the towel in. We didn't and you just got to find a way to do it anyway."

Simms overthrew Mowatt on the next play. The boos started again. The Giants settled for a 29-yard Allegre field goal.

"All I remember is a fan screaming behind me, 'This is a game we're supposed to win!'" Simms said, re-creating the whiny voice.

Bavaro had gone to the locker room for an x-ray. The report was he had chipped a tooth. He came back out to the field and planted himself in front of Parcells, not saying anything.

"He's pushing me. He just wants to go play," Parcells said.

Bavaro reentered the game and caught a touchdown pass before halftime.

On the third play of the second half, Andy Headen and Lawrence Taylor met eight yards behind the line of scrimmage, tackling Wilson. Headen received credit for the sack. LT stood over the quarterback, jawing at him.

The stat sheet has Taylor listed with seven tackles, but he dominated the game. He'd bury Wilson into the turf on one play. Drop back in zone pass coverage on the next. He even lined up wide, giving the look of man-to-man coverage on a wide receiver. The Saints tried to run away from him, but he consistently chased down running backs, catching them on the opposite side of the field before they reached the line of scrimmage. This is the game in which Taylor sprinted down the line to make a lasso tackle of Rueben Mayes, sliding on the Astroturf and popping up in one motion to celebrate with a quick finger point.

After the Headen sack, Mark Collins received the Saints' punt at the 43-yard line. The rookie cornerback lost his helmet on the return, but he kept going. He ran into a pile of players, taking two shots to the head. He gained six yards and was slumped over on the ground. He couldn't walk straight when trainer Ronnie Barnes came out to assist him off the field.

When Collins's play began to displace veteran corner Elvis Patterson, he had trouble with Patterson's friend Andy Headen. Collins muffed and then recovered a punt in the preseason game at Atlanta. Headen grabbed him as they came off the field. "What the fuck are you doing?"

"Motherfucker, get your hands off me," Collins said, pushing Headen as he responded. "I'm going to kick your motherfucking ass."

The incident happened in plain view of the coaches and the sidelines. Headen backed off a bit. But back in New Jersey, while Collins rode a stationary bike in the weight room, Headen came in and said something to the rookie. "You better make a move now. We could fight right now. I don't give a shit."

Linebacker Robbie Jones walked by and backed Headen off. "Andy, you better get along, man. He's got them crazy eyes, and he headstrong."

After that, Collins had no problem with Headen. Against the Saints, the rookie made his first start at cornerback. When he returned that punt without a helmet, he was looking to impress Parcells, particularly because he had heard Parcells didn't want to draft him. He referred to himself as a George Young pick.

"Now, was that a smart move on my point to keep running? Probably not. Not a career-making move. But I did it. I went down. I got concussed . . . Trying to impress the team, impress the coach, and make a play."

He spent the night in the hospital being evaluated, and he gained the respect of his teammates after they were done laughing at him for the crazy move.

Parcells knew what he saw had an impact on the team. "Players respect that kind of stuff. I don't need to say anything to it."

New York added a second Allegre field goal after Collins's punt return. In the fourth quarter, the Giants finished the comeback when Simms connected with Mowatt for a four-yard score.

"I don't know how we made the comeback, but I love the warm, humid, early fall days. It was perfect football weather, that's what I remember," Simms said.

The Giants ran 76 plays to the Saints' 47. Typical of Giant Football, they held the ball for almost thirty-nine minutes, more than a quarter longer than New Orleans.

Bavaro finished the game with seven catches for 110 yards and a touchdown. Further examination showed he had broken his jaw. What he felt floating around in his mouth wasn't a loose tooth. It was his jaw, disconnected from its hinge. He had his mouth wired shut, but the public report remained a chipped tooth.

As odd as it might seem, the next week in St. Louis, Bavaro, with his mouth shut down, had the best meal of his life. He ordered eggplant parmigiana and spaghetti, put it in a blender, and drank it through a straw.

18

ROLLING

Wellington Mara walked around the outskirts of the Giants Stadium turf. Players began entering the field through the tunnel. Once the action picked up, the Giants co-owner and team president set up his backless fold-up golf stool. Off to the side, he watched practice.

"He just loved being out there. Loved to see what our schemes were on defense. Or what we were featuring on offense that week, which player was being featured in the game plan. Looking at how the coaches taught their individual units. He loved watching the offensive line. That was probably his favorite thing," said his son John Mara.

Wellington sat in on draft meetings. He liked hearing about the prospective players, and he enjoyed the scouts' stories from the road.

One year, he was late for a predraft scouting meeting to have a mole removed from his face. He said he would return at 1:00 P.M. Soon, he sent word that he would be even later. He arrived back at the facility at 6:00 P.M., his face marked from the procedure. "Here's a guy who's apologizing to the scouting department for missing a meeting, and he's the doggone owner," said Jerry Shay, the team's director of college scouting.

In '86, the seventy-year-old father of eleven still attended Catholic Mass every day, alternating between Church of the Resurrection in Rye, New York, and Our Lady of Sorrows, fifteen minutes away in White Plains. The public's view of him had started to change. During those embarrassing losing years, he had been hung in effigy at the stadium. Fans held rallies against him. He received an urn filled with the ashes of burned tickets. He received letters filled with hate and criticism, and, as long as they weren't obscene, he responded to every one of them. "As much as you disagree with their reasoning or as illogical as they can be, if they care enough to sit down and write a letter to you, you have to give them the courtesy of a response. That was always his feeling," John Mara said.

Winning spurred the change in the fans' feelings. At the end of the 1981 regular season, the Giants beat the Cowboys 13–10 in overtime. The Jets beat the Packers the next day, sending the Giants to the play-offs, but before that Jets win happened, Big Blue had secured a winning record and had played itself into postseason contention.

The Maras watched that Cowboys game from the lower press box at Giants Stadium. The elevator they needed to use to get down to the locker room was out of service. They stepped out into the mezzanine concourse and walked the cement spirals down with the rest of the crowd. "That would've been a dangerous walk a year or two before that for him. But instead we're walking down there and people are saying, 'Way to go, Mr. Mara.' And they're slapping him on the back. It was a happy crowd, and that was something we were not used to experiencing in Giants Stadium. I'll remember that walk forever," John Mara said.

With George Young in place to handle the football decisions, it freed Wellington from dealing with contracts. He could take a paternal approach with the players. If they were coming back from an injury, he'd ask how they were feeling. He'd ask personal questions, too, checking in on how their families were doing. After games, he went from locker to locker, patting players on the back and thanking them for their effort.

Mara had served in the navy, so when Phil McConkey showed up at training camp in '83, he called the free agent "Commander." He never used McConkey's first name. When McConkey made the team in '84, Mara promoted him, calling him "Captain." "It was a bond we shared as naval officers, and it always made me feel a little special," McConkey said.

Sometimes after practice, defensive back Herb Welch would sit next to Mara. The owner would ask about Welch's father, who was a truck driver in California.

"You know, I like coming over here and sitting next to you because it feels like I'm sitting on a dock with my dad fishing. And it's just really calming," Welch said.

After the opening-week loss to the Cowboys in '86, Wellington felt deflated. It came from his hate for losing to Dallas coupled with the high expectations for the Giants that year. As the team started to win games, he became more optimistic, but the team had a problem—something Mara's jettisoned navy captain could fix.

McConkey didn't see much of the field in Green Bay. He ran down on the punt and kickoff teams. He never played a down at wide receiver. When Green Bay's Turk—the staffer responsible for telling cut players to see the coach—told McConkey to meet with head coach Forrest Gregg, McConkey figured he was done, out of football again.

Gregg put him on the phone with Parcells. McConkey had been traded back to the team that released him the Monday before the season started. "Those Packers drive a hard bargain. I had to throw in a couple of clipboards with a blocking dummy to get you back," Parcells said.

Back in the Giants' locker room, McConkey slid his green nameplate with the Packers logo into the slot above his locker. It was a reminder of the mercurial reality of pro football. At Parcells's request, he wrote a quote on the chalkboard in the middle of the locker room. It was something he said to Parcells when he spoke to him from Green Bay.

"The grass is always greener . . . my ass." It stayed there for the rest of the year.

On his first day back, McConkey met with Parcells in the head coach's office. Parcells told him the team's return game was in shambles. It was true. It had suffered in McConkey's absence. Parcells told McConkey the team could've traded for Henry Ellard from the Los Angeles Rams, but the coach chose McConkey.

"Parcells, master manipulation. I know it's not true. I know he's blowing smoke up my ass."

The Giants would've had to have given up a top-draft choice for a player like Ellard. For McConkey, they gave up a late-round choice.

McConkey listened and thought about the last time he was in Parcells's office, the day he was cut. McConkey felt he had the best training camp of his career, but Parcells told him, "You know, you're just not the same. If you didn't have that name on the back of your jersey, I wouldn't know it was you."

You're full of shit, McConkey thought. *Just tell me that you want younger guys. You got younger guys, and they were better than me. Just tell me that. Don't tell me I wasn't any good, because I was better than I've ever been, and I know it, and you know it. I'm not five years old.*

Yet, for all the mistrust of Parcells's words, McConkey left his return meeting feeling motivated. Whatever Parcells said, it worked. "I walk out there, and I feel like I'm going to run through brick walls for this guy and this team."

McConkey felt like it was a pat on the back. "It's an indirect way of saying, 'We really need you. I need you. You're valuable.' You don't say it that way, but I knew what he was trying to do, even though I knew he was bullshitting me."

McConkey made a point to speak to Parcells about one experience from his time in Green Bay. He had to tell him about the ultra-intense, militaristic position coach he had with the Packers, Tom Coughlin, who was also Joe Morris's offensive coordinator at Syracuse. "The guy was relentless."

The Giants went to St. Louis to face the winless Cardinals. Under a bright, sixty-seven-degree day at Busch Stadium, the teams exchanged 17 punts in a dismal affair. McConkey was the biggest yard gainer for New York, totaling 128 yards on seven punt returns and two kick returns. Punter Sean Landeta kicked the ball nine times, averaging 47.9 yards per boot and landing three of them inside the Cardinals' 20-yard line.

The Giants won 13–6. Big Blue's defense put together another dominating performance, holding the Cardinals to 83 yards rushing on 32 carries. They sacked Neil Lomax seven times with Lawrence Taylor, Leonard Marshall, and Carl Banks posting two sacks each.

The offense struggled. Phil Simms completed only 8 of 24 passes for

104 yards. St. Louis held Joe Morris to 53 yards on 17 carries. The G-Men averaged 7.4 yards per drive—not even a first down—and they only had two drives last longer than five plays. They lost the time-of-possession battle, holding the ball for thirteen and a half fewer minutes than the Cardinals. Their lone touchdown was set up by a 32-yard pass interference penalty that came on a reverse pass from wide receiver Bobby Johnson that was intended for Stacy Robinson. The most important offensive play probably came from nose tackle Jim Burt, and it happened after the game.

In the middle of the field as the players mingled, and before they headed to their respective locker rooms, Burt sought out his old University of Miami teammate, Ottis "O. J." Anderson. At the start of the game, Anderson was the eleventh leading rusher in NFL history, but his carries and playing time had dwindled under new Cardinals coach Gene Stallings. Parcells gave Burt the directive to have a conversation with Anderson.

"What do you think about playing for the Giants?"

"Come on, Virgil, that's not going to happen," Anderson said, referring to Burt with a nickname based on a character from *The Andy Griffith Show.*

"But, what if?"

"Virgil, there's no way that the Cardinals are going to trade me to the Giants in the middle of the season."

Burt understood Anderson's cautious response. "I wouldn't believe myself, either, because I'm always playing a practical joke, but I was serious this time."

Before they parted ways, Anderson gave his final answer: "I'd love to be a Giant."

Trades typically happen on Tuesdays, the players' day off. This gives them time to travel to the new city and start with the team midweek. Anderson heard nothing on his off day. The Cardinals were playing at Tampa Bay that weekend, so he went ahead and made plans to have dinner with Buccaneers linebacker Hugh Green on Saturday. Anderson went to work Wednesday and noticed he wasn't mentioned at all in the offensive game plan meeting.

Anderson was about to start the blitz pickup drill at the beginning of practice when a Cardinals player personnel man asked him to come off the field. He had been traded from the 0–5 Cardinals to the 4–1 Giants. "I went from the outhouse to the penthouse."

In Anderson's first game as a Giant, New York hosted the Eagles in week 6. Anderson saw some game action on the Giants' first possession, catching a swing pass, though it went for minus one yard.

On the next play, Phil Simms put on a display of strength. He stood in the shotgun on third down and 10. The Eagles blitzed. Simms rolled out to his left. Defensive back Elbert Foules applied pressure. Simms pump-faked. It froze Foules momentarily. The quarterback continued moving left. Then he stopped and began to cock his arm back. Foules overran him, but as he passed by, he grabbed hold of Simms's waist. Simms continued his throwing motion as Foules spiraled down Simms's body. Most of Foules was behind Simms, but as the defender swirled down Simms's lower body, he was draped himself on the quarterback's left leg, one hand pulling at Simms's waist and the other grasping a fistful of pants and yanking them down a bit at Simms's rear end. With the defender hanging off him, Simms delivered a 12-yard strike to Solomon Miller for the first down.

The drive stalled three plays later, and the first quarter ended without either team scoring. On the Giants' first play of the second quarter, Simms hit Mark Bavaro for a four-yard pass. The tight end's body bent backward on the tackle from linebacker Mike Reichenbach. Bavaro took himself out of the game. On the Giants' bench, he slumped over and writhed a bit. On the next play, Joe Morris hit the sideline and went untouched for a 30-yard touchdown. After the score, medical staff cut tape off Bavaro's ankle.

When Reichenbach fell on Bavaro to make the tackle, the weight came down on Bavaro's right big toe, bending it backward. This shattered the sesamoid bones, which act as a kneecap in the ball of the foot. Bavaro didn't have surgery to remove the bone fragments until the following year. He spent the season with them floating about, causing constant irritation. He used different orthotics. His cleat had to be cut certain ways to provide some relief. "It was a mess," he said.

Later in the second quarter, the Eagles lined up for a second-and-four play from the Giants' 5-yard line. With about six minutes to play in the half, quarterback Ron Jaworski crouched under center. Lawrence Taylor lined up just inside the left hash mark. The center hiked the ball to Jaworski. In 2.3 seconds, Taylor leaped over a would-be cut block from Keith Byars. Clearing the prostrate rookie running back, LT zoomed to Jaworski, steamrolling the quarterback from the blind side at the 12-yard line outside the opposite hash mark. Jaworski had little idea the hit was coming. LT popped up to his knees, shooting finger guns at the heap of quarterback that lay before him. The Eagles settled for a field goal, their only points of the game.

If Jaworski had anyone to blame for the hit, it might have been Eagles first-year head coach Buddy Ryan. The rest of the NFL had become resolved to the fact that a running back couldn't block Taylor. Ryan thought otherwise and left his quarterback to be protected by a rookie playing in his sixth game.

LT had tormented the Eagles throughout his career, and this game was no different. Of his 132.5 career sacks, 25 came against Philadelphia, the most against any single team. By the middle of the week before facing the Giants, former Eagles tackle Jerry Sisemore would break out in sweats. He'd have trouble sleeping at night.[1]

Quarterbacks had to know where LT was before they snapped the ball. This became so much of a mental game when one quarterback couldn't locate No. 56, he called time-out. Turns out, Taylor had subbed out of the game.

In the first game against the Eagles in '86, Taylor collected four sacks, giving him 7.5 on the season. Leonard Marshall added two, giving him 5.5 on the year. Combined, LT and Marshall had more sacks than ten NFL teams. The defense dominated the Eagles, holding them to 117 total yards and just nine first downs. Jaworski and backup quarterback Randall Cunningham combined to go 9 for 28 for 98 yards passing, but they lost 40 yards on six sacks. The G-Men bounced back from the 13-point effort in St. Louis, beating the Eagles 35–3. Simms ran for a score and completed 20 of 29 passes for 214 yards and two touchdowns. The offense gained 394 yards and ran 78 plays, 27 more than the Eagles. Holding the ball for 39:33, New York nearly doubled up Philadelphia in time of possession.

Up 21–3 late in the third quarter, the Giants executed a fake field goal. Backup quarterback Jeff Rutledge completed the 13-yard scoring pass to linebacker Harry Carson. The crowd chanted "Harry! Harry!" after the captain scored his second career touchdown.

Late in the game, defensive end George Martin missed Parcells on a Gatorade shower attempt, but cornerback Elvis Patterson finished the job.

In week 7, the 5–1 Giants traveled across the country to Seattle. They were three-point underdogs to the 4–2 Seahawks. Big Blue went through its walk-through the day before. Four hours before the game, Parcells stood at the edge of the Kingdome tunnel, leaning against the wall, sipping coffee. He had led the Giants to five wins in a row for the first time since 1970.

On the fourth play of the Giants' second drive, Simms hit running back Lee Rouson on a dump pass that went for 11 yards. During the play, left tackle Brad Benson took a shot from Seattle's Jeff Bryant. It was a routine blow that can happen between linemen. This one happened to slit open the skin on the bridge of Benson's nose. Benson stayed in the game. Splotches of blood spread across his face. Five plays later, he was called for a false start. Three plays after that the Giants punted and Benson went to the sidelines. Medical staff took a look at the cut. They decided to sew it back up. The Seahawks' drive lasted only five plays. The stitches weren't finished when the offense took the field. Parcells looked back at Benson and screamed at him to get back on the field. He ran out with the needle hanging on the thread and the cut open. The cut wouldn't heal for the rest of the season.

The Giants won the time-of-possession battle 34:42 to 25:18. They ran 19 more plays than Seattle and outgained the Seahawks 307 yards to 218. Joe Morris rushed 116 yards on 24 carries. These stats made it look like Giant Football, but Simms threw four interceptions and gave up a fumble. The offensive line allowed seven sacks to a team that only had nine total coming into the game. Jacob Green beat right tackle Karl Nelson for four sacks.

"Took some big hits that day. I'm sure that day was the most frustrating all year for the coaches because I made some great plays. But some really routine things they told me all week, I went against the grain on them there," Simms said.

In the second quarter, Simms threw a perfectly timed pass along the right sideline, dropping it to Solomon Miller in stride at the 6-yard line before the receiver took it to the end zone on the 32-yard scoring play. Simms also threw first-half interceptions that were picked off at the Seattle 4- and 5-yard lines.

"Inside the 20," said Giants offensive coordinator Ron Erhardt, "we stank."[2]

Even with the mistakes, the Giants' offense took over at their own 34-yard line, down 17–12 with 2:24 to play. They drove to the Seattle 22-yard line. Simms hit Solomon Miller with a pass at the 8-yard line, but Miller dropped it. Two plays later, Miller had a step on cornerback Terry Taylor, and Simms overthrew him in the end zone. On the next play, with less than a minute to go, Simms's pass for Bobby Johnson was intercepted at the 10-yard line.

"A game we should've won. We had a better team than they did. We just didn't do enough. They really probably outcoached us and outplayed us that day," Parcells said.

After watching the game film on Monday, Simms had a quick conversation with guard Billy Ard.

"You know, Bill, the worst part about yesterday's game?"

"What's that, Phil?"

"I was really on."

"What do you mean, you're on? You're on crack. You threw four interceptions."

While Ard found Simms's analysis comical, there was also something endearing about the quarterback's take. "His confidence level was always high. It's great. I liked that."

If players partied, the nights to go out were Mondays because they had off on Tuesdays, and Fridays because Saturday practices were walk-throughs.

This was the New York area in the mid-1980s, and the Giants entered night-clubs with a certain level of celebrity.

"The party scene was up off the chain," said safety Terry Kinard.

Clubs hosted specific events for the Giants, and women interested in football players flocked to them. Each year, when the team broke training camp, Club 88 in East Orange, New Jersey, hosted a Giants party.

"If you chose to," said Kinard, "there was anything and everything you wanted to get into."

During the season, Carl Banks, Andy Headen, Pepper Johnson, offensive lineman William Roberts, and wide receiver Lionel Manuel might start off the night with DJ Burt at Club 88. The group would split apart and, if they lasted into the wee hours of the morning, hook up again at some spot across the Hudson River in Manhattan.

"There just always was a party or somewhere to go to all the time, and we went to a lot of places," said fullback Maurice Carthon.

Manuel would break off and hit Club Zanzibar in Newark. Roberts would stay in East Orange and head to the Peppermint Club, while the rest of the crew made its way into New York City.

Sometime before sunrise, those who lasted would close out the evening in one of a few New York City spots: Studio 54, the China Club, or Palladium. Once they were in Manhattan, they'd end up in the same places as the New York Rangers and the hard-partying '86 New York Mets.

"We were all one big clique in that time. That part of it was phenomenal," Banks said. "New York City in the '80s was a lot of fun. You would run into whoever. You'd party with Run-DMC. You'd party with anybody."

At Studio 54, DJ Frankie Crocker had one party for the Giants and Jets. It wasn't the type of thing for wives or girlfriends. "It was one of those wild, wild parties where you'd have sex with a lot of different girls in one night," said linebacker Byron Hunt.[3]

Sean Landeta was big at the China Club. By all accounts, the punter was a first-team All-Pro ladies' man. "He was the playboy, the team's playboy; he was famous for dating these celebrities and models, and he had all kinds of stories," said kicker Raul Allegre.

"Well I'll just say this, I was like any normal young single guy that was lucky to be playing in the city I was playing in at the time," Landeta said.

The punter never had to wait in line at the China Club, even on Monday nights when it was celebrity night. *The National Enquirer, Entertainment Tonight,* and *People* magazine would all have cameras there to catch a glimpse of Madonna, Eddie Murphy, Hulk Hogan, or any other celebrity.

A few years later, Landeta met Jon Bon Jovi at the China Club. Landeta found out the Jersey rocker was a huge Giants fan. He worked it out with Parcells for Bon Jovi to visit practice. Eventually, this led to Bon Jovi being credentialed during the 1990 season as an incognito team photographer.

During the grind of training camp, Landeta would have the film crew splice in pictures of pretty fans with the footage players had to review each day. "We're watching film, and the next thing you know, these three beautiful women show up in our film session," Banks said.

On the Friday nights before away games, the players packed up whatever they needed to travel with and put it in their cars. They parked in the Giants Stadium lot. When the night ended, which could be two or three hours before they needed to be back at the facility, they'd sleep in their cars and pay the ball boys to wake them up.

"Don't go home and try to sleep for two hours and try to show up at the facility, 'cause you end up missing the flight or you get fined for being late," Banks said.

For home games, Parcells had the team stay at a hotel in Upper Saddle River. "Everybody's shit was locked up on Saturday night. Bill had us locked," Carthon said.

In week 8, the Giants faced the NFC-leading Washington Redskins at home on Monday night. About twenty miles away, over at Shea Stadium in Queens, some of the Giants' social scene buddies, the New York Mets, were playing the Boston Red Sox in game 7 of the World Series.

The Mets forced an improbable game 7 when a ground ball from Mookie Wilson squeaked through Bill Buckner's legs, allowing Ray Knight to score the game-winning run in the bottom of the tenth inning on

Saturday. Rain postponed the game from Sunday to Monday night, which meant it was played opposite *Monday Night Football*.

On the opening drive, Big Blue used up five minutes, covering 11 plays and 57 yards. The Giants fed the Redskins a healthy dose of Joe Morris, who ran the ball six times for 47 yards. A Raul Allegre 37-yard field goal put the G-Men up 3–0—the same lead as the Red Sox, who scored three runs in the top of the second inning.

Taylor, who had a pinched nerve in his shoulder, had been pacing back and forth on the Giants' sidelines before kickoff. Washington had acquired George Rogers in 1985, so this game was a matchup between Taylor and the one player taken ahead of him in the '81 draft. Rogers came into the contest with 672 rushing yards, more than 150 yards ahead of Morris, the Giants' leading ground gainer.

To Taylor's delight, Big Blue shut down Rogers. Washington ran its counter trey from their 45-yard line in the first quarter. Leonard Marshall grabbed Rogers's leg. Jim Burt hit him from behind while Carl Banks and Harry Carson met Rogers head-on. By the time the running back hit the ground on the one-yard loss, linebacker Gary Reasons and cornerback Perry Williams had joined the action. That's more than half the defense swarming the run. Taylor didn't make the play, but he leaned back at his waist, pumping both fists in the air after seeing what his teammates had done. Rogers was a nonfactor on the night, gaining 30 yards on 16 carries.

Morris continued to slash through the Redskins. He picked up 48 more yards on five carries, including an 11-yard touchdown run as the Giants drove 80 yards on nine plays to take a 10–0 second-quarter lead. Two and a half minutes into the second frame, Morris already had 90 yards.

With 1:37 to play in the half, Jay Schroeder crouched under center at the Redskins' 42-yard line. Out of nowhere, the crowd roared. Redskins left tackle Joe Jacoby, the man lined up across from LT, started to move. The refs flagged him for a false start. The burst of noise had nothing to do with anything at Giants Stadium. The fans in the stands reacted to the Mets' Ray Knight hitting a solo home run, giving New York a 4–3 lead in the bottom of the seventh inning. Thousands of fans at the football stadium had their faces planted on battery-operated mini TVs, or they had headphones on their ears, playing the radio broadcast of the World Series.

Taylor sacked Schroeder for a 13-yard loss. The Giants called time-out to make sure they got the ball back before the half ended. During the break, the crowd erupted again. The Mets' Lenny Dykstra singled to right field and advanced to second base on a wild pitch.

Phil McConkey received the punt at the Giants' 32-yard line, and the crowd broke out with noise for a third time.

"And now what's happening?" asked Frank Gifford, who was handling the ABC broadcast with Al Michaels.

"Well, the Mets are getting at least another run as Evans gets the ball back in and Dykstra just scored," Michaels said.

The Giants took a 20–3 lead in the third quarter when Bobby Johnson ran under a 30-yard Simms pass in the end zone. On the game broadcast, Michaels spoke about Johnson being in and out of Parcells's doghouse. There had already been an article in *The New York Times* about an ankle injury hobbling Johnson. He caught seven passes for 105 yards and two touchdowns in the opener. In the next six games, he only caught seven passes total, not registering a catch in three of those contests. He had hurt his ankle in the first game, but by this time, Johnson had become a full-fledged crack addict.

It had gotten to the point where it was the first thing he needed after practice and the last thing he needed to do before he went to sleep at night. Early on, he tried to stop. He gave it up for a month or two, but when he was reintroduced to it, he kept wanting more. When Cleveland Browns safety Don Rogers died of a cocaine overdose, Johnson's thought was to go get high. He never used publicly. After games, he would go out with his teammates and hang out a little, but he left to go home and get high. He didn't feel the need to use when he showed up in the locker room. Part of him thought he looked fine to everyone else, but another part knew that was a lie. "You might think you're not looking different and acting different, but people know."

His touchdown against the Redskins came four plays after a Darryl

Strawberry home run gave the Mets a 7–5 lead in the bottom of the eighth inning. By the time the Mets won the World Series, the Redskins narrowed the Giants' 17-point lead to a field goal.

LT had sacked Schroeder on the Giants' 42-yard line only to have the quarterback come back on the next play to throw a touchdown pass to Gary Clark, making the score 20–17, Giants. LT came off the field barking. "Goddamn it. Goddamn it," he said with his helmet off and his face covered with sweat.

Five plays into the next Giants possession, "METS WIN!" flashed across the yellow-lit scoreboard. Simms tried to quiet the raucous crowd. Brad Benson picked up a false start penalty.

The Redskins adjusted their game plan in the second half. Schroeder finished the game completing 22 of 40 passes for 420 yards. He threw for 313 of those yards in the second half. Gary Clark, Washington's five-foot-nine receiver, collected 11 catches for 241 yards.

With 4:06 left in the fourth quarter, the Redskins tied the game at 20. Big Blue answered back with another Morris-fueled drive. Running off right tackle, Morris picked up 34 yards, bringing the ball to the Redskins' 22-yard line. He lay on the field, banged up, but because of the two-minute warning, he didn't have to come out of the game. On three more carries, he picked up the rest of the yards and scored the game-winning touchdown. He finished the night with two touchdowns and 181 yards on 31 carries. The Giants won 27–20, and it created a three-way tie in the division. The Giants, Cowboys, and Redskins each had 6–2 records.

After the game, Parcells's NFL head coaching record stood at 30–29–1. He had become a winner, and his career record would never dip below winner's status again.

Six days later, the Giants welcomed the Cowboys to the Meadowlands on a gray, humid, fifty-eight-degree day. The turf at Giants Stadium bore a new logo at midfield. A red circle with a white silhouette of New Jersey was accompanied by the words NEW JERSEY MEADOWLANDS in white letters. The game was being marked as the tenth anniversary of the stadium. In the tug-of-war for the team's geographic identity, the logo was New Jersey pulling the rope in its direction.

About ten minutes into the game, Dallas had the ball at the Giants' 35-yard line. Quarterback Danny White took a five-step drop back. He relaxed his body. He dropped the ball low on his torso as he looked upfield for a receiver. *Wham*. Carl Banks came around the right side, untouched. He lowered his helmet into White's chest and flattened the quarterback. The ball left White. Jim Burt recovered the fumble as the quarterback lay splayed out on his back. White left the game. He had broken his wrist.

Over the next two seasons, White would start nine games and play in fourteen before ending his career. White and Banks—both radio broadcasters for their respective teams—talk now, but for years, White didn't speak to the linebacker. They saw each other once at a Super Bowl, and White said, "You ended my career," and kept walking by Banks.

The play has less meaning for Banks. It's not one that sticks out in his career. "For me, it was all in a day's work."

The Giants held off the Cowboys, winning 17–14 as Rafael Septién missed a 63-yard field goal with thirteen seconds left. Statistically, it was a struggle. Dallas outgained the G-Men 408 to 245 yards. The Cowboys held the ball for eight and a half minutes longer and ran fourteen more plays. Phil Simms had a dismal day. He completed 6 of 18 pass attempts for 67 yards, and he had one interception. The Giants only threw three passes in the second half. Parts of the home crowd chanted, "We want Rutledge!" calling for Simms's backup.

Morris posted another spectacular day, rushing for 181 yards on 29 carries and scoring two touchdowns. "Parcells's philosophy was he wanted to dominate and just grind 'em all out," Morris said.

With banged-up receivers, Morris knew he would carry the load against Washington and Dallas. It had also gotten to the point where he had a rhythm with his blockers. On sweeps to the outside, Bavaro or Mowatt would cave in the end of the defensive line, giving Morris a clear path to the sideline and the opportunity to cut the play upfield. The Giants also ran a play called 36 Flow. The guard pulled and turned upfield, followed by Carthon, both clearing an alley for Morris. The five-foot-seven back could change direction, making sharp cuts into holes without losing speed.

"Those holes were big, man. I think a lot of guys could've ran for 180 that day. I really do. But he was perfect for us. Low-built. Strong. Holes were there, and he hit them," said guard Billy Ard.

In his first four games of the season, Morris scored three touchdowns and averaged 3.9 yards per carry while gaining 333 yards. In the four games after the trade for Ottis Anderson, Morris gained 547 yards, scored five touchdowns, and averaged 5.3 yards per carry.

Slowed by a hamstring injury, Anderson didn't play that much, but the trade had done its job. "It just motivated the hell out of Joe," Anderson said. "Joe had one of the best years he ever had rushing the football."

After Banks knocked Danny White out of the game, the Cowboys would go 19–52 in the next four and a half seasons until they returned to the play-offs in 1991. While Dallas was an older version of its once perennial play-off self, the back-to-back wins in a six-day stretch over the divisional nemeses gave the Giants momentum.

"We were rolling then," Parcells said.

19

FOURTH AND 17

Phil Simms didn't say anything. His wife made a big meal. She always cooked after games, but now the couple sat at their kitchen table in silence.

"The Dallas game was as bad as it ever got. We won the game, but, my God. I was shot. Just shot. I couldn't concentrate on the plays because I couldn't trust the players. I didn't trust the receivers."

Simms had thrown for 67 yards against Dallas, throwing one interception and completing only a third of his 18 attempts. The Giants' offense pulled back on the passing game in the second half, giving Simms just three throws. Injuries to the receiving corps inhibited any formation of chemistry with the quarterback. Players with typically reliable hands dropped passes. Simms second-guessed throwing the ball to them. As a result, he held the ball longer than he should have. "If I had just stayed with the guy I was supposed to stay with, he would've been wide open for a big play. I turned and looked to the other guy who was covered. No matter what we did, it was not going to work."

Simms posted a 22.2 quarterback rating that day. It was—and always would be—the worst rating in his 164-game career.

The Giants beat the Eagles 17–14 in Philadelphia the next week, but Simms didn't fare much better. There were more drops, five of them. He was intercepted twice and posted a 29.6 passer rating, completing 8 of 18 attempts for 130 yards.

"Even though we won and were 8–2, I couldn't have cared less. It felt like we were 2–8."

Bill Parcells could see Simms's confidence was shaken. "We really didn't have much firepower outside. We were using Zeke [Mowatt] and Mark [Bavaro]. We were using them a lot together. The press was on Phil's ass."

He called Simms into his office. "You've got your team in first place. You've just finished beating three division teams. I just want you to go out there and be aggressive. Take chances, and let's try to win this thing."

In Parcells's view, it was critical that Simms know the head coach wanted a quarterback to be aggressive, not a ball control game manager.

"Look, I think you're a great quarterback, and the way you got to be great was by being fearless out there, and resilient. Don't worry about the things you can't control, like drops. Be yourself."[1]

Late in the day, when only a few people were still at the facility, Bill Belichick stopped Simms in the hallway outside the locker room. Belichick told Simms he saw him putting work in every day. "You're a really good player. I have great faith in you. Just do your job."

The Giants flew to Minnesota to take on the 6–4 Vikings and quarterback Tommy Kramer. The Minnesota quarterback had thrown 21 touchdowns already. He had a 95.2 rating—good for second in the NFC—and his 2,613 passing yards were the second most in the NFL.

The night before the game, kicker Raul Allegre grabbed dinner in the team hotel with starting inside linebacker Gary Reasons. After hitting his first four field goals in New York, Allegre missed a field goal in each of the last five games. He had missed kicks, including a 29-yarder he should've made, and because of that, he told Reasons he didn't feel like he was part of the team.

"What do you mean?" Reasons asked.

"Until I have a game in which I make a lot of field goals or the game winner at the end . . . until I do that, I will not feel part of the team."

The next day, with less than three minutes to play in the first half, Allegre had kicked three field goals and given the Giants a 9–6 lead.

Simms looked different. He moved with fluidity in the pocket. Stepping up in the face of pressure, still taking hits, but delivering passes. He completed 11 of 15 throws in the first half for 173 yards. One of the incompletions was a touchdown that came off the hands of Joe Morris, who had run a seam pattern into the end zone. Simms even rushed for 16 yards on two carries.

With the ball at their own 22-yard line and fifty-five seconds left in the half, the Giants and Simms stayed aggressive. After two straight completions, Simms added a third on an 18-yard pass over the middle to Bobby Johnson. Simms pushed the hurry-up offense, running up to the Vikings' 37-yard line. "Same play! Same play!" he yelled amid the din of the Metrodome.

Left tackle Brad Benson took this to mean the ball would be snapped on the second sound, just as it had been on the play before. As Simms came to the line of scrimmage, he yelled, "Same play!" again and Benson moved, drawing a false start penalty.

When the refs marched off the penalty, Parcells started screaming at Benson, "Fuck you." And Benson gave it back to him. The penalty forced Allegre into a 60-yard attempt, which he missed as time ran out in the half.

The anger between Parcells and Benson led them to be separated at halftime. Benson stayed out of the offensive meeting. He stood in the shower area, away from Parcells.

After the Giants went three and out on their first possession of the second half, the Vikings took the lead on an 11-play, 79-yard drive. Kramer ended it with an eight-yard touchdown pass to fullback Allen Rice. Allegre added his fourth field goal of the day, but Minnesota had the ball and a 13–12 lead heading into the fourth quarter.

Every time Kramer broke the huddle, he looked for No. 56. "That was the toughest thing about the Giants, figuring out where that sombitch was."

Kramer knew all the blocking schemes, but LT changed that because teams had to assign an extra blocker to him. "No one person can block him."

On the Vikings' second play of the fourth quarter, Kramer stood in the shotgun with a running back on each side of him and three wide receivers at the line. Taylor faked a rush to the outside and then stunted up the middle. Kramer threw a three-yard pass over the middle to flanker Leo Lewis, and the quarterback took a hit from Taylor. The play-by-play sheet says Kramer jammed his thumb. He had a different experience. His hand shook uncontrollably. "My thumb got bent back to my goddamn forearm," he said. He was done for the game.

Taylor led the NFL in sacks, coming into the game with 14.5. He added two more against the Vikings, but hits like the one against Kramer never showed up on a stat sheet. The Giants battered signal callers. Kramer was the eighth quarterback New York knocked out of the game since the start of the '85 season, and it was the third week in a row this Big Blue Wrecking Crew sent the starting quarterback to the sidelines with an injury. "The Giants' basic defensive philosophy is this: Kick the shit out of them," Taylor said.[2]

The Vikings punted the play after Kramer injured his thumb. The Giants drove 70 yards to take the lead. Bobby Johnson picked up the final 47 yards, first on a 22-yard reverse, which was followed by a 25-yard touchdown catch.

Wade Wilson replaced Kramer and Minnesota answered immediately, driving 80 yards in six plays. Wilson hit Anthony Carter for a 33-yard touchdown, giving the Vikings a 20–19 lead.

After a 17-yard Phil McConkey punt return, the Giants' offense took over at their 41-yard line with 2:14 left in the game. Simms threw deep down the right sideline, unable to connect with Stacy Robinson. On second down, Simms avoided a blitz and threw a dart over the middle to Johnson, who picked up 14 yards. After the two-minute warning, Simms found O. J. Anderson for a two-yard dump pass. On second and eight, Simms looked for Johnson but came up empty. With seventy-eight seconds to play, the Giants called time-out before facing a third down and eight.

Simms stood in the shotgun. Running back Tony Galbreath lined up to his right. Johnson was wide left with McConkey in the slot. Bavaro stood in a two-point stance, shading the left tackle, and Robinson was right.

The Metrodome crowd stood and made enough noise to drown out the nearly ever-present Viking horn.

Simms took the snap. The Vikings sent six players. Simms backpedaled. He tried to avoid the sack from Doug Martin, George's brother. He flicked the ball toward Galbreath but was called down on a nine-yard loss. Simms, his chin strap unbuttoned, rolled his neck around and headed to the sidelines. The Giants called time-out to discuss their options for fourth and 17.

Parcells and wide receivers coach Pat Hodgson were on the field, talking to offensive coordinator Ron Erhardt, who was above the field in a coach's box. They picked a play: Half Right W-Motion 74 X In. Hodgson offered the wrinkle of adding motion. They'd move McConkey before the snap, forcing the Vikings to show what type of defense they were in.

On the sidelines, maneuvering to get a good view, defensive line coach Lamar Leachman stood, perched on the Giants' bench. As the offense broke the huddle, Simms told Johnson to be alert; he might have to throw to him late in the play.

"I was just supposed to run like a clearout," Johnson said. "I actually wasn't in the play."

The crowd noise forced Simms under center. Galbreath was offset to the left, behind him. Bavaro was set back, shading the right tackle. Bobby Johnson lined up wide right. Robinson stood flanked out to the left. McConkey started in the left slot and came in motion. He was in front of Bavaro when Simms called for the snap. McConkey ran a seam route upfield. Galbreath released out of the backfield to the left. Bavaro, the team's leading receiver, stayed in to block. Simms looked left to Robinson. Nothing. He scanned the middle of the field. Nothing. The Vikings rushed three, running a stunt with nose tackle Mike Stensrud looping to the outside and Doug Martin cutting inside. Bavaro picked up Stensrud, who bull-rushed the tight end, getting by him. Stensrud hit Simms just as the quarterback released the ball to the right.

McConkey drew attention from cornerback Issiac Holt, who couldn't recover as the ball spiraled toward the sideline. Johnson had run up the sideline, getting behind Holt and stopping in front of safety John Harris. Johnson found an open spot and stopped 22 yards downfield. Before Johnson even made the catch, McConkey, standing about at the 23-yard line, raised his hands that the play was made.

Simms, meanwhile, saw the completion from the ground. After being hit, he was left to peek through the arms and legs of the offensive and defensive linemen around him. He raised his arms and gave a couple of celebratory pumps before putting his hands to his helmet.

Leachman forgot he stood on the bench. He walked forward as if he were on the ground.

"He took maybe one step and just went down, *boom,*" said Maurice Carthon.

"Several of us saw this—it was a hysterical moment!!" Belichick said.

The Metrodome fell quiet. Johnson didn't offer any big celebration. He clapped his hands together as he jogged back to the huddle.

The play did make LT a believer in Simms. That had not always been the case. Taylor thought Simms was a selfish player, out for his own stat line earlier in the quarterback's career.

"I'm sure Lawrence looked at me and thought I was some little rich white boy," Simms said. "I really believe he thought that. I doubt to this day that he has any idea about how I grew up or that I came from a family of eight children and how we lived."

Whatever impression Taylor had, it changed with the fourth-down completion. "From that time on, I felt if we're going to win a champion-ship, if we're going to excel as a team, it was going to be behind the arm of Phil Simms. He became my man, right there," Taylor said.[3]

The reception put the ball at the Minnesota 30-yard line. After a Vikings offside and three Morris runs, Allegre lined up for a 33-yard field goal with fifteen seconds to play. He nailed it. Then he ran a few steps and leaped into the air with arms stretched out wide. Gary Reasons wrapped him up in a hug.

"Do you now feel part of the team?"

"Yes," Allegre said.

The Vikings used up the remaining twelve seconds lateraling the ball to each other on the kick return. The Giants won 22–20.

"We wouldn't say it aloud. We wouldn't say it in public, but it was almost like divine intervention from that point on. We knew that we were destined to win," said George Martin.

The whooping and cheering sounded off in the postgame locker room. Parcells touted his quarterback to the media. He even kissed Simms on the cheek.

"It was like the only endorsement he gave me in his whole career. He never did that," Simms said.

Simms finished the day with 310 yards passing, connecting on 25 of 38 attempts. He completed passes to eight different receivers along the way. "It's my favorite game in my career, not because of the fourth and 17, but because I played the way I really wanted to play."

He threw two interceptions in the game, but he didn't let the miscues dull his confidence. "Let's go out there and fight them again. It was a very physical game. I took some hellacious hits in the game, and it's just the way I wanted to play. That's who I wanted to be every week."

When Benson walked by Parcells boarding the plane back to New Jersey, the coach and player exchanged glares. Benson sat in the back, having a beer with Simms. A trainer interrupted them to let Benson know Parcells wanted to see him. Simms offered Benson some luck as the left tackle walked the aisle to the front of the plane.

Parcells greeted Benson with, "Sit down. Want a drink?"

"No. I'm all right," said Benson, thinking he didn't want to stay there long enough for the flight attendant to make a drink. He just wanted to get back to his little haven in the back of the plane.

"Listen, I was a little rough today. I'm willing to say I'm sorry," Parcells said.

"Well, I'm sorry, too."

"You know you're one of my guys. You're one of my lunch pail guys."

They spoke for ten minutes. Benson did take a seat. He felt like it was a great pep talk from his coach.

"We're okay, right?" Parcells asked, closing up the chat.

"We're okay."

"Good. Okay. You can go back. Thank you."

Benson stood up to leave. Parcells took his hand. "Oh, one more thing. You ever jump offsides like that in a crucial situation, I'll cut your ass."

Bill Parcells was named head coach of the Giants in December 1982. He was 41-years old. (JIM REME)

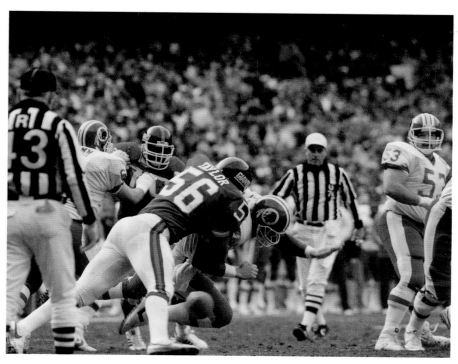

Lawrence Taylor with the strip-sack of Washington quarterback Jay Schroeder. (JERRY PINKUS)

Phil Simms drops back to pass against the 49ers in the divisional round of the playoffs. (JIM REME)

The Giants picked Mark Bavaro with the 100th pick in the 1985 draft. (JIM REME)

Coming out of Morehead State, Phil Simms was the No. 7 overall pick in 1979. (COURTESY OF MOREHEAD STATE UNIVERSITY ATHLETIC MEDIA RELATIONS)

Defensive Coordinator Bill Belichick uses his board while talking to his unit. (JIM REME)

Lawrence Taylor and Leonard Marshall were a nightmare for the left side of offensive lines. (JIM REME)

Cocaptain George Martin played 14 seasons with the Giants. He presented Bill Parcells for induction at the Pro Football Hall of Fame. (JIM REME)

Hall of Fame middle linebacker Harry Carson went to nine Pro Bowls. (JIM REME)

Carl Banks and Jim Burt gather around to listen to Bill Belichick on the sidelines. (JIM REME)

Before he became the head coach, Bill Parcells served as the Giants defensive coordinator. (JIM REME)

Joe Morris took a handoff from Phil Simms and darts upfield. (JIM REME)

Punter Sean Landeta watches as Parcells is about to feel the cold, wet rush of a Gatorade bath. (JERRY PINKUS)

Lawrence Taylor on the attack. (JIM REME)

Before Super Bowl XXI, General Manager George Young talks to CBS sideline reporter Will McDonough. (JERRY PINKUS)

The linebackers, Carl Banks, Gary Reasons, Harry Carson, and Lawrence Taylor, about to be announced at the Super Bowl. (JERRY PINKUS)

Carl Banks, the No. 3 overall pick
in the 1984 draft. (JIM REME)

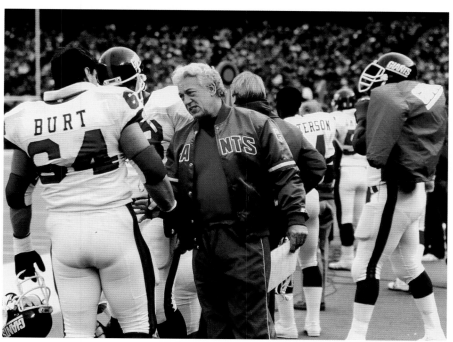

Jim Burt talks to defensive line coach Lamar Leachman during a game. (JIM REME)

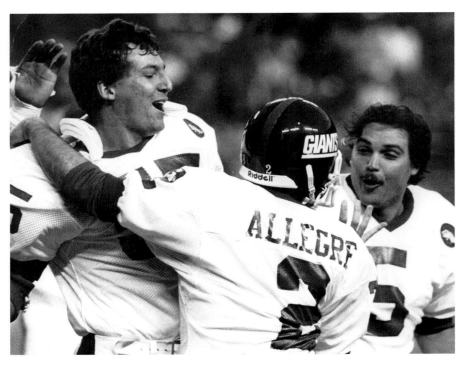

After hitting the game-winning field goal at Minnesota, Raul Allegre hugs Gary Reasons and gets a high five from Sean Landeta. (JERRY PINKUS)

Belichick and Carson go over some defensive strategy. (JIM REME)

Mark Bavaro is about to drag Hall of Famer Ronnie Lott for 14 yards. (JERRY PINKUS)

Special Teams Coach
Romeo Crennel. (JIM REME)

Guard Billy Ard has a drink on the sidelines. (JIM REME)

Four-fifths of the Suburbanites—*(clockwise left to right)* Karl Nelson (63), Billy Ard (67), Bart Oates (65), and Chris Godfrey (61)—watch the defense thump the Packers in week 16 of the '86 season. (JIM REME)

Jim Burt throttles Joe Montana, knocking the quarterback out of a divisional round playoff game. (JERRY PINKUS)

Brad Benson shoves Washington's Dexter Manley in a pivotal late-season match-up between the NFC East rivals. (JERRY PINKUS)

Phil McConkey, Mark Bavaro, and Phil Simms head out to watch the movie *Platoon* on Saturday before the Super Bowl. (COURTESY OF PHIL MCCONKEY)

Phil McConkey warms up at midfield of the Rose Bowl before the Super Bowl. (COURTESY OF PHIL MCCONKEY)

Mark Bavaro holds up Phil McConkey after McConkey lived his dream and caught a touchdown in the Super Bowl. (COURTESY OF PHIL MCCONKEY)

Giants team president and co-owner Wellington Mara received the Lombardi Trophy from NFL Commissioner Pete Rozelle *(left)* and then he spoke to Brent Mussburger. (JERRY PINKUS)

The Rose Bowl scoreboard when time ran out in Super Bowl XXI. (COURTESY OF PHIL MCCONKEY)

Mark Bavaro goes for a drive while in Hawaii for the Pro Bowl. He was one of eight Giants named to the Pro Bowl after the '86 season. (COURTESY OF MARK BAVARO)

20

BUTTON-PUSHER

On Monday after the Vikings game, Bill Parcells walked into the locker room with a clear, calculated message for his team.

He knew the comeback win in the closing seconds at Minnesota boosted the squad's confidence. The Giants were 9–2. They shared the division lead with Washington. At the same time, all of this meant nothing.

"Okay, boys, the season's starting right here. You might as well start over, because you've got a lot of games to win between now and the championship. You've got eight you've got to win to get to where you want to go."

He never wanted his players to be complacent. Parcells knows he has a reputation as a button-pusher, but to him, that's not accurate. "You just follow your own way of doing things."

One of those things was placing a rock in his shoe during practices. Just in case he needed a reminder to be uncomfortable, he had it with every step. Even though he made a point to lift Phil Simms up before the Minnesota trip, there were plenty of critical jabs thrown at the quarterback. One day, out of nowhere, Parcells walked into the weight room and interrupted Simms's workout. He told the quarterback he had been watching film.

"You know, Simms, we just can't throw slants because you just can't throw them."

What, are you shitting me? It's a five-yard throw, Simms thought before politely disagreeing.

Parcells said he couldn't call plays with slants in them anymore, abruptly turned his back, and walked out.

"I don't know what he studied in college, but if you told me it was psychology, that'd make sense," Simms said.

Parcells reached Lawrence Taylor in other ways. In practice, he'd talk up Taylor's counterparts, Washington's Dexter Manley or Tampa Bay's Hugh Green. During one film session, Parcells showed 49ers guard John Ayers manhandling Taylor on a play. Parcells clicked the rewind button and showed it again. The coach didn't say anything. He rewound and showed it again, and again, until Taylor walked out of the room. Later in LT's career, Parcells put a plane ticket for New Orleans in Taylor's locker. He told Taylor to fly there and send back the Saints' No. 56, Pat Swilling, because Swilling did a better job than Taylor against the Giants' upcoming opponent.

The offensive line didn't receive any cozy treatment. Looking less like hogs and more like a group ready for orange slices at halftime, they were dubbed "the Suburbanites." They wore collared shirts, carried briefcases, and had jobs or academic pursuits in the off-season. Brad Benson owned a car dealership. Billy Ard worked as a stockbroker. Karl Nelson had an industrial engineering degree from Iowa State but he had started working in finance. Bart Oates and Chris Godfrey pursued law degrees, which they put into practice after their playing days.

Parcells called Godfrey "Tunnel" because the guard would lock in on an assignment with tunnel vision and, in Parcells's view, miss blocking another player.

"You know, Godfrey," Parcells said while working out in the weight room, "you're the kind of guy who'd be walking through the canyon and you wouldn't see all those Indians gathering above the canyon."

"Billy, if I was always looking up in the sky, I'd never get anywhere," Godfrey shot back.

Oates, by his own account, felt like the default center. The Giants spent $100,000 to get him out of his USFL contract and join the team. They needed him after Kevin Belcher's career-ending injury. "Kevin had a mean streak. He was physical. He was a Parcells player. I wasn't the big, strong, dominant-type guy that Parcells wanted in the middle, but I was the only thing that was available."

Parcells stood in the offensive huddle during practice, doling out a steady stream of jabs.

"Oh, Brad, another hubcap fall off?" he said, taking a shot at Benson and referencing the car dealership.

"It's okay, Karl, Heidi will have cinnamon on your bread pudding when you get home," he'd say to Nelson, referencing his wife after the tackle made a mistake.

Once, he called Godfrey "Biscuits." "Because you're soft and fluffy looking," he explained.

"Nah, you call me that because I'm your bread and butter, and you know it," Godfrey said.

Parcells didn't mind if a player came back at him. As long as you had some standing, you could get away with it, and he'd actually appreciate it. If the players could take what Parcells dished out, he believed he'd have to take it in return. "I mean, yeah, we would have good dialogue back and forth. They knew they weren't crossing the line. Our team had a personality. They did not get rattled. They didn't pout much. They were very committed to trying to win."

When the Giants took the field at home in week 12 against the Broncos, Phil McConkey burst out of the tunnel, sprinting down the sideline to the opposite end zone. He waved a white towel, rousing the crowd. It had become a tradition, something that evolved since McConkey returned from Green Bay.

For McConkey, the sprint released the pent-up nervous energy. It was something he did every game, but in his first game back at Giants Stadium, he noticed something different. This time, in the pregame versus the Eagles, he could hear the crowd. It was as if they were responding to him. He looked up and gave a nod. The next home game was the Monday night game against Washington. The crowd reacted again. McConkey waved. Six days later against Dallas, McConkey made the dash and pulled out the white towel that hung from his waist. He waved it in the air as he ran, beckoning the crowd to come alive with noise. They did. "I'm just relating to the fans, getting them into the spirit, and getting them emotional because I know what it's like on the other side of that."

Parcells never wanted attention-seeking self-aggrandizers. The towel-waving display might have fit into that category, but Parcells responded to it by patting McConkey on the back after the wide receiver finished igniting the stands. "He wouldn't even have to say anything. If I had come off the field after doing that, all it would have taken was that look from him, I never would have done it again," McConkey said.

The Broncos came into the Meadowlands with a 9–2 record. Even though the teams hadn't played each other in six years, they had familiarity with each other. When the NFL schedule came out, it pitted all the NFC East teams versus the AFC West squad. At the NFL off-season meetings, Parcells reached out to Dan Reeves. He asked to have the coaching staffs meet and exchange scouting reports on their division rivals. Reeves thought it was a great idea, and both teams went through it. A few years later, the league prohibited this practice.

On the first play of the second quarter, the Giants tied the game at 3 on a 31-yard Raul Allegre kick. The 16-play, 63-yard scoring drive was aided by a trick play. The Giants initially lined up in punt formation on fourth down and five at the Denver 44-yard line. Backup quarterback Jeff Hostetler went in motion and crouched under center with running back Lee Rouson and punter Sean Landeta set behind him. Hostetler handed the ball to Rouson, who gained eight yards and the first down.

Late in the quarter, the Giants had two one-play drives. A 15-yard completion to Stacy Robinson ended in a fumble, which Denver turned into a second Rich Karlis field goal, putting the Broncos up 6–3. Running back Tony Galbreath fumbled on the next Giants play.

With John Elway at the controls and the Denver offense 41 yards away from the end zone, the Broncos seemed poised to increase their lead. Four plays into the drive, Elway had Denver at the Giants' 13-yard line with a minute left. On first down, the Denver running backs lined up in the I-formation behind Elway. They motioned to a split set behind the quarterback. Elway called for the snap. He faked a handoff up the middle to Sammy Winder. In one motion, he finished his five-step drop back, set his feet, and threw a swing pass to the right flat intended for running back Gerald Willhite.

Defensive end George Martin had been pushed upfield, behind the pass. Trying to regain his balance after an attempted cut block, all Martin could do was leap in the air, reach back, and stop the ball with his gloved right hand. Martin's momentum spun him away from Elway, toward the sideline. He bobbled the ball and pulled it into his chest, completing the spin. He intercepted the pass at the 22-yard line and headed toward the end zone. With Elway in pursuit, Martin held the ball out, faking a pitch to Lawrence Taylor. Elway tried to bring Martin down, but the defensive end tossed the quarterback aside like a man handling a child's doll. Elway twirled to the ground near midfield. Martin locked eyes with Taylor and faked another pitch. "He was demanding it. He was begging for it," Martin said.

"It's the best play I've seen a defensive player make in football, ever," Parcells said.

Harry Carson came barreling through the scene, blocking Broncos center Billy Bryan. Denver running back Sammy Winder ran ahead of Martin, and it looked as if he would bring Martin down.

Rookie cornerback Mark Collins was in pass coverage in the end zone when he saw Martin make the interception. Collins thought about the big-play defensive pot. It had grown to four figures from players paying into it for being late for meetings and getting called for penalties. Collins sprinted from the end zone, starting more than 20 yards behind the play.

He caught up to Martin around the 18-yard line and dived at Winders's hip, sending the Bronco to the ground. Martin hurdled the prostrate player and charged into the end zone, where Taylor dragged him to the ground with a clothesline celebration tackle that saw the defense and some offensive players join the pile.

Martin collected the big-play pot for the touchdown, and Collins grabbed $200 for his block. When the defense watched the play in film sessions, Bill Belichick gave Collins's hustle special attention. "That was the biggest play of my NFL career, in my thirteen years. That was it," Collins said.

The Giants led 10–6 at the half. Field goals accounted for the only second-half points until Elway led the Broncos on a nine-play, 73-yard touchdown drive to tie the game at 16 with 1:55 to play.

After the Denver score, Phil Simms tossed the ball on the sideline a few times under the cloudy, gray sky on the fifty-degree late-autumn day. He spread his legs and rotated his upper body, stretching as he waited for the kickoff. The Giants took over at their own 29-yard line. On the first play, Broncos linebacker Karl Mecklenburg applied the pressure as Simms looked for Galbreath on a failed screen pass. On second down, Freddie Gilbert beat Brad Benson and sacked Simms for an 11-yard loss. The G-Men called time-out. It was third down and 21 at their own 18-yard line with 1:35 on the clock.

Simms lined up in the shotgun. The offensive line gave him time. He pumped once, stepped up in the pocket, and hit Bobby Johnson in stride over the middle. Johnson took two steps to gain 24 yards before taking a helmet-to-helmet shot from safety Dennis Smith. The hit cracked Johnson's helmet. Simms pushed the offense in the hurry-up. McConkey ran over to help up Johnson. Simms called out the play. McConkey tried to get his attention to let the quarterback know not to throw to Johnson. "He's in a daze. Today it'd be criminal," McConkey said. "But in the '80s, you lined up and kept playing."

Simms handed the ball off to Galbreath for a seven-yard gain. On the next play, he dumped a seven-yard screen to Galbreath, but the Giants lost 10 yards because Karl Nelson was called for holding. The clock stopped with fifty-seven seconds left.

The Giants had the ball at their own 39-yard line on second down and 13. Simms stood in the shotgun. McConkey saw something Simms had pointed out to him earlier in the week. On their off days, Simms and McConkey would lift weights and watch film. McConkey was working out when Simms called him to look at something. The Broncos would line up as if they were blitzing, figuring the offense would make a sight adjustment and run shorter routes. When the ball was snapped, the Broncos wouldn't send everyone on the blitz. They'd have defensive backs ready to pounce on the shorter routes. Smith, the safety, lined up in front of McConkey and showed blitz. On the snap, Smith charged at the quarterback. Galbreath stayed in the backfield and planted Smith on the ground. The second level of Denver defenders didn't blitz. They moved up as if McConkey cut his route short, but he didn't make the sight adjustment. He ran a deep seam route, blowing past the defender. Simms lofted the ball to McConkey, who caught it at the Denver 26-yard line and brought it to the 15 before being tackled.

Simms extended both arms in the air and pumped his fists. Johnson ran over to McConkey to congratulate him. "I did it! I did it!" is what Johnson heard McConkey say. When the two receivers spoke about the play more than two decades later, they laughed because McConkey had said, "I didn't sight adjust! I didn't sight adjust!"

The 46-yard catch was the longest play for the Giants of the season. After two plays to force Denver time-outs, Allegre booted a 34-yard field. The Giants won 19–16, and Harry Carson dumped Gatorade on Martin, Big Blue's lone touchdown scorer on the day. That night, McConkey went to a club. He spotted a crush of his, an MTV VJ. He spoke to her. "Man, what a day."

In week 13, the Giants headed to San Francisco to play the 49ers on Monday Night Football. Quarterback Joe Montana returned to play his first game since the season opener. He was four weeks removed from spinal surgery. Like the Giants and the Redskins, the 7–4–1 49ers were in a race for their division title with the Rams.

The 49ers jumped out to a 17–0 halftime lead. San Francisco had 229 yards of offense. Montana carved up the Giants' defense with short passes. He was 17 of 24 for 145 yards without a single pass completion for more than 15 yards. They held the ball for more than nineteen minutes.

Part of the edge San Francisco had offensively in starting games is that head coach Bill Walsh scripted the team's first 15 plays.

"We didn't handle the script and start of the game well. I didn't do a good job," said Bill Belichick.

Simms threw two first-half interceptions, and Joe Morris was held to two yards on six attempts. The 49ers came into the game focused on stopping the run. On New York's first play, San Francisco lined up six defenders on the defensive line. Seven swarmed to Morris on a three-yard loss.

"In the first half, they're lining up nine guys in the box. Ronnie Lott is almost in our backfield. He's playing safety, and we can't get anything. That's because Ronnie Lott is up on the ball. Throw the fucking ball," said Billy Ard.

When the G-Men threw the ball in the first half, Lott made plays there, too. The Giants drove the 49ers' 23-yard line in the second quarter. Simms put the ball on Stacy Robinson as the receiver crossed over the middle. Lott broke up the play, drilling his helmet and shoulder into Robinson's chest. The ball flung in the air and landed incomplete. Robinson lay facedown on the ground for a moment. The receiver bent over on one knee by the time three of the Giants' medical personnel attended to him. He left the game and was replaced at receiver by Jeff Hostetler. The backup quarterback had taken the approach of doing anything to get on the field. He played special teams and had already blocked a punt in week 10 at Philadelphia. On the next play, Simms threw to Hostetler in the end zone. He made the catch, but it was out of bounds.

The half ended, and in an unusual occurrence, Simms was the first player in the locker room. Typically, he trotted in with the middle of the pack. By the time the quarterback stepped in there, Parcells was waiting for everyone.

"Simms, what'd we miss, two field goals?"

"Yeah."

"We're moving the ball. We could score on these guys."

Parcells did not give halftime pep talks. He wasn't a "Win one for the Gipper" guy. That's what made halftime in Candlestick Park different. He addressed the entire team.

"Men, when are we going to say, 'It's enough'? It's enough. We can beat these sons of bitches. We've got time to win the game. We're going out, and we're going to get after them, and defense, you've got to hold these guys down the rest of the way."

The mood in the locker room shifted. "I was so uplifted. It was incredible," Simms said.

Big Blue came out in the second half and played a near-perfect quarter of football. Even though he lacked the results on the scoreboard, Simms felt like he was throwing the ball well. On the Giants' first play of the second half, he dropped the ball over the shoulder to Bobby Johnson at the San Francisco 31-yard line, but Johnson caught it out of bounds. On the next play, second and 10 from the San Francisco 49-yard line, Simms looked right and saw a wide-open out pattern during his pre-snap read. At the last moment, a defender covered it. Simms dropped back, pumped right. He couldn't throw it there anymore. He held the ball and looked to the center of the field for another option. "Son of a bitch, where is he? Where is he? And I just threw it, and he caught it. And the rest is what it is."

Mark Bavaro found a spot in the middle of the field at the 40-yard line. He caught the pass and turned to run. Michael Walter was the first to arrive, crashing into Bavaro's body at the 37-yard line and then falling to the turf. At nearly the same moment, Riki Ellison dived at Bavaro and slid away. Lott hopped on Bavaro at the 32-yard line. The future Hall of Famer's grip turned into a bear hug at the 28-yard line. Bavaro kept him on for the ride. Eventually, four 49ers hopped on. Bavaro's teammates Joe Morris, Bart Oates, and Maurice Carthon tried to push the pile forward. Carrying

1,130 pounds of NFL players, Bavaro fell to the ground at the 18-yard line. He picked up 31 yards, carrying at least one person for nearly half of it.

"Just doing my job. It was bad tackling by the 49ers. I didn't try any harder on that play than I tried on any other play as a player. Go watch it. Study it. It's horrendous tackling. They don't wrap up. They don't try to drag you down. Ronnie Lott? I don't know what Ronnie Lott was doing. He never did that again for the rest of his career, it was so embarrassing to him."

Since none of the 49ers had wrapped up his legs, Bavaro thinks if his teammates didn't join the mass of bodies, he could've carried Lott and Co. all the way into the end zone.

Two plays later, Simms connected with Morris for a 17-yard touchdown pass. On the Giants' next drive, Parcells made the call to go for it on fourth and two at midfield. The Giants ran Morris to the right side for the second consecutive play. On third down, the 49ers stopped him for no gain. On fourth, he picked up 17 yards, rushing for more yards in one play than the Giants did all night. On the next play, Simms hit Robinson for a 34-yard score. Ottis Anderson added a one-yard touchdown run on the Giants' third possession of the quarter, giving New York a 21–17 lead it wouldn't surrender. The Giants could've tallied 28 points, but Bavaro fumbled at the 49ers' 6-yard line, ending Big Blue's final possession of the quarter.

In those fifteen minutes, Simms completed 11 of 13 passes for 198 yards. In that one quarter, he threw for more yards than the combined total amount he passed for in those brutal Dallas and Philadelphia games. He finished the night with 388 yards through the air.

The defense shut down San Francisco. The 49ers didn't get a first down and only gained 20 yards in the third quarter. Montana threw an interception while completing 2 of 8 passes for nine yards.

"Once we settled down, San Francisco couldn't do much. Their advantage in a lot of games was their fast start. After that, we always felt that we had the advantage," Belichick said.

With the win, the Giants were 11–2 and the first team in NFL history to have a six-game winning streak without any of the victories decided by more than a touchdown.

The Giants only managed 13 yards on the ground at San Francisco. Back at the Meadowlands, the offensive line worked out in the weight room. Parcells made a point to visit them and unveil his new antagonizing nickname: Club 13.

21

SEPARATION

Click. Click.

The sound meant it was on. Lawrence Taylor had buckled his chin strap during practice. The terrorizing in-game effort he gave came next.

"I got to work you this week, dude," Taylor said across the line of scrimmage to Brad Benson. "Parcells is, you know, up my ass. We all want to do well."

Normally, Benson, the left tackle, faced a second-stringer. It might not even be a linebacker or a defensive end. It could be a body that went through the motions, running the same scheme as the upcoming opponent. When he heard LT's rationale, all he could think was, *What a teammate,* in an eye-rolling tone.

What Taylor failed to mention was that Benson's assignment at Washington was Dexter Manley. The Redskins' defensive end had taken the NFL lead in sacks with 17.5, one more than Taylor. In the first meeting between the two teams, Manley sacked Simms twice.

That the thirty-year-old Benson had made it to a tenth year in the league was an accomplishment on its own. "It's a known fact that Ray Perkins wanted to run Brad out of there. Bill Austin, the line coach under Perkins, blamed Brad for everything, like he was some sort of dog," said Jim Burt.[1]

Benson, along with George Martin and Harry Carson, were the lone remaining Giants who had witnessed The Fumble. Benson had come to New York as a free agent after New England dropped him in 1977. He was never supposed to be a starter. Jeff Weston was pegged for that role in '79, but Benson started 10 games that year. In '84, the Giants drafted William Roberts, whose trajectory to supplant Benson was slowed by injury. When Parcells became the head coach in '83, he hired Tom Bresnahan as the new offensive line coach. Bresnahan spent two seasons in New York and switched Benson from playing right-handed to playing left-handed. It made a difference. Gradually, the confidence that had been shaken under Perkins and Austin returned, and Benson maintained a starting spot.

Benson's nemesis in Washington never seemed to have a problem with confidence. In the days before the showdown, Manley spoke to the media, sitting at his locker wearing red-and–electric blue Spiderman tights and a matching jacket. The six-foot-three 257-pounder was in the midst of his fourth consecutive double-digit sack season. Already that season, he told reporters he would "ring Joe Montana's clock." In '85, he promised to "knock" Chicago Bears running back Walter Payton "out of the game."[2] Redskins head coach Joe Gibbs had asked Manley to quiet the chatter, but the defensive end said he had a "vendetta" against Benson.

The Giants tackle didn't take the bait. "Sure, I'm nervous about facing Manley," Benson said. "I'd be lying if I said I wasn't. I've never gotten this much attention in my life. It's like I was a quarterback or something."[3]

For the entire week of practice, Taylor, Martin, and Leonard Marshall worked Benson continuously.

"That son of a gun, he literally worked himself into perfection. I've never seen a guy work as hard in practice as Brad Benson, and he brought it to Dexter Manley," Martin said.

Other teams developed special schemes to block Manley. They'd send a tight end cracking down on him from the slot, or they'd assign extra blockers to double-team him. The Giants would do neither.

"Benson gets him all by himself," said Phil Simms. "That's our style, and I'll tell you something. I'm not worried."[4]

The Giants had some injuries to address heading into Washington. Burt's back problems kept him out of the San Francisco game. He wouldn't play against the Redskins. Hostetler, the backup quarterback, who lined up at receiver, broke his left fibula trying to catch a pass against the 49ers. Cornerback Mark Collins broke his left hand in two places. Phil McConkey broke his right thumb on a kickoff return. The fracture was at the base of the thumb. The Giants and McConkey contemplated surgery and inserting pins to reset the bone, but if that happened, McConkey was done for the year. He opted to wear a cast instead.

New York and Washington led the NFC East with 11–2 records. They had both clinched play-off spots. The outcome of this game would propel one toward the divisional crown and send the other one to the wild card round.

"It was a great rivalry. People don't appreciate it as much. We went against them. They were good. They had a great coach. They had good players. They were together for a long time just like our guys," Parcells said.

The Giants arrived in Washington on Saturday, the day before the game. Benson's parents and two of his brothers met him there. His brother Troy couldn't make it because he was in his rookie year with the New York Jets. Benson's parents saw the nervousness in their son. "I was just a wreck," he said.

Before the Giants had meetings at the team hotel, Benson and his family visited Arlington National Cemetery. They walked part of the vast final resting place for hundreds of thousands of men and women who served in the country's military. Amid the rolling green hills and white marble headstones, Benson found some calm.

When the offensive line met at the hotel, the unit's coach, Fred Hoaglin, offered a confession. The six-foot-four Hoaglin, who carried more heft than his 250-pound playing weight, stood before his players. He had mocked Redskins defensive tackle Dave Butz to a reporter from Green Bay. He said the six-foot-seven, 291-pound tackle had a pumpkin head. His comments made the paper and traveled back east. It was unusual for the soft-spoken Hoaglin to make negative comments.

In speaking to his players, he started out contrite, but then he switched gears. "Well, I'm gonna tell you the truth, the guy does have a pumpkin head. Maybe I really did mean it. Dexter Manley and Charles Mann, I'm sick and tired of all this. You guys have something I don't have anymore; you can still play." His eyes filled with tears, and he walked out of the room.

Benson had never seen his coach like this. The mini-speech left him exhilarated. "There was no doubt about it, they were gonna get an ass whooping," he said.

After warm-ups on Sunday, McConkey ducked into the locker room. With the cast on, he mishandled kicks during the week of practice. Now, it had to go. A trainer cut it off and wrapped the thumb with some medical tape. "It's got no protection, no needles, no shooting up. The Giants didn't believe in shooting us up. No drugs. Nothing," McConkey said.

Parcells and Simms walked side by side from the locker room to the baseball dugout that led up to the turf at Robert F. Kennedy Memorial Stadium. Parcells stopped his quarterback just before the steps up to the field.

"Boy, you ready?"

"Yeah. I'm ready, Bill."

Out of view from the fans, they heard the rancorous din of the crowd. Simms buckled his chin strap because you didn't walk out onto the field at RFK without protecting your head from any object that might be thrown.

"You know, Simms, they hate us so much down here, they love us," Parcells said.

Simms gave his head coach the obligatory laugh a boss gets when he makes an odd comment, but the quarterback understood what the coach was saying. In the next moment, they walked up the steps and the barrage of insults hailed down on them from the Redskins' fans. "It was just great. I loved it. I loved going on the road and having people yell at you because that means you're doing well," Simms said.

After Benson took the field, he glanced up into the stands and saw a mannequin wearing his No. 60 with a noose around its neck.

Wellington and John Mara walked through the stands to get to an elevator that would bring them to the level of the stadium where they watched the game perched in a little open-air radio booth.

McConkey received the opening kickoff. He ran it back to the 18-yard line, where defensive tackle Dean Hamel promptly smashed into him. The hit from Hamel, who outweighed McConkey by more than one hundred pounds, landed squarely on McConkey's injured thumb. The pain he felt then made the initial injury feel minuscule. "I go down to my knees, and these involuntary tears are just streaming down my face." The tears smeared the eye black on his face. "It was a mess, and the pain was excruciating."

In the lead-up to the game, Parcells met with Simms to go over the offensive game plan; the head coach continued to encourage the quarterback to make big plays. "It's going to be an all-out attack," he told the quarterback. "We're going to go after them as hard as we can go. You think it's there, take a chance."

Simms liked it. He wanted to take the risk on big throws. "That's easy for me. That was the whole premise of the game."

The quarterback opened the offensive series hitting Bavaro over the middle for a 41-yard pickup. On his way back to the huddle, the tight end made the sign of the cross. On the next play, Simms went back to Bavaro, gaining 12 more yards. The Giants had first down at the Washington 29-yard line. Bobby Johnson had a step on Darrell Green, the NFL's fastest man. Simms underthrew the pass, and Green, a future Hall of Famer, intercepted it at the 4-yard line.

"One of the dumbest plays I've ever had in my career. But I just did it because, hell, I'll throw it up there and see who gets it."

Parcells glared and pursed his lips, pacing the sideline to meet Simms. The Giants had established momentum and given it away. "I know, 'Be aggressive,'" Parcells said to Simms. "Be a little careful, too."

The Giants opened the scoring on their first drive of the second quarter. Simms connected with Bavaro for nine yards to complete the 10-play, 77-yard, 4:14 march. The Redskins tied the game on a four-yard Kelvin Bryant run with 1:50 left in the half.

New York got the ball back, and Simms relished these situations. He loved Parcells's approach to the hurry-up offense. "He never played them by the book. It was never, 'Hey, let's just get down in field goal range.' His big thing was, 'Hey, throw it down there.'"

John Madden, who handled the game's broadcast duties with Pat Summerall for CBS, called Simms the best quarterback in the hurry-up offense, and Simms proceeded to prove him right.

In ninety-two seconds, Simms led Big Blue on a seven-play, 81-yard drive that culminated in a seven-yard touchdown pass to Bobby Johnson. The Giants went into halftime up 14–7.

While the score looked close, the game wasn't. The G-Men missed opportunities. A sure touchdown came off the hands of Bavaro, and a second underthrown ball to Johnson would have led to more points.

Redskins quarterback Jay Schroeder completed 8 of 20 passes and was intercepted three times. The defensive line often shifted just before the snap, not giving Schroeder time to readjust his protection or change the play. On one play, Carl Banks followed the Redskins' tight end in motion. LT would typically switch to the spot Banks vacated when this happened. This time, he didn't. Banks and Taylor looked at each other and gave a slight nod. When the ball was snapped, Taylor, Banks, and Leonard Marshall rushed the quarterback from the same side. "Scared the shit out of Joe Jacoby," Banks said.

What happened next typified how the Giants' defense excelled. Taylor and Banks came off the field laughing about the rogue blitz. They spoke to Belichick about it. The defensive coordinator grabbed his board and drew a scheme based on it. In the second half, he drew a different scheme, and by the middle of the next week, knowing opponents would have seen the game film, Belichick devised a multitude of options from the look. The defensive coordinator's in-game communication with his players and subsequent adjustments made the playbook something that was in constant evolution.

At Washington, Taylor registered three sacks on the day and took over the league lead. He was part of the unrelenting barrage of defenders hurrying and hitting Schroeder and sending Washington's offense off kilter. The Redskins tried to adjust in the second half by throwing shorter passes, but that proved ineffective.

In the third quarter, New York added a 21-yard Raul Allegre field goal.

With 3:11 left in the same quarter, McConkey leaped in the air, stopping a Simms pass, and juggling it into a catch for a 16-yard touchdown. In the flurry of offensive players slapping McConkey's helmet in congratulations came No. 56, the lone defensive player to run to the corner of the end zone to join the celebration. The Giants were up 24–7.

Schroeder threw three more interceptions in the second half. He came into the game having thrown 11 all season, and he threw more than half that—six—at home against the Giants. The Redskins scored with about three and a half minutes to play on a 22-yard touchdown pass from Schroeder to Kelvin Bryant. This provided the final score, making it a 24–14 Giants win.

After the game, Wellington and John Mara left the radio booth. On their way to the visitors' locker room, they walked through the crowd in the stands. The fans recognized them and screamed obscenities, and John Mara remembered it as one of the happier postgame walks he took. The sound victory on the road against Washington bolstered his confidence in his team. "For me personally, it made me believe we were going to win."

After the string of close wins for Big Blue, the Giants showed a clear separation between them and their opponents. It was a divide that would only grow.

Bavaro caught five passes for 111 yards to go with his touchdown. He ended up on the cover of *Sports Illustrated,* an image of him dragging a Washington defender with the headline REAL GIANTS. Yet it was more than the stats that impressed Madden. "The greatest blocking job by a tight end I've ever seen in my life," the CBS analyst said.[5]

Simms always knew Manley was closing in when he heard the huffing, snorting sound the defensive end made as he came around the corner. The quarterback didn't hear much of it that day. Benson handled Manley. The Giants believed Manley was a momentum player. New York figured if he didn't make plays early in the game, frustration would set in. It did. In the third quarter, Manley shoved Benson after a play. The Giants tackle had none of it, knocking Manley back with a two-handed chop right in the middle of the chest. On the next play, Benson caved in Manley, blocking him on the outside shoulder and burying him into the ground. The camera showed Benson on the sideline midway through the fourth quarter, his nose bandaged and bloodied from the unhealed cut that was first opened two months ago at Seattle.

"This guy's really done a job. He did a job all day today. I think he's done a job all season for this Giant team, but they're the last to get the accolades when you hand them out," Madden said.

This was the day Benson stopped being a journeyman lineman. His play and Madden's praise changed everything for him.

"Everybody has pivotal points in their life, in their careers, and that was one of them for me. One of the biggest things that ever happened to me in my life was that football game, right there."

For his effort, Benson became the first lineman ever to be named the NFC Offensive Player of the Week. Part of winning the award meant Benson, who owned a Jaguar dealership, was given a Mercedes to drive for the week. He went on to become a member of the All-Madden team. He was one of eight Giants selected to play in the Pro Bowl. Taylor, Carson, Bavaro, and punter Sean Landeta were named starters. Benson, Burt, Morris, and Leonard Marshall were reserves.

Days after the win in Washington, Benson's wife, Lisa, called the Giants' facility around lunchtime. Brad took the call in an office off the locker room. The social worker from Golden Cradle Adoption Services had called the Bensons' home to let them know they could come get their baby boy. They had been waiting three and a half years for a child. Lisa wanted Brad to pick her up at their home in Tuxedo, New York, and they would get the child together. Benson had to talk to Parcells about missing practice. He called up to the head coach's office.

"Bill?"

"Yeah."

"You know that my wife and I applied for adoption for this baby and everything like that."

"Yeah."

"Well, the baby's here."

"Well, what does that mean?"

"What does that mean? It means, like, I got to go."

"Oh, you can't wait until afternoon practice is over to go?"

Benson mentioned how he hadn't missed practice in forever.

"That's exactly the point," Parcells said.

Benson repeated that he had to leave.

"You do what you have to do."

An irritated Benson left the Meadowlands. *Mr. Compassionate,* he thought about Parcells. The head coach had a similar approach when Joe Morris's wife gave birth the day before the Eagles game in October. Parcells advised Morris to stay at the team hotel. Morris left. Saw the baby and came back with celebratory cigars. Benson and his wife picked up Tyler, their baby boy. After they brought him home that night, the phone rang. It was Parcells. He asked Benson if everything went well with the baby. It had. Then Parcells asked to speak to Lisa. "Soothes everything over," Benson said.

TAKING THE WIND

Harry Carson grabbed the Gatorade bucket. He moved low to the ground like a jungle cat stalking its prey.

Carson approached the edge of the field. Bill Parcells turned around, saw No. 53, and sidestepped Carson. The home crowd let out a burst of noise, and about half the drink splashed down on the Giants' head coach. His blue Giants parka half-drenched, Parcells stood, hands in his pockets, headset off, smiling.

About a minute remained in the Giants' week 16 trouncing of the Green Bay Packers. The week before, New York had beaten the St. Louis Cardinals 27–7. The 55–24 win against the Packers clinched home-field advantage in the play-offs for the G-Men. They had finished the regular season with a 14–2 record, winning nine straight games.

After dumping the Gatorade jug, Carson made a circle, coming back around to the edge of the sidelines. This time, he wore a wide smile and shook Parcells's hand. The thirty-three-year-old team captain, who had seen the worst of the Giants' bumbling years, had not always sported a joyous look.

He came to the Giants as a project, a fourth-round pick in '76. He played defensive line, not linebacker, at South Carolina State. "I spent a good part after being drafted hanging out with the shrink because he had to determine whether I could make the adjustment," Carson said.

By his third year in the league, Carson became a Pro Bowl player. A couple of years later, when Lawrence Taylor showed up as the ballyhooed number-two overall pick, it irritated Carson. "I understood his talent level, but he sort of leapfrogged everybody from a salary perspective. I was sort of pissed because he leapfrogged me, and I wasn't happy with my contract."

Carson asked to be traded at different points in his career. He spoke about leaving football to join the air force. What made Carson so different, and an enigma in comparison to most of his contemporaries, was that he was really good at football, but he didn't love it. "I happened into football. It wasn't that I wanted to play football all of my life. Most of the guys had dreams of playing in the NFL. I did not."

The first day Carson played football, he quit the team. He started practice with the freshman team in high school, and he turned in his equipment before the first session ended. He hadn't done any conditioning to prepare. He eased his way into the game playing for a local Boys & Girls Club and went back out for the high school team the following year. His main motivation in playing the sport was the attention it garnered from girls. He was senior class president in high school and earned a college football scholarship, but after a disagreement with his coach, he quit the high school team with three games left in his senior season.

He had to recalibrate his priorities after his first year at South Carolina State. "I almost flunked out my freshman year because I got this whole girl thing and football and classes all mixed up. It scared me because I could've lost my scholarship."

He had grown up seeing black men work all week and get drunk on payday, arriving home with empty pockets. "I remember having our lights turned off and being evicted." That wasn't going to happen to him. He earned a degree in education. Now, the eight-time Pro Bowler was on the precipice of professional success that seemed unimaginable during most of his career in New York, and yet, he wasn't going to get caught up in the moment.

"One of the things that had always been instilled in us as players by

Parcells and Belichick was to manage our excitement. Don't get too high after a win. Don't get too low after a loss."

David Fishof, the agent, had dinner with a few of his Giants clients at an Italian restaurant on Route 17 near the stadium. With the G-Men cruising into the play-offs, Fishof encouraged his clients to take full advantage of their football star status and their proximity to the media capital of the world.

The mid-'80s were ripe for caricature-driven marketing of athletes. The defending Super Bowl champs, the '85 Chicago Bears, had set a tone for this. They crossed over into pop culture with their song and music video, "The Super Bowl Shuffle." Of course, the team's quarterback, Jim McMahon, had national endorsement deals with Taco Bell and Honda scooters. Charismatic backup defensive tackle William "the Refrigerator" Perry starred in a national McDonald's ad while his teammates, the guys who started, served as extras. Even a Bears backup wide receiver had a regular radio spot.

William Roberts, Lionel Manuel, and Andy Headen spearheaded the group that recorded and made a very low-budget music video, "We're the New York Giants." It saw some airtime on MTV and had a small release as a 45 vinyl record. The video opened with eight players running from the tunnel onto the turf in an empty Giants Stadium. They danced in sync in the clothes they wore to the facility that day. They sang lines such as "We are the New York Giants / Don't you know we're great / Football is our business / Pasadena, we can't wait." Not surprisingly, it didn't have the same mass appeal as "The Super Bowl Shuffle."

Other songs sprouted up. A parody of the number-one Bangles hit "Walk Like an Egyptian" turned into "Walk Like a Giant."

Phil McConkey, one of Fishof's clients, capitalized on his opportunities. "McConkey was luckily a victim of everything Phil Simms turned down," Fishof said.

Parcells incessantly busted his chops for being an attention-seeker. In the middle of the locker room, the head coach announced McConkey as the number-one self-promoter, having taken the spot from Jim Burt and Sean Landeta.

"I was never going to let it get out of control. And he wasn't going to let it get out of control. So, I understood where he was coming from," McConkey said. "But all those things, what did they take? They took a few minutes here and there."

McConkey developed a relationship with the crew at Z100. He had started listening to the station at training camp when he was trying to make the team as a free agent. Now, during the '86 season, he started doing regular appearances on the morning show.

Fishof's office at 1775 Broadway in New York City was a floor below MTV. This provided the entry point for McConkey to meet the VJs and eventually appear on a celebrity version of *Remote Control,* the game show that helped launch the careers of actors and comedians Adam Sandler and Colin Quinn.

As the Giants made their play-off run, McConkey wrote a diary with Steve Serby of the *New York Post* and appeared in an ad for the *Post*'s competitor, the *New York Daily News* with Simms, Burt, Benson, and Billy Ard.

"I worked extremely hard, but listen, I got cut once before that. And I knew I was going to get cut again," McConkey said. "I still was in the weight room. And I still did everything I needed to do and more. But I enjoyed being a pro football player on and off the field. I thoroughly enjoyed it. And I'm glad I did."

In the wild card round, the Washington Redskins defeated the Los Angeles Rams 19–7. The NFL restricted divisional rivals from facing each other in the next round. This meant Washington would head to Chicago to play the Bears and the Giants would host the San Francisco 49ers, the NFC West champs.

On the Tuesday before the game, Lawrence Taylor was named the Associated Press NFL MVP. Taylor remains just the second defensive player to be named MVP and the first since the Vikings' Alan Page won the award fifteen years earlier. LT's forty-one votes more than doubled those of the runner-up Eric Dickerson, who grabbed seventeen. Miami Dolphins quarterback Dan Marino finished third with nine votes. Two of Taylor's teammates elicited MVP attention. Running back Joe Morris finished fourth with five votes, and tight end Mark Bavaro was among a group of five players who received one vote each.

Taylor finished the season with 20.5 sacks, one and a half shy of the record set by New York Jets defensive end Mark Gastineau. For the third time in his career, Taylor was named the Defensive Player of the Year, receiving seventy-four of the seventy-nine votes for that award.

After he received the honors, Taylor did something he had hardly done all season. He spoke to the media. As the regular season drew to a close, Taylor began interacting with the press, but he would only take football questions. This time, he spent an extended period taking questions from reporters.

He credited Parcells's media blockade with taking the pressure off him. "He was the big reason I had a good year this year, not having to deal with the press."[1]

Without naming anyone, he spoke about people doubting him being a source of motivation for his play. "A lot of people were hoping I would fall flat on my face and wouldn't recover. I didn't fall on my face. Anytime somebody says I can't do something, it ticks me off."[2]

He wouldn't talk about his substance abuse, but he did offer words that reinforced an image of his daredevil style. "I'm just a plain wild dude," he said. "I live life wild. I play wild, but I do it all my own way. I don't really care what other people expect of me or what I'm supposed to do or how society says I'm supposed to do certain things. I do it my way and try to get the job done that way."[3]

Oddsmakers installed the Giants as three-point favorites against the 49ers, but broadcasting from the sidelines at the sunny but subfreezing Meadowlands, CBS's Jimmy "the Greek" Snyder picked San Francisco to win 27–24 on a late-game Ray Wersching field goal.

The Giants failed to get a first down on the game's opening possession. Joe Montana and the 49ers took over at their 37-yard line. In three plays, they moved the ball to midfield. Montana dropped back on second down and 10. He hit wide receiver Jerry Rice in stride on a slant pattern from the right side. Rice cut across the field and left the Big Blue defense behind. With nothing impeding Rice's path to the end zone, the future Hall of Famer inexplicably lost control of the ball at the 27-yard line. The fumble went bouncing toward the end zone. Rice tried to recover it, but lost control as Giants defenders caught up and pounced on him. Finally, amid a flurry of mostly blue jerseys, safety Kenny Hill recovered the ball in the end zone. A touchback. What could have been a 7–0 lead for the 49ers turned into the Giants' ball at the 20-yard line.

Eight plays and five minutes later, Simms threw a laser to Bavaro on a 24-yard seam route for New York to take a 7–0 lead. As Simms celebrated with some raised-arms fist-pumping behind the line of scrimmage, Taylor came off the bench, grabbing and slapping the quarterback in congratulations.

The Giants' defense quickly forced the 49ers into a third down and six at their own 45-yard line. LT rushed Montana, who lofted a pass to Dwight Clark that was broken up at the Giants' 33-yard line by Perry Williams. Taylor raced more than 30 yards to slap Williams on the helmet for making the pass breakup.

When the 49ers got the ball back, Wersching did add a 26-yard field goal to make the score 7–3 Giants at the end of the first quarter.

Midway through the second quarter, safety Herb Welch picked off a Montana pass intended for Jerry Rice. On the next play, Joe Morris took a handoff to the left side. He made a quick cut back behind a wall of Giants blockers and darted 45 yards to the end zone. The Giants were up 14–3 and Morris had already rushed for 110 yards in the game. The offensive line obliterated the Club 13 moniker from the regular season meeting at San Francisco.

The rout was on.

San Francisco had driven to the Giants' 9-yard line before kicking their first-quarter field goal. They would never get remotely close to scoring again. They crossed midfield once more, never moving the ball past the Giants' 40-yard line.

Big Blue scored on its next possession, using 12 plays to drive 57 yards in nearly five minutes. On fourth down and six, the Giants lined up for a 45-yard field goal. Before the snap, Big Blue shifted into a shotgun set with Jeff Rutledge moving from holder to quarterback and kicker Raul Allegre flanked out wide as a receiver. Rutledge dropped a 23-yard pass to a wide-open Bavaro for the first down. Four plays later, Simms stood in the pocket until the last possible moment. A charging Dwaine Board drilled his helmet into Simms's chin as the quarterback threw a strike to the right corner of the end zone, where Bobby Johnson made the catch for the score. The quarterback lay on the turf, chin strap unbuckled, slowly getting up as Taylor once again came to offer congratulations. Burt and Bavaro checked in on the passer as he made his way to the sidelines. The Giants built a 21–3 lead with less than a minute to play in the half.

On the second play of the 49ers' ensuing drive, Montana dropped back from the San Francisco 18-yard line. He looked left for Jerry Rice. He brought his arm back to throw, and as he delivered the pass, Jim Burt throttled him, knocking Montana off both his feet and hitting him with such force that the quarterback bounced off the turf after landing with the full force of his body on his left shoulder. LT picked off the underthrown pass at the 34-yard line and zoomed back to the end zone. The Giants were up 28–3. A crumpled Montana stayed on the ground for more than two minutes. With a 49ers staffer on each arm, the wobbly legged quarterback went directly to the stadium tunnel and into the visitors' locker room.

Sports Illustrated's Paul Zimmerman acutely observed that if the Giants stuck to the letter of the law with their Gatorade tradition of dousing the coach when the game was in hand, Parcells would have spent the second half soaking wet. The Giants scored three more touchdowns in the third quarter to make it 49–3, but the game had long been decided by then.

In the third frame, Simms threw two touchdowns: a 28-yarder to McConkey and a 29-yarder to Zeke Mowatt. Simms finished 9 of 19, completing passes to eight different receivers, for 136 yards and four scores. Morris added a two-yard touchdown run. He ran for 159 yards on 24 carries that day.

The 49ers tallied nine first downs. Carl Banks had seven tackles, stuffing a San Francisco running game that gained 29 yards on 20 carries. The next day, Banks appeared on *Good Morning America*.

Parcells had spoken with Banks during the week about his play. He thought the linebacker was too tentative when the teams met in San Francisco. The head coach lauded the improvement in the play-off game before unloading a zinger. "Can you imagine? America woke up and saw that face," Parcells said. "Five thousand people in Nebraska couldn't go to work today. They had to call in sick."

After the game, Taylor was asked if the outcome would have been different had Jerry Rice scored instead of fumbling on the 49ers' opening possession. Taylor laughed and then said the score would've been 49–10 instead.

By the time the game ended, Montana had been transported across the Hudson River to the Hospital for Special Surgery in Manhattan. He was groggy and still had a headache when a visitor showed up with a twelve-pack of beer. It was Burt.

The G-Men were one win away from the team's first Super Bowl appearance. The Bears had finished the regular season with a 14–2 record, but the Giants wouldn't get a revenge match with the team that had ended their previous season. The Bears were no longer the Super Bowl Shuffling Bears. That change started when Buddy Ryan, the team's defensive coordinator, left to become the head coach in Philadelphia. It culminated in changes at the quarterback position. Injuries left Jim McMahon playing only five of the first eleven games of the season. In week 12, the Green Bay Packers' Charles Martin threw McMahon on his shoulder, pretending the cheap shot was a block during an interception return. McMahon returned to that game but didn't play again the rest of the season. Head coach Mike Ditka brought in Doug Flutie from the USFL. The diminutive Heisman Trophy winner would go on to have a quality NFL career, but he wasn't ready in Chicago. After the Washington Redskins' wild card win against the Rams, the Redskins went to Chicago. In the divisional round matchup, Ditka started Flutie, whom some of his teammates referred to as a midget. Washington won 27–13. Now, the Giants would face their divisional foe for the third time that season.

When the Giants lost to the Bears to end the '85 season, New York City mayor Ed Koch lost a bet to the mayor of Chicago. Koch sent cheesesteaks from Manny's, the restaurant down the road from the stadium. When the Giants won the wild card game against the 49ers in '85, Koch accepted a dozen steaks from San Francisco mayor Dianne Feinstein. This year, though, Koch changed his policy. He declined the bet with Feinstein. He referred her to the mayor of Moonachie—mispronouncing it "mah-NOO-chee" instead of "moo-NAH-key"—where Manny's was located.

Worse than that, before the Giants had even earned a spot in the Super Bowl, Koch said New York City would not host a parade for the team if Big Blue became the world champs. The city hosted a parade for the World Series champion New York Mets, but because the Giants moved to New Jersey and didn't pay taxes in New York, Koch refused. American Express stepped up and offered $700,000 for the cost of the tickertape parade, but Koch remained adamant that there would be no parade for the team from New Jersey.

Parcells followed a pattern on his commute to Giants Stadium. In the predawn darkness, he stopped at Elmer's in Upper Saddle River for a coffee with one cream and one sugar to go. A half hour later, he finished the drink and stopped at Christiana's in Wood-Ridge. There he bought two more cups of coffee with cream and sugar to go.[4]

By eight o'clock in the morning of the NFC Championship game, Parcells picked up the phone in his office and started dialing the National Weather Service phone number. The recorded message calculated the winds already blowing at ten miles per hour. An hour later, the winds picked up to fifteen miles per hour.

In the general manager's office, George Young called a friend and former coworker from the Baltimore Colts. Ernie Accorsi was the general manager of the Cleveland Browns. Accorsi's squad hosted the Denver Broncos in the AFC Championship game, which was the first game to kick off that day. Both men were nervous, but Young—never one for a pithy "good luck"—ended the call with, "I hope tonight we talk and we're both happy."

As the Giants' 4:00 P.M. kickoff drew near, Bobby Johnson had yet to show up in the locker room. He had been late to games before, but this was the NFC Championship, a chance to go to the Super Bowl. He stayed at the team hotel the night before, but when he woke up early in the morning, he went to his apartment, the place where he would use drugs. He ended up falling asleep there. "Next thing you know, it was a couple hours before the game. I'm like, 'Oh, my God.' I jumped in the car and just tried to get there as fast as I could."

Johnson found himself in the same traffic as the rest of the fans clogging the roads heading to the game.

"It was never worth it," Johnson said. "It just kind of got out of control, and like I said, next thing you know, it was time to get up."

He made it to the facility and ducked into the training room to get dressed. It had been written that Jim Burt and Lawrence Taylor started to beat Johnson. Both Burt and Johnson said that never happened. "No one laid a hand on him," Burt said, but it did get verbal, with players expressing their anger about Johnson's apparent lack of care for the team. Johnson said nothing back.

When Parcells made his final check on the weather, the winds had picked up to their greatest intensity. During the three-hour stretch of game time, twenty- and twenty-five-mile-per-hour winds whipped through the stadium with gusts in the first through fourth quarters recorded between thirty-five and forty miles per hour.

Harry Carson stood in the middle of the field for the coin toss. He had orders from Parcells to take the wind. Redskins guard Russ Grimm called tails when the referee flipped the coin in the air. It landed on heads. The

Giants kicked off to Washington, and Big Blue had the wind at their back for the first quarter.

Washington started with the ball at their 20-yard line after Raul Allegre booted the opening kickoff out of the end zone. Carl Banks and LT stopped Redskins running back George Rogers on two consecutive two-yard runs. Quarterback Jay Schroeder followed those up with an incomplete pass. On fourth down, punter Steve Cox took the long snap and shanked a 23-yard punt out of bounds into the wind. The Giants started inside Washington territory, and with the wind at his back, Raul Allegre gave the G-Men a 3–0 lead.

Against the rest of the NFL, the Redskins averaged 118.4 yards per game on the ground. Against the Giants, Washington had less than half that success, running for 52.5 yards per game. In the NFC Championship, head coach Joe Gibbs used a backup lineman as a tight end, sending him in motion to provide extra blocking against LT. After a Gary Reasons sack of Schroeder, Kelvin Bryant rushed for no gain. On third down, Schroeder scrambled right before unleashing a 51-yard cannon against the wind. It slipped through the hands of Gary Clark, the receiver who torched the Giants in October with 241 yards. Forced to punt again, Cox kicked it 27 yards, and the Giants took over at the Washington 38-yard line.

The Giants used up 4:37 on the eight-play drive that ended with Simms throwing an 11-yard touchdown score to Lionel Manuel. As the Giants drove to go up 10–0, John Elway and the Denver Broncos completed an improbable comeback against the Browns. Elway led The Drive, a 98-yard, game-tying scoring march at the end of the regulation. Denver won in overtime on a 33-yard Rich Karlis field goal.

At the Meadowlands, the Redskins got the ball back and managed to get one first down before Cox added his third 20-something-yard punt of the first quarter.

Washington forced New York to punt on its first possession of the second quarter. The last time Sean Landeta punted in wind like this, he whiffed against the Bears in Chicago. Six months after that game, Parcells, his mentor Mickey Corcoran, Simms, and offensive coordinator Ron Erhardt played a round of golf at Alpine Country Club. Standing on the sixteenth tee, Erhardt shook his head. "I can't believe he missed that damn ball."[5]

The blooper-reel miscue stayed in the minds of others, but not Landeta. It was the type of moment that could've crushed other athletes, but not Landeta. "It hasn't bothered me," he said in the off-season. "In five or 10 years, people will forget about it."[6]

Landeta turned around and had an All-Pro year in '86, averaging 44.8 yards per punt. He was a student of punting. In training camp, Landeta had conversations with Steve Belichick, the Navy assistant coach and scout and the defensive coordinator's father, about studies on the roll punts get when they hit the ground and on kicking into the wind. Landeta arrived at Giants Stadium two hours before kickoff of the NFC Championship. The weather forecasts throughout the week had predicted the wind. He walked the field gauging the conditions. He knew the idiosyncrasies of his home turf. He knew that when the flags on top of the scoreboard blew in one direction it meant the wind on the field blew in the opposite direction. He knew about the wind whirlpooling in one corner of the stadium. He noticed that at practice one autumn when leaves and stray pieces of papers swirled in the air for minutes at a time. On windy practices late in the week, Landeta would walk over and throw some paper into the corner. "It would get vacuumed in a circle and stay in midair, and we'd just stand there looking at it like it was magic."

He also knew that knowing all this stuff only meant so much. He'd have to deliver on game day. "You can practice in it. You can be a veteran. You can have all these things in place, but after all that, what matters is what happens in that five seconds when the ball's snapped to you and you kick it."

On his first punt into the wind, Landeta walloped a skyward 46-yarder that pinned Washington at its own 4-yard line. The Redskins moved the ball into Giants territory and set up for a 51-yard field goal. Jeff Bostic's snap skidded across the Astroturf through Schroeder's hands. Elvis Patterson was the first Giant to make a play for the ball, but Banks ended up with the recovery at the Washington 49-yard line.

Simms hit Bavaro for a 30-yard pass, which brought the ball to the Redskins' 17. It was Simms's second and final pass of the quarter. Three plays later, Joe Morris ran over right tackle for a one-yard score. He looked at a Redskins defender and declared, "It's over." The Giants were up 17–0.

With less than two minutes to play in the half, Phil McConkey slid to the ground fielding a punt at his own 27-yard line rather than letting the ball bounce deep into Giants territory. He hopped to his feet and returned it for five yards before Reggie Branch launched his helmet like a missile into McConkey's head. The battered navy veteran popped up like Rocky Balboa telling Clubber Lang, "Ain't so bad. Ain't so bad." With bloodstains on his left leg and the towel hanging from his waist, McConkey trotted to the sidelines waving his right hand in the air, pumping up the crowd.

As the teams left the field at the end of the half, Dexter Manley started talking to Brad Benson. Thus far, Benson continued to keep Manley in check as he had a month before in the pivotal matchup at Washington.

"I'm telling you, man, I'm going to get a sack in the second half. I'm going to get your ass," Manley said.

In between the finger-pointing and jabbering, they settled on a $500 bet. If Manley sacked Simms, he got the money. If Benson kept the defensive end at bay, Manley owed Benson.

The Giants chose the wind instead of receiving the kickoff in the second half. They spotted Washington a possession, and New York didn't score again in the game, but it didn't matter. The Big Blue defense continued to dominate. The G-Men shut out Washington, holding the Redskins to 190 yards of offense. Washington was 0 for 14 on third-down conversions and followed that with four failed fourth-down attempts.

"We had to stop the run and vertical passing game. They weren't going to beat us throwing check downs to the backs or crossing patterns. The deeper throws gave us a chance to rush," said Belichick, who wore a gray-hooded sweatshirt under a red faux-satin Giants jacket.

Whether by design or to save himself, Schroeder took enormous drop backs trying to throw the ball deep down the field. On one play, Carl Banks chased Schroeder 25 yards behind the line of scrimmage. The quarterback got the pass off, but even if he had completed it, it would've gone for a seven-yard loss.

"The wind was so violent. The ball wasn't flying the way it normally does. You're on the road. The crowd is a little excited," Parcells said. "You're getting a lot of pressure. That's a hard situation. That's almost an impossible situation."

The Giants ended up with four sacks. Schroeder became the next in line of quarterbacks the G-Men battered, but this was without LT, who sat out for most of the second half with a thigh bruise. Schroeder threw 50 passes, completing 20 for 195 yards. After those throws, though, any combination of Leonard Marshall, Jim Burt, Carl Banks, Eric Dorsey, Erik Howard, and George Martin collapsed on him. Knocked to the ground by Burt and Marshall after an incompletion late in the fourth quarter, Schroeder stumbled to one knee before waving his backup, Doug Williams, off the field. Schroeder stayed in the game but collapsed on the sidelines moments later. He had been concussed.

For the long-suffering Giants fans, the scene became euphoric. Their team was headed to the Super Bowl. They sounded foghorns. They popped bottles of champagne they had snuck into the stadium. When the Giants players motioned the crowd to get louder, it did. Papers started swirling throughout the stadium. Fans ripped pages from game programs, threw streams of toilet paper, and tossed newspaper pages into the gusting winds. It turned into a pop-up confetti storm.

Chris Mara watched the game with his father and brothers. They had made their way down to the field to take in a celebration that Giants Stadium had never seen before. "It looked like a tickertape parade, and I just remember looking up in the sky and giving Ed Koch the finger."

The scoreboard lit up with the message: THE GIANTS THANK THE GREATEST FANS IN THE WORLD.

Landeta averaged 42.3 yards on his six punts. He also attempted to act as the decoy, distracting Parcells while Carson tried to dump the Gatorade on him.

By now, CBS had built a graphic player bio for the jug. Instead of the cutout of a player's head shot, it was the orange cooler in the foreground of the New York City skyline. Parcells turned around and spotted Carson. The forty-five-year-old coach made a stutter step left and then right. He put his hands up, knocking the bucket back into a little spill on Carson before the contents were thrown toward the coach.

A few minutes later, a grinning Parcells pulled a water pistol out of his pocket and fired a few squirts at Carson.

When the game ended, a couple of Giants carried Belichick off the field on their shoulders. Burt climbed into the stands, swarmed by fans on the way to see his wife, Colleen. Pepper Johnson and William Roberts danced at midfield.

"Where's my $500?" Benson asked Dexter Manley.

"I ain't paying; you guys didn't throw the ball."

"We threw it enough. You didn't get your sack. You bet. You owe me money."

Simms only attempted two passes in the second half. Benson agreed to settle the wager by having Manley buy him a beer at the Pro Bowl.

Burt came down from the stands, autographed footballs, and waved his hands up to the roaring crowd as he headed to the locker room.

The turnaround that started after The Fumble had reached its penultimate point. Only Benson, Carson, and Martin remained from that infamous day. The Giants headed to the Super Bowl with just fourteen players who experienced the 3–12–1 disaster of Parcells's first year.

The Giants dusted off their play-off opponents by a total score of 66–3. In the two games, their opponents never got that close to the end zone. The 49ers and Redskins combined to run a total of seven plays inside the Giants' 30-yard line.

After the game, the Giants released a statement putting the parade controversy to rest. "The only logical place for a Giants celebration is here at Giants Stadium in the New Jersey Sports Complex."

For a fleeting moment, Parcells took in the scene. "I noticed it at the end. You notice it at the end. You're too busy while it's going on."

Within a few hours after leaving the field, his mind had already shifted. "You've got the Super Bowl coming up. You try to think about what you're going to do schedule-wise," he said. "After the game's over, your mind isn't thinking about the game. You're thinking about what's next."

23

"NOT GOING TO HAVE A DAY ON ME"

In his office at Giants Stadium, Bill Parcells kept elephant figurines. He had ten of them, and each one faced the door with its trunk raised up.

This was one of many superstitions bestowed upon him by his Italian mother. "I'm still a little bit of an elephant guy," he said decades later.

He never picked up coins if they were tails up.

His players made use of these two superstitions. When leaving his office after meetings, they'd not-so-accidentally bump an elephant, turning it away from the door. They'd place pennies tails up in the locker room.

Parcells's devotion to these beliefs compelled him to get United Airlines pilot Augie Stasio to fly the Giants from Newark to California for the Super Bowl. Stasio had flown the charter flights for the past two Super Bowl winners. Even though the G-Men had to switch from a DC-8 to a DC-10 because that's what Stasio flew, flying with Stasio was a no-brainer for Parcells.

The Broncos and the Giants had two weeks to prepare for Super Bowl XXI. A week before the game, the Giants left behind the frigid New Jersey winter weather for the sunshine and warm temps of Southern California. Phil Simms also left behind an awful day of practice. "As bad as I've ever seen him. He was throwing awful, the receivers were dropping the balls he did get near them—a nightmare," Parcells said.[1]

That changed for Simms on the West Coast. He didn't have to worry about the weather or losing his grip on a slick, nearly frozen football. "Maybe it's all psychological, too. I play in forty-mile-per-hour winds against the Redskins. We practice a couple days before we go and it's cold. We get to California and I'm like, 'Oh, my God, it's warm.' We're on grass, and I just felt so much more relaxed."

Billy Ard did not have the same experience as his quarterback. The Giants practiced at the Los Angeles Rams' facility the Monday after they arrived. The atmosphere was loose as the offense and defense lined up for the nine-on-seven drill. Typically, the offense started with a basic play, and the players gradually worked their way from about 85 percent speed to 100 percent. Rookie defensive lineman John Washington bent into his stance across from Ard. Center Bart Oates snapped the ball to Simms, and Washington exploded at 100 percent, stunning Ard and blowing up the play. Parcells went off on Ard, yelling at him. It was unusual. Brad Benson, Karl Nelson, they were constant victims of Parcells's barbs, not Ard. "I get embarrassed. I get pissed. Now, the rest of the practice I'm going like a maniac," Ard said.

Before Ard dropped down into his stance for the next play, he confronted Washington. "Now, what the fuck was that about?"

The rookie answered, talking in sped-up words. "I'm sorry. I had to do it. He told me not to say anything. Because I'm a rookie. I don't know."

That's when Ard knew Parcells had put Washington up to it. Ard didn't have a misty-eyed, nostalgia-driven week experiencing the Super Bowl. He went into a bunker mentality. "I don't say anything to anybody. I keep my mouth shut. I'm just like a little boy that Mom scolded, and I'm taking my blanket and I'm going away."

He practiced, worked out, ate, and then went back to his hotel room. Over and over, he had two things on his mind: Rulon Jones and Tom Glassic. Jones was the Broncos' All-Pro defensive lineman Ard would face on Sunday. Glassic was a former Broncos guard who happened to have attended Watchung Hills Regional High School, the same school as Ard. Glassic was the fifteenth overall pick in the 1976 draft. He started in Super Bowl XII against the Dallas Cowboys. On the way to sharing the game's MVP award, Cowboys defensive linemen Randy White and Harvey Martin toyed with Glassic that day. It was worse because of the NFL Films highlight video, which was replayed every year. "So fucking Tom Glassic got his ass kicked every year for the next hundred thousand years because they're always showing Super Bowl XII on TV and every year Randy White's the MVP."

This and the incident with John Washington shaped Ard's week of preparation. "No relaxing. No enjoying. No nothing because Rulon Jones was not going to have a day on me."

Tuesday was picture day. Tight end Mark Bavaro donned his uniform, stood for pictures, walked to the edge of the field, and left. The second-year pro had become a nontalker of mythic proportions. During game broadcasts, TV announcers joked that when he had his jaw wired shut during the season, nobody noticed because he never said anything anyway. John Madden told an anecdote about Parcells even being a little spooked by his quietness. Bavaro didn't rebuff the media. He avoided them. In an era before the NFL mandated that players speak to reporters, when the press entered the locker room, Bavaro headed to the weight room or someplace the media couldn't access. He'd have off-the-record conversations with them, but formal interviews brought discomfort to the twenty-three-year-old. "I just wasn't a big fan of the sound bites. Or, 'Give me your evaluation.' Or, 'What were you thinking on this play?' Still to this day, I'm not a fan of having my words out on public record for all eternity, half-thought-out, just because people need something to say on a subject I don't really care about or have a position on. I just didn't want to get in the game you play with the media."

Looking back, Bavaro views his stance as that of a shy, quiet, immature young adult. "If I had to do it over again, I think I would realize now they have a job to do, and I would probably just play the game and provide them some material."

On Wednesday of Super Bowl week, he had to talk, and because of his silence, he drew the biggest crowd of reporters. First, they wanted to know why he took off the day before. "It was Picture Day," he said. "I came down for my picture and left. It wasn't media day. Today is writers' day."[2]

He spoke quietly and gave succinct answers. *Newsday* wrote up the hour-long session comparing it to the pain of a dental visit. The *New York Post* printed it as a court transcript of Bavaro defending his quiet nature.

"I don't think I'd be able to do it today. I wouldn't be able to get away with it," said Bavaro, who, nearly thirty years later, can still rattle off the names of the Giants beat writers.

The players had downtime. Brad Benson, Bart Oates, and Chris Godfrey went fishing for bonito.[3] Running back Tony Galbreath carried around a video camera, recording material for a segment CBS used in its pregame show. In part of it, Bavaro and McConkey did a parody of the characters from the Bartles & Jaymes wine cooler commercials. In perfect casting, McConkey played the chatty character, and Bavaro played the one who said nothing.

Parcells had concerns about the temptations Southern California posed to his players. He hired security to keep an eye on them. "Not just Lawrence. I had a couple guys being watched pretty close," he said.

If Bobby Johnson was one of them, the wide receiver had no idea. "If he did have somebody watching me, it was undercover."

On Friday, Simms had a spectacular practice. He was so good, Parcells shouted to him to save some of it for the game. Belichick's defense had an up-close view of the display Simms put on.

"We knew we were good on defense. But in practice, Simms could kill us even when we were in perfect position. When Simms got into that zone, he was unstoppable—nobody knew it better than our defense," Belichick said.

Since they arrived in California, the Giants had been staying at the Westin South Coast Plaza in Costa Mesa. On Friday, to get away from the distractions at the team hotel, Parcells had everyone move to the two-star accommodations of the Howard Johnson in Pasadena.

That night, Jim Burt appeared on *The Late Show Starring Joan Rivers*. Simms and McConkey went out to dinner with actor and comedian Billy Crystal. Director Rob Reiner was supposed to join them but had to cancel.

Crystal asked Simms about the game plan, and Simms gave him the opening. Simms had met with offensive coordinator Ron Erhardt. He knew the Giants were going to come out throwing.

"I'm going to fake it to Joe Morris. I'm going to throw an in-cut to Lionel Manuel. He's going to be open. We know the defense," he told Crystal.

"Really?"

"Yes."

In the stands, watching the game, Crystal acted like a football genius to the people around him, and he'd go on to use the dinner story with Simms on the talk show circuit.

Later on Friday night, Simms spoke with his agent, David Fishof. Disney had approached him with an idea about having the game's winning quarterback look into a camera and say, "I'm going to Disney World." Throughout the week, Simms backed Fishof off the deal. He had no interest in it.

"I don't care. I'm not doing it. You start doing these things before the game, you're going to lose. You can't make deals like this before the game," Simms told Fishof.

"Well, John Elway said he'd do it."

"Well, I don't care what John Elway does. Good for him."

By Friday night, Disney came back with an offer that win or lose, they'd pay the quarterbacks. Feeling sufficiently comfortable that the terms didn't mess with the mojo of the game, Simms agreed to the deal.

On Saturday, Parcells canceled practice. He had thought about having a walk-through of the Rose Bowl, but streaks and superstitions won out. The Giants hadn't conducted a walk-through on the road since they had lost at Seattle. They had done one at Dallas for the season opener and lost. Before going to Seattle, they did walk-throughs at the Raiders and Cardinals and followed them up with mediocre showings.

Simms, Bavaro, and McConkey went to see *Platoon* at a local movie theater. After the movie, the team met at 9:00 P.M. Parcells told them tomorrow's game would be the highlight of their athletic lives. He charged them with doing everything they could to help the team win. "If you don't do that, you're going to look in the mirror someday, and you're going to remember that you didn't, and it's going to be hard to get rid of that memory."

Curfew was 11:00 P.M. Bobby Johnson, Tony Galbreath, and Maurice Carthon rolled dice in a hotel room. LT walked by, and they let him in on the action. In about twenty minutes, Taylor won a few thousand dollars.

"Oh, this guy is lucky at dice," Carthon said.

Johnson had a different take. "We put $100 down there. We might only have $600. He put $100 down, and he might have $10,000 left. It makes the game a lot easier."

Whether it was luck or a hefty bankroll, Taylor walked away with his teammates' money.

Raul Allegre had been nervous all week. The kicker kept thinking that the Super Bowl was the type of game that could be great for his career or it could ruin it. The night before the game, he couldn't fall asleep. He turned on the TV, and he and his roommate Sean Landeta watched *Saturday Night Live*. Joe Montana and Walter Payton were hosting. They watched Payton introduce a music video, "We Are Kickers." It was a parody of the Bears' "Super Bowl Shuffle," and Dana Carvey came on the screen in a blue jersey with a white No. 2 outlined in red piping.

"I am Raul / I'm kick machine / I play for seven different team."

The kicker who had been out of football, helping build bridges in Indiana at the beginning of the season, had become worthy of a nationally televised comedy skit.

"You're a character on *Saturday Night Live,* I mean, you're big," Landeta said.

Seeing Carvey's version of himself eased Allegre's mind. "I laughed so hard. It helped me relax, and I was able to go to bed."

Over in Joe Morris's room, tight end Zeke Mowatt kept him up, asking him one question. "Joe, you think we gonna win? 'Cause if you don't win it, you may not ever get it back."

Mowatt understood the fleeting nature of the game. Before the knee injury wrecked his '85 season, he was on a trajectory to be an elite tight end. He spent months rehabbing to come back as a backup to Bavaro in '86.

The Giants were nine-point favorites, but it didn't stop Mowatt from wondering if the team's Pro Bowl running back thought they'd win. The hype around the game focused on the matchup between the Giants' defense and Broncos quarterback John Elway. The number-one overall pick from the historic 1983 quarterback class had a rocket arm and could break open plays with his mobility. He had led the Broncos on a nearly impossible comeback win in the AFC Championship game at Cleveland.

"And I kept saying, 'Joe, you think we gonna win?' And I know Joe was sick and tired of me saying that."

24

"WHAT IT WAS ALL FOR"

SUNDAY, JANUARY 25, 1987

Harry Carson woke up in the Howard Johnson in Pasadena, 2,500 miles and more than a decade away from his Florence, South Carolina, childhood.

He spent the last two weeks batting away thoughts about the Super Bowl. He wanted to treat it like any other game. "Otherwise, you go nuts," he said.

In a matter of hours, the middle linebacker would be the lone Giant standing at midfield in the Rose Bowl, representing Big Blue for the coin toss at Super Bowl XXI.

Lying in bed that morning, the thoughts flooded his mind. "You replay everything," he said. "You start to question how is it that I got from there to here."

He thought about how he quit football on his first day of practice in high school. In eleven NFL seasons, he had become one of the best in the league at his position. He stood on the sidelines when the Giants hit rock bottom with The Fumble. He heard fans call him a bum. He read about his head coach questioning his leadership. And now he'd play for the chance to be a world champion.

His mind drifted from the nostalgia to the responsibilities of the day. He started thinking about the game plan, about his responsibilities in the defense. Was his family all set with their tickets? "There's a hodgepodge of stuff running through your mind."

Bill Parcells contemplated wearing a suit and tie for the game. He ended up going with navy blue pants and a gray sweater with two horizontal red stripes framing GIANTS, which was written in blue. At 6:45 A.M., he met trainer Ronnie Barnes in the hotel coffee shop. They took a 7:30 cab toward the stadium. Security didn't allow the taxi to drive right up to the stadium. Parcells and Barnes had to walk the last block. Joe Morris joined them after security turned his cab away, too.

Parcells walked the field when he arrived at the Rose Bowl. He scouted the sun's trajectory because he didn't want it in his receiver's eyes. He checked the end zones, which were tight to the stands as safety Herb Welch, who played his college home games there for UCLA, had told him. While he looked around at the venue, which would seat more than 101,000 fans, he thought about the place where he had started coaching twenty-two years earlier. "You could fit the whole stadium of Hastings College into one little section of the stands here."[1]

He went back to the locker room. Morris didn't talk much before games, but he and Parcells spoke about the running back's time at Syracuse. They also had to handle some official business. Parcells had received a letter from the league about Morris's uniform. He had been wearing the same beat-up game pants since he exploded for 181 yards against the Redskins on Monday night in October. The NFL wanted him to wear new pants. He wore new pants at Dallas and Seattle, both Giants losses.

"Joe, you gotta wear old pants," said Parcells, the devotee of superstition.

"Bill, I got it covered."

Morris asked an equipment staffer for new pants. He slipped new pads into them and took the field to warm up. He rolled around in the grass about twenty times, scraping dirt and grass stains into the white pants. Morris went back into the locker room and changed back into the old pants, knowing no one would be able to tell the difference.

"That was a pretty good idea," Parcells said.

"Mm-hmm," said the quiet running back.

After attending a short Catholic Mass and eating a pregame meal at the hotel, Brad Benson, Chris Godfrey, and Phil Simms shared a taxi. "I feel real good. I'm throwing fastballs today, guys. I'm telling you, I feel great," Simms told his linemen during the ride.[2]

Simms bought twenty-six tickets at seventy-five dollars apiece for the people in his life. His oldest brother, Dominic, sat next to their father, Willie, at the 7-yard line of the Rose Bowl.

Broncos head coach Dan Reeves became annoyed during the player introductions. Denver was the first team introduced. Reeves wanted his team in the middle of the field to greet the defensive starters when they were announced. The league told him he couldn't do it. The Broncos stood on the sidelines and watched their teammates run onto the field, one by one.

Phil McConkey led most of the Giants onto the field, sprinting and waving his towel. The G-Men stayed out there, forming a path of high fives for the defensive starters to run through.

The league gave Parcells the same message it sent Reeves. The Giants' coach gave a different response: "Fine me if you want to. We're going to do what we did all year."

"I should have done that, too," Reeves said. "I mean that really irritated the hell out of me."

Of the twenty-two New York starters on offense and defense, only three were first-round draft picks—Simms, Taylor, and Carl Banks. Six of the starters were free agents, and one—Kenny Hill—came to New York through a trade. Of the seventeen drafted players, the average draft slot was the middle of the fourth round. The last player introduced as a starter was Herb Welch, a twelfth-round choice in '85, pick No. 326, eleven spots away from being a free agent. He ran onto the field, shooting finger guns at the camera.

Brooklyn-born singer Neil Diamond delivered a sixty-six-second rendition of the national anthem. He left the field via the Giants' sidelines. Parcells told him he did a good job, and Diamond told the coach he was pulling for Big Blue because of his Giants' roots.

The Broncos won the toss and elected to receive the ball. At Giants

Stadium in November, John Elway threw for 336 yards and rushed for 51 in the 19–16 loss. He started the Super Bowl scrambling away from LT for 10 yards and a first down.

The Giants were sweating already. It was hot, seventy-eight degrees. The G-Men hadn't been in a game above sixty degrees since they had played inside the Metrodome in Minnesota in week 11, eight games ago. The only other time the Giants played in weather this warm was the last time they were in the area, playing the Raiders in week 3.

Facing a third and seven two plays later, Broncos wide receiver Mark Jackson beat Giants cornerback Elvis Patterson for a 24-yard pass play. Denver had moved the ball to the New York 39-yard line. On third and two from the New York 31-yard line, Carl Banks made his third tackle of the drive, stifling Sammy Winder for no gain. "During the play-off run, if you could ever be in a zone, I was in it," Banks said.

After hearing Raiders defensive end Howie Long talk about studying game film, Banks studied an inordinate amount of tape. "I had a feel for how Denver was going to play. Not exact plays, but I had a feel for every-thing they could do. So when I got into that game, I don't think there was anything they could do that I wasn't ready for," Banks said.

His third-down stop of Winder forced Rich Karlis to kick a Super Bowl record–tying 48-yard field goal. Denver took a 3–0 lead.

The Giants took over at their 22-yard line. Simms could hear the heavy, nervous breathing in his huddle. When he broke the huddle, he saw Denver defensive players taking big gulps of air, too. "That was a lot for everybody to handle," Simms said.

He opened the game as he had promised Billy Crystal. He faked a handoff to Morris and hit Lionel Manuel over the middle for 17 yards. On the eighth play of the drive, Simms lined up under center at the Denver 23-yard line. Bavaro shifted from the right side to the left. Oates snapped the ball. Simms dropped back and released the ball in less than two and a half seconds. Bavaro ran his man up the seam. When he turned in, Simms had put the ball on him at the 6-yard line. Defensive back Randy Robbins was on top of Bavaro but still couldn't make the play.

"Nobody in football would've thrown that pass except us. They really almost had the perfect defense on, and I just threw it right in there. I didn't even hesitate," Simms said.

On first and goal, New York went without wide receivers. Tackle William Roberts came in as a third tight end. Zeke Mowatt went in motion left. Simms gave a little hesitation fake right to Morris. The play action drew Denver safety Steve Foley. Mowatt streaked across the back of the end zone wide open. Simms held the ball for less than three seconds before hitting Mowatt for the touchdown.

The Giants used up more than a third of the quarter, driving 78 yards on nine plays. Simms was 6 for 6 for 69 yards.

On their next possession, the Broncos came back and took the lead on a four-yard rushing score from Elway. "We gave up a TD on the stupid bootleg, which everyone knew was coming," Belichick said.

The first quarter ended with Denver up 10–7, and neither quarterback had thrown an incomplete pass.

On the second play of the second quarter, Simms threw his first incompletion. It was a pass intended for Phil McConkey, who fell down on the play. Simms's brother Dominic rose from his seat screaming at the referee.

"I was interfered with," McConkey said. "I faked the crap out of this guy, and he throws his legs out to get in my way 'cause he's totally going the other way, and I go down. No interference call, and I'm livid."

After Sean Landeta booted a 59-yard punt into the end zone, Denver took over at its 20-yard line. Highlighted by a 54-yard pass to Vance Johnson, Elway drove the Broncos to the Giants' 1-yard line. On first down, Elway rolled right. With no receivers open, he tucked the ball to run it in, but Taylor tackled him for a one-yard loss. On second down, Carson stuffed a Gerald Willhite run up the middle for no gain. On third down, Carl Banks saw something that looked familiar. He remembered during the regular season game that the Broncos' only touchdown came in a similar situation: a Sammy Winder sweep. In the Super Bowl, Elway pitched left to Winder, and Banks came down the line of scrimmage, swallowing Winder in a tackle for a four-yard loss. After being three feet away from going up 17–7, Denver had to settle for a field goal, but Karlis missed the 23-yard attempt. After tying the record for the longest make, he set the record for the shortest miss.

With 3:33 to play in the half, the Broncos had the ball at their own 15-yard line. The Giants flushed Elway out of the pocket, and Leonard Marshall caught him from behind for the sack and a two-yard loss. A replay review of a second-down incompletion to Clarence Kay took more than two minutes. This allowed defensive end George Martin to hatch a scheme of his own. Before breaking the huddle, Martin told rookie nose tackle Erik Howard to disregard whatever Martin said at the line of scrimmage. Martin grabbed Howard's face mask for emphasis.

About to put his hand in the ground, Martin said, "Erik, me-game." It was a fake stunt call meant to dupe the offensive line into thinking Martin would loop into an inside rush. "Erik, did you hear me? Me-game. Me-game."

As soon as the ball was snapped to Elway in the shotgun, Martin started into a stunt. When the offensive tackle slid down to beat Martin to the spot, the twelve-year veteran charged into an outside rush. Howard applied pressure up the middle, forcing Elway toward Martin, who wrapped up the quarterback for the safety. The Broncos' lead had been cut to 10–9.

With sixteen seconds left in the half, Karlis missed another gimme field goal, sending a 34-yard attempt wide right. The Broncos could have been up between 24–9 and 16–9, but they headed to halftime up by 1.

In six quarters of football, George Martin had scored more points against Denver than the Giants' offense, but Big Blue went into the midway break without a worry.

"I didn't think anything of it," Simms said of the score.

He sat down at halftime with offensive coordinator Ron Erhardt. "Well, everything we're trying, it's there. I don't see any reason to try anything different," Simms told him. "Ron, we're cool, man. Just keep calling them."

There was no big halftime speech from Parcells. The sun went down. The temperature cooled. And the stadium played Jersey-born crooner Frank Sinatra from its speakers.

"Halftime is always so daggone long during that thing. And when we come out on the field, they're playing 'New York, New York,'" Reeves said.

The Giants received the second-half kickoff, and Lee Rouson returned it to the 37-yard line. In three plays, the Giants gained nine yards. They sent the punt team on the field. Backup quarterback Jeff Rutledge lined up in the fullback spot with Landeta behind him awaiting the snap. The Giants shifted into an offensive set. Rutledge went under center with Rouson and Maurice Carthon moving to the backfield. Throughout the season, the Giants had tinkered with the punt unit, looking to catch opponents off guard.

"If you can get them to think that the punt team is coming on and you can keep some of your offense out there, then you could run an offensive play against a punt return team, and chances are they're not going to be ready to defend the play," said special teams coach Romeo Crennel.

The Giants used a code word for this: ARAPAHOE. The acronym stood for A Run, A Pass, A Hit On the Enemy. Special teams coordinator Romeo Crennel called out ARAPAHOE on the sidelines, and players repeated the call to each other. It didn't mean there had to be a fake. It meant if the opponent didn't adjust and the personnel on the field believed a first down could be converted, they'd run a simple run or pass.

The Broncos had seen a form of this look from the Giants when they played during the regular season. After starting in punt formation and motioning into a regular offensive look, backup quarterback Jeff Hostetler handed the ball to Rouson for a first down in that game. Reeves had spoken to defensive coordinator Joe Collier about keeping the defense on the field.

Rutledge scanned the Denver defense. The middle linebackers stayed back. The quarterback glanced over at Parcells, who gave a slight nod to go for it. Rutledge kept the ball and ran over the right guard, picking up two yards and the first down.

"They still executed the fourth-down play, and we were prepared for that. And that was a big play in the game," Reeves said.

Five plays later, Simms waited for the ball in the shotgun at the 13-yard line. In 2.41 seconds after the snap, Simms released a spiral that landed on Bavaro at the 2-yard line. The tight end ran a short post and went into the end zone untouched. He dropped to one knee and crossed himself.

He had made the sign of the cross on the football field before in his career, but this was the first time he did it in the end zone. This wasn't any end zone, either; this was genuflecting under the world spotlight of the Super Bowl. "I could never not do it again. So then I would do it even if it was just halfhearted. You could tell I wasn't really interested in it, but I had to do it, because what happens if you don't do it?" Bavaro said.

Big Blue grew its 16–10 lead to 19–10 on a 21-yard Raul Allegre field goal. Seizing the momentum, the Giants called a trick play late in the third quarter. Morris shuttled it into Simms. The quarterback looked to Parcells as if he heard a mistake.

"Run the fucking play that Joe brought in," Parcells said from the sidelines.

It was a flea-flicker. "We put that in, in week 1, and we worked on it every freaking week," Morris said, but they never used it.

"Don't worry, I'll get the ball to you," Morris said to Simms.

The trickery worked. Simms pitched the ball to Morris, who pretended it was a run and then pitched the ball back to Simms. The Denver defense bit on the run by Morris.

"I'll never, ever, for the rest of my life lose that image of the defensive backs running helter-skelter in the secondary after they realized they had been caught and they're trying to get back into position. It was like the clowns getting out of a Volkswagen," said McConkey, who broke open downfield.

Simms dropped the ball to a wide-open McConkey at the Denver 20-yard line. He raced down the sideline, leaping head over heels over Mark Haynes. McConkey's body ended up in the end zone. From his knees, he raised both arms triumphantly, thinking he had fulfilled his boyhood dream and scored a touchdown in the Super Bowl. He didn't. Officials marked him down at the 1-yard line. Morris took the ball in for the score on the next play.

The Giants had taken control of the game in the third quarter. They built a 26–10 lead and held Denver to 13 yards of offense in less than three minutes with the ball.

New York scored on its first possession of the fourth quarter. On third and goal from the 6-yard line, Simms took the shotgun snap and backpedaled three steps before drilling the ball to Bavaro, who got sandwiched between two defenders in the end zone. The ball popped loose, and Bavaro's best friend on the team, McConkey, trailed the play, dropping to his knees and catching the dislodged pass. He did a high-step backpedal and then jumped into Bavaro's arms. The undersized kid from Buffalo did live his dream. He scored a touchdown in the Super Bowl.

The Giants were up 33–10. Soon CBS started showing sideline shots of the Gatorade buckets. There was time left on the clock, but the game was over. The players knew this.

The ricochet touchdown catch by McConkey was Simms's last pass of the game. He'd run 22 yards to set up a two-yard Ottis Anderson touchdown, which made the score 39–13. Simms completed all 10 of his passes in the second half for 165 yards and two scores. He finished the game going 22 of 25 for 268 yards and three touchdowns. His 88 percent completion percentage remains a Super Bowl record, as does his single-game passer rating of 150.92.

"Simms had a perfect day. There's a reason Simms had a perfect day. We gave him the perfect amount of time," said Ard.

Rulon Jones, the man Ard stewed over in his hotel room during the week, finished with a nondescript four tackles.

Harry Carson didn't drink in the moment just yet. "For me, it was, 'Okay, let's get Parcells with the Gatorade.'"

Carson went into deep cover, donning a yellow stadium security coat before pouring the Gatorade on Parcells.

Denver added a meaningless touchdown to cap the scoring at 39–20.

On the sidelines, Jim Burt started to have flashbacks of his life. "My dad picking me up, taking me at four o'clock in the morning to play hockey in Canada," he said.

He started thinking about the guys he made the journey with. "It's hard. There are a lot of things that people have to give up, and you can't be worried about your health. You gotta lay it on the line . . . You terrorize your body, and you practice Wednesday, Thursday, Friday and practice all year. I mean, you're beating yourself up, and your fingers are halfway over here, this one's over here. You're dealing with all that stuff, but you love it."

Burt had taken off his jersey and shoulder pads, and his five-year-old son joined him on the sidelines. Sure, this was Burt's dream, but he started thinking about the people in his life. "You don't win it for yourself. You do it for your parents and for your brothers and sisters, your aunts and the uncle who helped you out when you couldn't help yourself. All the people who changed your diapers."

On the bench, Bobby Johnson cried. Not because he was emotionally moved by a sense of accomplishment. His tears flowed because he knew this was his last game as a Giant. No one had said anything to him, but they didn't need to. His drug-fueled behavior would no longer be tolerated. "I'm gone, man," he told his pal Tony Galbreath.

Carl Banks finished the game with 10 tackles. He pressured Elway, and his highlight-reel run-stopping tackles blunted any chance Denver had to build momentum. Leonard Marshall finished the game with two sacks, four tackles, and a pass deflection. "I definitely thought Banks and I were going to end up co-MVPs of that game," Marshall said. "I was happy for Phil. He had the day of his life throwing the football."

Simms's blistering passing earned him the MVP. Leaving the field, he turned to a camera and became the first player to say, "I'm gonna go to Disney World."

Parcells stood in a crowded locker room, surrounded by the men who had collectively accomplished what was once believed to be unthinkable. The organization that had been a laughingstock had proved it was the best.

"The rest of ya life, men, nobody could ever tell ya that you couldn't do it, 'cause you did it."

Twenty simple words that captured the truth.

This is the team that brought winning back to the one of the NFL's flag-ship organizations.

In the locker room, Wellington Mara accepted the Lombardi Trophy from NFL commissioner Pete Rozelle. Co-owner Tim Mara didn't join Wellington on the dais. George Young had come in and smoothed out the football operations, but the family divide remained.

When Wellington stepped down from the award ceremony, a couple of the players took Wellington into the showers and turned the water on above him. "They did it probably as gently as possible. He willingly went along with it," said John Mara.

On the ride out of the stadium, Belichick let the championship soak in. "Three years after turning down the job in Minnesota, sitting in the front of the bus next to Bill on the drive from Pasadena to our hotel, was a highlight of my coaching career. We had a good team. I was coaching a great defense, and we won in New York. When I came to the Giants in 1979, no one ever said they were a Giants fan without putting the words *long-suffering* in front of the word *fan*. I never heard those words again."

Simms put together one of the greatest performances by a quarterback on the biggest stage his profession has to offer, but he gets neither nostalgic nor introspective about it. "Maybe that was enough to keep me from being one of those bitter ex-players. 'God, I should've done this. Should've done that,'" he said nearly thirty years later. "It probably takes away some of the sting of my career, getting hurt. Missing a chance here and there where we probably could've maybe gone to the Super Bowl and we didn't do it. So the fact that I got to go to the one I did and I played well, it takes a little bit of the frustration from the other stuff away."

The night of the Super Bowl, his reaction wasn't much different. His family made its way up to his hotel room. His brother Dominic shared a bottle of champagne with LT when the linebacker stopped by to see the quarterback. Simms was signing footballs and shirts from a group of vendors who had descended on his room.

Dominic gave his younger brother a hug and shook his hand. "He was very stoic," Dominic said as his voice wavered as he tried, but failed, to choke back his emotion. "I mean, this was the best thing that ever happened.

"What people don't understand about athletes is they give up so much to get where they are. Phil didn't do all this stuff. He was always working to get better and better, and now he's made it. That's what it was all for."

GENERATIONS

Just like he did in 1979 when the club hired general manager George Young, less than a week after the Super Bowl, NFL Commissioner Pete Rozelle had to intervene on an issue with the Giants.

This time, Rozelle shut down talks between the Atlanta Falcons and Giants head coach Bill Parcells. Young had already told Parcells's agent, Robert Fraley, that the coach wouldn't be allowed to have talks with the Falcons about being the team's coach and general manager. Fraley went to the commissioner, who knocked down the idea, too.

Parcells and Young were able to work together, but the relationship never recovered from the incident in '83 when Young made overtures to Howard Schnellenberger. After Parcells's flirtation with the Falcons, it became Young's turn to be distrustful. Later, Young would tell his close associates that Parcells was the "most duplicitous" man he'd ever met.

At the end of the Super Bowl season, Parcells had two years left on his contract. He went an entire year without signing an extension. He left open the possibility that he might leave the Giants, but in February of '88, he signed a deal through the 1991 season.

There would be no Super Bowl repeat in 1987. Big Blue started off 0–2. Then the players' strike happened. The Giants went 0–3 with replacement players. They'd finish 6–9, but the 0–5 start set the course for the G-Men to go from world champs to last place in the NFC East in one season.

After missing the play-offs in '88 with a 10–6 record, the Giants went 12–4 in '89 and hosted the Los Angeles Rams in the divisional round. The visitors forced overtime. LA won the coin toss, and four plays into the extra period, Rams quarterback Jim Everett completed a 30-yard touchdown pass to Flipper Anderson, stunning the Giants Stadium crowd.

The following year, the Giants and Parcells did get their second Lombardi Trophy.

After leading the Giants to an 11–2 record in the first thirteen games of the '90 season, Phil Simms hurt his right foot in week 14. He didn't play the rest of the year. Jeff Hostetler, the quarterback who played wide receiver and special teams in '86, stepped in as the starter.

The Giants played the 49ers in San Francisco for the NFC Championship. Leonard Marshall crushed Joe Montana, sending him out of the game. With less than three minutes to play, Lawrence Taylor recovered a Roger Craig fumble, which led to Matt Bahr's game-winning field goal in the closing seconds. After the 15–13 win, the underdog Giants faced the Buffalo Bills in Super Bowl XXV. Ottis Anderson, who came to the Giants from the in-season trade in '86, won the game's MVP as Big Blue upset Buffalo 20–19.

"I'm not going to say I'm just as proud of the second Super Bowl, but I'm pretty damn proud of it," Simms said. "I'm glad I've got two instead of one. Maybe I didn't feel that. I think what bothered me in '90 is when it was all over that I got no credit. It was like I never played. That was a little bothersome."

By the time the '90 season arrived, things were different. Jim Burt was a 49er. He tweaked Ronnie Lott so much before a regular season Monday night tilt with the Giants that Lott and Simms went face mask–to–face mask, jawing at each other on the field after the game.

Phil McConkey was out of the league in '90, but Parcells did hire the receivers coach from Green Bay that McConkey had told him about. Tom Coughlin took over the same role with the Giants in '88, McConkey's last year with the team.

After the Super Bowl XXV win, Coughlin used the postgame locker room to recruit players for the collegiate head coaching job he had taken. He handed players like Mark Bavaro a phone and had them talk to some of his Boston College targets.

After the season, Bill Belichick became the head coach of the Cleveland Browns. He led the Browns to their last play-off win, a 20–13 victory over a Parcells-coached New England Patriots team.

In his second head coaching gig, Belichick has etched himself into legendary status, leading the New England Patriots to six Super Bowls and winning four of them. His only losses in the Super Bowl have come against Giants teams coached by Coughlin.

In May 1991, four months after the Giants beat the Bills, Parcells stepped down from his head coaching post. He immediately went to work as a studio analyst for NBC.

Belichick was already gone, but George Young didn't believe Belichick would be a good head coach. He wanted Coughlin, but Coughlin wouldn't renege on his deal with Boston College. Young went with the cerebral choice, elevating Ray Handley to head coach.

After the Super Bowl in '86, religion crossed with superstition for Mark Bavaro. He had been a daily communicant, but now he was a Super Bowl champion in New York who went to Mass every day. This was newsworthy, and the once private practice became a public image he had to uphold.

While he got taped in the visiting locker room at Veterans Stadium in Philadelphia, teammates popped in and crouched to the floor. They peeked through a gap between the wall and the floor that gave them a view of the open shower room for the Eagles' cheerleaders.

The women giggled. "Stop looking at us."

"You know how bad I wanted to look, right?" Bavaro said. "How many times do you get to watch professional cheerleaders shower in an open shower? But I didn't do it—not because it was morally wrong but because I feared the repercussions of what might happen in the game by not being faithful to my beliefs."

After the Super Bowl XXV season, the Giants cut Bavaro. They said his knee wasn't healthy enough to allow him to play. He wanted to remain on the roster and spend the year getting healthy. He wanted half his $750,000 salary, and if he couldn't play the following season, the Giants wouldn't owe him anything. If he could play the following year, he'd take the rest of his salary then.

George Young said Bavaro would be paid if he could play. Since he couldn't, the tight end would get about $60,000 after being waived because of the injury.

Wellington Mara stepped in. He offered to give Bavaro half his salary to not play at all. Bavaro became stubborn. "I don't want to take it under those circumstances. I only want to take it if I'm working toward coming back to play, and I'll take the other half as my salary the next year when I play."

Mara told him to go home, talk to his wife, and think about the offer.

Bavaro called his old mentor Don Hasselbeck.

Hasselbeck asked Bavaro to go to the bank and take out $10,000 in small bills. "Go back to your house. Put it in a big pile in your living room. Then sit on your couch. Look at it for a little while. Then I want you to jump in it. Roll around in it. Throw it up in the air, and then just imagine that, that the pile will be ten times bigger. And then make your decision."

Bavaro looked at his wife. "Do you think they'll still give it to me?"

They did. Bavaro sat out 1991. He received a check in the mail every Monday during the season.

He played for Belichick in Cleveland in 1992 and finished out his career with two seasons in Philadelphia.

Bobby Johnson never played another down in the NFL after the '86 season. He made it to the Giants' training camp in 1987. On the practice field that August, he found out he had been traded to the San Diego Chargers. He didn't make the team.

His drug use worsened. He became homeless. He slept on park benches. In June 1994, the man who caught the most important pass in the Giants' '86 season lost three fingers on his right hand in a work accident at a pencil factory. A couple of years after that, he walked into his mother's home in Smyrna, Tennessee. "Son, you look terrible. You look terrible," she said, and she started crying.

Johnson never went to rehab, but he ended his drug use after that visit to his mother. He has been sober since. He doesn't look back at his time in the NFL with any bitterness. He loves the Giants and Parcells. He calls it a happy ending "because I'm alive."

Harry Carson entered the Hall of Fame in 2006. He continues to act as the team captain. He organized the twenty-fifth reunion of the Super Bowl XXI team, which had near-perfect attendance from the players and coaches. He checks in on his teammates' health. He takes them to doctors' appointments, ensuring that their battered football bodies get certain neurological checkups as they age.

Lawrence Taylor missed the first four games of the '88 season because of a failed drug test. His final double-digit sack season came in 1990. He played three more seasons, retiring after the '93 campaign. His life after football has included grappling in the main event at WrestleMania, an arrest for allegedly buying fifty dollars' worth of crack from an undercover cop in 1998, induction into the Pro Football Hall of Fame in '99, a role in the 1999 film *Any Given Sunday*, a cameo appearance in *The Sopranos* in 2004, and registering as a sex offender in 2011.

After two seasons, Ray Handley was out as the head coach. Dan Reeves, who had interviewed for the position as a Dallas Cowboys assistant in 1979, took Handley's spot in 1993.

Coaching Phil Simms in the wind and elements of Giants Stadium gave Reeves a new appreciation for the quarterback who beat him in Super Bowl XXI.

"Seeing him throw the football in Giants Stadium, I told him, 'Man, you ought to be in the Hall of Fame right now,'" Reeves said.

In Reeves's first year, Simms completed more than 60 percent of his passes, threw for more than 3,000 yards, and posted an 88.3 passer rating, the third highest of his career.

The solid numbers made the radio report sound even stranger to Simms. He was in his car, driving to play golf on an off-season Sunday, when he listened to a reporter talking about how the Giants might get rid of him. His first thought was that the reporter should be fired for putting out such an inaccuracy.

When Reeves called him into the office in mid-June, Simms figured he was going there to sign some autographs. The coach told the thirty-eight-year-old passer the Giants were going to cut him. "I was just astounded," Simms said. "I just remember thinking, *What am I going to tell my wife?*"

Simms went into another room and met with Wellington Mara. The Giants' owner told Simms if he still wanted to be a Giant, Mara would make it happen.

Two years earlier, George Young had used a supplemental draft pick on Duke football product Dave Brown. He had appeared in three games and thrown seven passes, but Young pushed for Brown as the future. Simms had the realization his time was done in New York. He declined Mara's offer.

Mara held back tears announcing Simms's release. He publicly voiced his disagreement with Young's move to let go of the franchise quarterback.

Before it became official, Mara had gone to Young with a piece of paper and notes on restructuring three contracts in order to keep Simms. The Giants would have owed Simms $2.5 million, and the salary cap had just come into existence. Young went forward with the move to cut Simms, concerned that restructured contracts brought trouble in the future.

John Mara drove his father home that day. "He was so angry and upset about that because he loved Simms," John Mara said. "I don't think his relationship with George was ever quite the same after that."

George Young's belief in Dave Brown didn't pay off. Brown posted a 23–30 record with the Giants. He threw 46 interceptions against 35 touchdowns in three seasons as the full-time starter.

In 1997, Young's final year with the Giants, Brown became a backup, and Young won NFL executive of the year for the fifth time in his career. New York clinched the division, beating Washington in the final home game. On the field after the game, Young sat alone on the bench. He entered the coaches' room and thanked Jim Fassel, the last head coach he hired, and then Young cried.

At the Giants, Young was replaced by Ernie Accorsi, his friend from the Baltimore Colts. Young brought Accorsi into the organization as an assistant general manager four years before Young left the Meadowlands.

Young took a job with the League office until 2001. In the fall of that year, Bob Patzwall, who played high school football for Young and became his broker, drove Young to a hospice facility in Baltimore. The cerebral general manager suffered a short battle with Creutzfeldt-Jakob disease, which attacks brain function.

Bill Parcells almost came back to the Giants in 1997.

After four years of Dan Reeves, John Mara initially offered the job to Michigan State head coach Nick Saban.

"'He's the best candidate that I've ever interviewed for a head coaching position.' That was George's quote," Mara said. "He repeated that quote on several different occasions."

Saban mulled over the offer. He wasn't comfortable with the organizational structure. He wanted to have more control than the Giants were willing to give a head coach. The two sides never came to an agreement on how it could work. "It was a mutual thing where we decided to walk away. It was on friendly terms," Mara said.

Meanwhile, the idea of bringing Parcells back for another stint had been brewing for a while. Parcells had left New England, but he still wanted to coach.

"Parcells definitely wanted to come back, and he made it known that he wanted to come back. And George was dead set against that," Mara said.

By now, the Giants also had a new co-owner in Robert Tisch. He had misgivings about Parcells. Tisch didn't know him and Young had strong recommendations against hiring him.

While a series of conversations had been ongoing between the Maras and Tisch, Young popped into John Mara's office. Young had Jim Fassel waiting by the phone at a nearby hotel. The Maras knew forcing a head coach on a co-owner would be a bad move. John gave Young the go-ahead to offer Fassel the job.

"I later joked, and I'm only half-kidding—this is the first time in my life I ever saw George sprint down the hallway to a phone," Mara said.

Within minutes, Tisch called John and told him if they really wanted Parcells, they should hire him. John called down to Young's office. No answer. He ran down the hall to catch him.

When he arrived in the doorway, Young had just offered Fassel the job, and as a matter of business policy, the Giants wouldn't pull back the offer.

Parcells ended up coaching in Giants Stadium in '97, but it was for the Jets. When asked about the possible return to Big Blue, he said it wasn't a possibility. "They didn't want me back there."

When Parcells speaks about the '86 team, he makes it a point to use *we*. After leaving the Giants, he coached the Patriots, the Jets, and the Dallas Cowboys. He liked the players in those other places. He built lasting relationships with them, but it wasn't the same as it was with the Giants. It never could be.

"They're the ones who kinda got me over the hump," Parcells said. "We really went through it together. Me trying to make my way in the business and them trying to make their way, and then collectively trying to make the Giants winners again."

By the time he left Big Blue, he had won two Super Bowls. Every franchise he entered thereafter was getting an elite coach. In New York, he became that coach, and it was a shared experience with the Giants players.

"They've seen it all. They've seen me come from nothing to something, and I've seen them do the same thing. To where we could accomplish something together that, for a little while, was pretty good. Those guys were good."

Did they like playing for him at the time? Did they enjoy the nonstop barbs and the gauntlet of competition he created?

"He wasn't the most pleasant guy to play for when you're playing for him, but when you look back, there's not a guy that's going to say, 'I don't respect the man, and the man didn't get me to where I played my best,'" said center Bart Oates.

In 2013, when Parcells entered the Pro Football Hall of Fame, he could've selected any of the hundreds of former players and coaches he worked with to present him. He picked a member of the '86 team, co-captain George Martin.

When the 112 million people tuned in to CBS for Super Bowl 50, they listened to Simms call the game. Parcells narrated a pregame feature for CBS. The kicker—yes, even the kicker!—from the Giants' first Super Bowl team was part of the NFL's golden Super Bowl. Raul Allegre handled Spanish-language broadcast duties.

These Giants with the Gatorade splashes, quarterback sacks, and "I'm gonna go to Disney World," they made a place for themselves in the history of the game.

"We've been fortunate enough to win three Super Bowls since then and be in a fourth. But that one was special to me, and for my family, for the opportunity to see my father finally accept the Lombardi Trophy and see our organization go from the very bottom of the league and a laughing-stock to one of the more respected organizations in the league. I can't describe to you what that meant to us," John Mara said.

Wellington Mara died in 2005 at the age of 89. Since his death the Giants, under former Parcells assistant Tom Coughlin, won two more Super Bowls.

In January 2015, Phil McConkey was having cocktails at Sparks Steak House in New York City. The fifty-seven-year-old was still svelte, but the thick, wavy black hair from his playing days is now gray and close cropped. The Tony Orlando–style mustache is long gone. Ed Abbot still recognized him, though.

Abbot's family have been season ticket holders since the Giants' first game in the Meadowlands in 1976. In Giants Stadium, they had the first four seats in row four of section 111, behind the Giants' bench.

Abbot had to interrupt McConkey. He had to introduce his son to the Giant. Abbot was so moved by the chance meeting he wrote McConkey an e-mail the next day. He thanked McConkey for his military service and for sprinting out of that tunnel and waving that white towel before games. "We watched you and your teammates the way many don't have the opportunity to, and we saw the joy, heartache, frustration, and elation . . . You made being a fan so incredibly enjoyable."

This is the team that has been passed on to generations. This is the team upon which the modern foundation of winning Giant Football was built.

GIANTS 1986
REGULAR SEASON AND PLAY-OFF SCHEDULE

09/08/1986 (Mon)	@ Dallas	Texas Stadium (Irving, TX)	L 31–28
09/14/1986	San Diego	Giants Stadium (East Rutherford, NJ)	W 20–7
09/21/1986	@ LA Raiders	Los Angeles Memorial Coliseum (Los Angeles, CA)	W 14–9
09/28/1986	New Orleans	Giants Stadium (East Rutherford, NJ)	W 20–17
10/05/1986	@ St. Louis	Busch Memorial Stadium (St. Louis, MO)	W 13–6
10/12/1986	Philadelphia	Giants Stadium (East Rutherford, NJ)	W 35–3
10/19/1986	@ Seattle	Kingdome (Seattle, WA)	L 17–12
10/27/1986 (Mon)	Washington	Giants Stadium (East Rutherford, NJ)	W 27–20
11/02/1986	Dallas	Giants Stadium (East Rutherford, NJ)	W 17–14
11/09/1986	@ Philadelphia	Veterans Stadium (Philadelphia, PA)	W 17–14
11/16/1986	@ Minnesota	Hubert H. Humphrey Metrodome (Minneapolis, MN)	W 22–20
11/23/1986	Denver	Giants Stadium (East Rutherford, NJ)	W 19–16
12/01/1986 (Mon)	@ San Francisco	Candlestick Park (San Francisco, CA)	W 21–17
12/07/1986	@ Washington	RFK Stadium (Washington, DC)	W 24–14
12/14/1986	St. Louis	Giants Stadium (East Rutherford, NJ)	W 27–7
12/20/1986 (Sat)	Green Bay	Giants Stadium (East Rutherford, NJ)	W 55–24
01/04/1987	San Francisco	Divisional Round, Giants Stadium (East Rutherford, NJ)	W 49–3
01/11/1987	Washington	NFC Championship, Giants Stadium (East Rutherford, NJ)	W 17–0
01/25/1987	Denver	Super Bowl XXI Rose Bowl (Pasadena, CA)	W 39–20

ACKNOWLEDGMENTS

The idea for this book was hatched over a burger with Scott Gould and Marc Resnick in one of those farm-to-table joints in New York City.

Those gentlemen have shepherded the process of making the idea a reality. Scott Gould, my agent at RLR, has been a true confidant as the manuscript came to fruition. Thank you.

Marc, thanks for helping to guide the narrative through a plethora of source material and always providing a listening ear and tremendous counsel. I offer an enormous thanks to the entire team at St. Martin's Press: assistant editor Jaime Coyne; jacket designer Jimmy Iacobelli; marketer John Nicholas; production editor Ken Silver; production manager Eric Gladstone; publicist Joe Rinaldi; and marketing director Laura Clark.

Thanks to the Giants organization, particularly the media relations staff for accommodating my research requests. The New York Giants are a first-class outfit, and the media relations department exemplifies that. Very specific thanks to Pat Hanlon and Phyllis Hayes for always providing quick answers to the questions I'd send their way. Thank you also to Michael Eisen, who let me borrow the clip book his father made for him from his 1986 coverage of the Giants for *The Daily Record*.

Thanks to the media relations offices at Morehead State, the University of Notre Dame, Syracuse University, and the University of Oregon.

I had no relationships with any of the Giants' coaches or players from the 1986 team before I started this project. Thank you, Scott Kowalkowski and Gary Boesch, for putting in good words and opening those doors.

Thank you also to Chip Namias for that and for your work to let football fans and the football world know about this book.

Thanks to Stacey James of the New England Patriots and Amy Palcic of the Houston Texans, your fulfilling my interview requests made this book better.

Special thanks to Robert Patzwall. I'll never forget our tour of Baltimore. We had to stop the car twice: once to move a turtle aside; and another time when a knife-wielding man chased another man into a park on Greenmount Avenue.

To Anthony DeVincenzo and Andrew Watkins, thanks for those very first reads. They were very helpful.

To the Keane family of Avon, thanks for the accommodations on my research trip. To all the Keanes and the Zeringues—always grateful for all your love and support.

To Dennis Joyce, our friendship continues to be a tremendous support to my output.

On the home front, I can't thank Mary Derin and Elizabeth Barca enough. You're a safety net when we need it.

To Bella, Gracie, Bryant, and Jerry, thanks for sharing in the excitement and everything else that comes with having a dad who writes books.

Beth—you get the ineffable thanks for joining me on all this.

AUTHOR'S NOTE

My first interview for this book took place in Baltimore. I went there to find out about George Young, the general manager who transformed the culture of the New York Giants. Young died in 2001. To discover who he was, I visited his roots. Robert Patzwall, who played football for Young at Calvert Hall High School and later became Young's broker, gave me the tour. We visited Young's final resting place, stopping the car so I could pick up and move a turtle across the road as we drove up to the mausoleum. We also spent time in Baltimore's Tenth Ward, where Young grew up. Driving out of Charm City, Patzwall slammed the brakes on Greenmount Avenue. He stopped short of hitting a man who ran into traffic, crossed the street, and sped into a park. Following closely behind was another running man. The second man carried a knife while pursuing the sprinter.

I interviewed a lot of people for this book; all of them provided a less harrowing experience than the chase across Greenmount Avenue.

I spoke to Bill Parcells for a couple of hours. I interviewed NFL legends Don Shula and Ernie Accorsi. Both are a treasure of information on the NFL and George Young. From a golf course, Mike Ditka gave me a few minutes on the play-off game between the Chicago Bears and the Giants. In between answers, he took a break to hit a golf shot. When I played the recording back, my seven years of caddying experience tell me just from the sound of the club striking the ball Ditka was happy with the shot. Ray Perkins spoke to me about his time as the Giants' head coach and his hiring of two critical assistants for Big Blue: Bill Parcells and Bill Belichick.

Former coach Dan Reeves has an interesting place in this book. He was a top candidate to become the Giants' head coach in 1979. He was the opposing head coach in Super Bowl XXI, and he is the Giants' coach who cut Phil Simms. We spoke about all of it.

Bill Belichick answered a series of questions through e-mail. He was candid, and he is fond of the double exclamation point.

The lack of personal information on Phil Simms made me curious, and the more I found out, the more I became intrigued. Here is a guy that in his most pressure-filled moment of performance played the greatest game a quarterback had played in the Super Bowl. Almost thirty years have passed, and his performance in Super Bowl XXI still stands as one of the best. Yet he came out of nowhere—Morehead State. He was maligned by fans, slowed by injuries, and so on, and so on, and he kept bouncing back. How did he get there? How did he have the wherewithal to keep coming back from the injuries and battle back against the criticism?

I interviewed the man who recruited him out of high school to Morehead State. I spoke to the track coach at Morehead who wanted Simms to throw the javelin. I spoke to the daughter and the widow of the former FBI agent–turned–NFL scout who was the first Giants representative to watch Simms play.

Simms was physically tough. The game film shows that. Quarterbacks don't take hits like they used to, and Simms stood in there until the last possible moment taking shots and delivering passes.

Eventually, I spent two and a half hours interviewing Simms at his home office in New Jersey. At one point, we stopped talking about his career because I had to ask about his lack of introspection. He doesn't overthink or overanalyze his situation. He doesn't wax nostalgic about his life. Never did. I have little doubt it's part of why he succeeded. It's all performance. For him, it's all about getting in the weight room, training, and getting on the field to compete. He was more interested in beating his competition than being liked or what anybody thought of him. He didn't stand back and wonder, *How did I do that? Let's talk about it.* He just did it and kept doing it.

The Giants' Hall of Fame owner Wellington Mara died in 2005. In order to gain insight on his perspective and experience with the fall and rise of the organization, I interviewed his sons, John and Chris. I spent more than an hour with John, the current team president, in his office at the franchise's facility. I spoke to Chris, who was a scout for most of the period covered in this book, via phone. The Giants' players were also able to broaden the picture of Wellington based on their personal interactions with him.

I spoke to a plethora of players from the '86 team and some who were with the Giants before that Super Bowl season. I spent hours with Carl Banks, Mark Bavaro, Harry Carson, George Martin, Jim Burt, Phil McConkey, Brad Benson, Leonard Marshall, Joe Morris, and many others. I spoke to opponents and game officials, too.

There is one main player whom I did not interview. His agency did take questions on his behalf, but Lawrence Taylor did not participate in this book.

To flesh out this story, I pored over newspaper and magazine articles from the 1970s through the 2000s and read through the books listed in the bibliography. I also rewatched the game broadcasts from the '86 season as well as other key games that defined the Giants' championship run.

As a guide, when reading quotes, if they are not referenced in the notes, they come from original reporting for this book. The exception to this are quotes from an interview subject who was speaking to multiple reporters. After reviewing multiple daily newspapers, these quotes, which appear in the text mostly as postgame comments, were seen in multiple publications.

BIBLIOGRAPHY

Burt, Jim, and Hank Gola. *Hard Nose: The Story of the 1986 Giants*. San Diego: Harcourt, Brace, Jovanovich, 1987.

Callahan, Tom. *The GM: A Football Life, a Final Season, and a Last Laugh*. New York: Three Rivers Press, 2007.

Carson, Harry. *Captain for Life: My Story as a Hall of Fame Linebacker*. New York: St. Martin's Press, 2011.

Carson, Harry, and Jim Smith. *Point of Attack: The Defense Strikes Back*. New York: McGraw-Hill, 1987.

Izenberg, Jerry. *No Medals for Trying*. New York: Macmillan, 1990.

Lewis, Michael. *The Blind Side: Evolution of a Game*. New York: W. W. Norton, 2006.

Marshall, Leonard, and David Klein. *Leonard Marshall: The End of the Line*. New York: New American Library, 1987.

McConkey, Phil, Phil Simms, and Dick Schaap. *Simms to McConkey: Blood, Sweat, and Gatorade*. New York: Crown Publishers, 1987.

New Jersey State Commission of Investigation, public hearing held February 18 and 19, 1992.

Parcells, Bill, and Nunyo Demasio. *Parcells: A Football Life*. New York: Crown Archetype, 2014.

Parcells, Bill, and Mike Lupica. *Parcells: Autobiography of the Biggest Giant of Them All*. New York: Bonus Books, 1987.

Robustelli, Andy, and Jack Clary. *Once a Giant, Always . . . : My Two Lives with the New York Giants*. Boston: Quinlan Press, 1987.

Simms, Phil, and Vic Carucci. *Sunday Morning Quarterback*. New York: It Books, 2004.

Taylor, Lawrence, and David Falkner. *LT: Living on the Edge*. New York: Warner Books, 1987.

Taylor, Lawrence, and Steve Serby. *LT: Over the Edge*. New York: HarperTorch, 2003.

NOTES

1 THE FUMBLE

1 Greg Garber, "Pisarcik Eager to Set Record Straight; Others Aren't," ESPN.com, December 2, 2008.

2 Al Harvin, "Patriots Gain 19–17 Victory," *New York Times*, November 20, 1978.

3 Michael Katz, "Dryer, the Ex-Giant, Reflects, Laughing," *New York Times*, December 3, 1978.

2 THE BOOKMAKER'S TEAM IN A PAINFUL PERIOD

1 Arthur Daley, "A Pioneer Passes," *New York Times*, February 18, 1959.

3 PURE MAYHEM

1 Dave Anderson, "Quarterback Giants Traded Away," *New York Times*, December 9, 1978.

2 Andy Robustelli and Jack Clary, *Once a Giant, Always . . . : My Two Lives with the New York Giants* (Boston: Quinlan Press, 1987).

3 Ibid.

4 FUMBLE FALLOUT AND THE FAMILY FEUD

1 Michael Katz, "20 Seconds Left as Eagles Win," *New York Times*, November 20, 1978.

2 John Branch, "For One Bad Call, One Big Toll," *New York Times*, February 3, 2015.

3 "Sports World Specials: Why Was It So, Joe? So Much for a Streak Not . . ." *New York Times*, November 27, 1978.

4 Michael Katz, "Giants' Old and Young in Disarray," *New York Times,* November 30, 1978.

5 Michael Katz, "Giants' Owners Assailed," *New York Times,* December 9, 1978.

6 Andy Robustelli and Jack Clary, *Once a Giant, Always . . . : My Two Lives with the New York Giants* (Boston: Quinlan Press, 1987).

7 Ibid.

8 Michael Katz, "Feuding Giants to Seek Coach," *New York Times,* February 10, 1979.

9 Michael Katz, "Maras' Feud over Staff Erupts," *New York Times,* February 9, 1979.

10 Ibid.

5 THE COMPROMISE CHOICE

1 Michael Olesker, "Remembering Young for His Discipline, Sentimentality," *Baltimore Sun,* December 11, 2001.

2 Frank Deford, "A Former High School Teacher Has Made the New York Giants Winners," *Sports Illustrated,* December 16, 1985.

3 Ibid.

4 Gary Myers, "Young, the Compromise Who Never Did," *New York Daily News,* December 10, 2001.

5 Michael Katz, "George Young Is Appointed General Manager," *New York Times,* February 15, 1979.

6 Dave Anderson, "Always Hire a Guy You Know," *New York Times,* February 23, 1979.

7 Michael Katz, "Perkins Appears to Be Giants' New Coach," *New York Times,* February 22, 1979.

8 Paul Zimmerman, "Awww, C'mon, Ray, the Giants Won! Give Us a Smile," *Sports Illustrated,* October 15, 1979.

9 Bill Parcells and Nunyo Demasio, *Parcells: A Football Life* (New York: Crown Archetype, 2014).

6 FINDING WHITEY

1 Phil McConkey, Phil Simms, and Dick Schaap, *Simms to McConkey: Blood, Sweat, and Gatorade* (New York: Crown Publishers, 1987).

2 Ibid.

3 Michael Katz, "Giants Defend 'Value' in Choice of Simms: Perkins Optimistic Giants Selections," *New York Times,* May 5, 1979.

7 A BRONCOS SEASON TICKET HOLDER

1 Bill Parcells and Nunyo Demasio, *Parcells: A Football Life* (New York: Crown Archetype, 2014).

2 Bill Parcells and Mike Lupica, *Parcells: Autobiography of the Biggest Giant of Them All* (New York: Bonus Books, 1987).

3 Ibid.

4 Parcells and Demasio, *Parcells: A Football Life.*

5 Ibid.

6 Parcells and Lupica, *Parcells: Autobiography.*

7 Ibid.

8 Michael Katz, "Giants Test Simms in a Workout: Pisarcik Overweight Free Agent Impresses," *New York Times,* May 11, 1979.

9 Dave Anderson, "Report Card on a Rookie QB," *New York Times,* October 8, 1979.

10 Ibid.

11 Ibid.

12 Parcells and Lupica, *Parcells: Autobiography.*

13 Ibid.

14 Michael Katz, "Perkins's Tough Road to Success," *New York Times,* July 30, 1979.

15 Will McDonough, "Patriots May Be Fined for Sweep of Dolphins," *Boston Globe,* December 19, 1982.

16 Paul Zimmerman, "Awww, C'mon, Ray, the Giants Won! Give Us a Smile," *Sports Illustrated,* October 15, 1979.

17 Michael Katz, "Giants Falter in 2d Half, Lose, 27–14," *New York Times,* September 10, 1979.

18 Michael Katz, "Perkins: No Giant Shakeup," *New York Times,* September 11, 1979.

19 Michael Katz, "Perkins, Players Differ on Carson Benching," *New York Times,* September 25, 1979.

20 Katz, "Perkins's Tough Road."

21 Zimmerman, "Awww, C'mon."

22 Ibid.

23 Michael Katz, "Players Are Pained by Perkins's Attitude: Gravelle Now a Free Agent 'Rest Is the Worst Thing,'" *New York Times,* October 18, 1979.

24 Malcolm Moran, "Raiders Defeat Giants by 33–17," *New York Times,* December 22, 1980.

25 McDonough, "Patriots May Be Fined."

8 "GOT MY LATHER GOING"

1 Lawrence Taylor and David Falkner, *LT: Living on the Edge* (New York: Warner Books, 1987).

2 Doug Looney, "Kickin' Up Their Tar Heel," *Sports Illustrated*, October 27, 1980.

3 William Wallace, "Taylor Shapes Up as the Giants' Top Pick," *New York Times*, April 12, 1981.

4 Ibid.

5 Frank Litsky, "Taylor Says Giants Made Him Welcome," *New York Times*, April 30, 1981.

6 John Papanek, "Another Campbell May Be Coming," *Sports Illustrated*, August 3, 1981.

7 Taylor and Falkner, *LT: Living on the Edge*.

8 Jim Burt and Hank Gola, *Hard Nose: The Story of the 1986 Giants* (San Diego: Harcourt, Brace, Jovanovich, 1987).

9 Ibid.

10 Ibid.

11 Ibid.

12 Ibid.

13 Taylor and Falkner, *LT: Living on the Edge*.

14 Lawrence Taylor and Steve Serby, *LT: Over the Edge* (New York: Harper-Torch, 2003).

15 Taylor and Falkner, *LT: Living on the Edge*.

16 Taylor and Serby, *LT: Over the Edge*.

17 Dave Anderson, "The Weekend That Could," *New York Times*, December 15, 1981.

18 Michael Katz, "Taylor: In Back of the Surprise," *New York Times*, December 21, 1981.

19 Ibid.

20 Ibid.

9 EUPHORIA

1 Lawrence Taylor and Steve Serby, *LT: Over the Edge* (New York: Harper-Torch, 2003).

2 Ibid.

3 Lawrence Taylor and David Falkner, *LT: Living on the Edge* (New York: Warner Books, 1987).

4 Ronald Sullivan, "N.F.L. Says Players' Cocaine Use Could Threaten Integrity of Game," *New York Times,* June 27, 1982.

5 Don Reese, "I'm Not Worth a Damn," *Sports Illustrated,* June 14, 1982.

6 Michael Demarest, "Cocaine: Middle Class High," *Time,* July 6, 1981.

7 Sullivan, "N.F.L. Says."

8 Taylor and Serby, *LT: Over the Edge.*

9 Michael Janofsky, "Drug Report Cites Cowboys," *New York Times,* October 3, 1985.

10 Frank Litsky, "2 Giants in Battle," *New York Times,* August 12, 1982.

11 Frank Litsky, "Simms Frustrated by Erratic Line Play," *New York Times,* August 24, 1982.

12 Ibid.

13 Will McDonough, "Patriots May Be Fined for Sweep of Dolphins," *Boston Globe,* December 19, 1982.

14 Frank Litsky, "Parcells Sidelines New Role," *New York Times,* December 20, 1982.

15 Bill Parcells and Nunyo Demasio, *Parcells: A Football Life* (New York: Crown Archetype, 2014).

16 McDonough, "Patriots May Be Fined."

17 Parcells and Demasio, *Parcells: A Football Life.*

10 FIRE PARCELLS, PLAY FOR TRUMP

1 Thomas Rogers, "Scouting; The Parcells Way," *New York Times,* April 30, 1983.

2 Frank Litsky, "Giants Get Kinard, Safety, as Top Pick," *New York Times,* April 27, 1983.

3 Lawrence Taylor and Steve Serby, *LT: Over the Edge* (New York: Harper-Torch, 2003), 66.

4 Frank Litsky, "Heaviest Giant Is Making Slow Progress," *New York Times,* July 31, 1983.

5 Michael Katz, "Brunner Is Named to Start in Opener," *New York Times,* August 30, 1983.

6 Dave Anderson, "Absolution for Brunner," *New York Times,* September 5, 1983.

7 Taylor and Serby, *LT: Over the Edge.*

8 Ibid.

9 Bill Parcells and Nunyo Demasio, *Parcells: A Football Life* (New York: Crown Archetype, 2014).

11 GANGSTER

1 Bill Brubaker, "Taylor Has It All—Including a 'Substance' Problem," *Washington Post*, April 7, 1986.
2 Bill Parcells and Nunyo Demasio, *Parcells: A Football Life* (New York: Crown Archetype, 2014).
3 Jane Gross, "Giants Waive Scott for Not Following Club Policy," *New York Times*, July 21, 1984.

12 THE BIRTH OF "PARCELLS GUYS"

1 Peter King, "Taylor Played Out of Control," *Newsday*, February 16, 1986.

13 GATORADE AND AN EXORCISM

1 News Services, "Carson Back in Camp," *Washington Post*, August 17, 1984.
2 Phil McConkey, Phil Simms, and Dick Schaap, *Simms to McConkey: Blood, Sweat, and Gatorade* (New York: Crown Publishers, 1987).
3 Ibid.
4 Ibid.
5 Ibid.
6 Ibid.
7 Ibid.
8 Frank Litsky, "Giants Win by 19–7; Jets Defeat Browns," *New York Times*, October 15, 1984.
9 Craig Wolff, "Giants Try to Forget Losing Past," *New York Times*, September 2, 1984.

14 "HEY, PARCELLS, YOU GOT TO FIND A WAY TO BEAT THOSE GUYS"

1 Dave Anderson, "How the Giants Lifted Their Game," *New York Times*, January 11, 1987.
2 Jim Burt and Hank Gola, *Hard Nose: The Story of the 1986 Giants* (San Diego: Harcourt, Brace, Jovanovich, 1987).
3 Frank Litsky, "Bengals Triumph on Giant Mistakes," *New York Times*, October 14, 1985.
4 Luke Mullins, "The Oral History of Joe Theismann's Broken Leg," *Washingtonian*, September 29, 2015.

5 Ibid.

6 Lawrence Taylor and Steve Serby, *LT: Over the Edge* (New York: Harper-Torch, 2003).

7 Vinny DiTrani, "Taylor's Descent Traced to 1983," *Record* (Bergen County, NJ), February 16, 1986.

8 Christine Brennan, "Giants Face a Nemesis; New York Plays 49ers Again in Postseason," *Washington Post,* December 28, 1985.

9 Vinny DiTrani, "Refrigerator Gets Deep-Six," *Record* (Bergen County, NJ), January 3, 1986.

10 Frank Litsky, "Bears Pound Giants, 21–0, in Wind and Cold," *New York Times,* January 6, 1986.

15 REHAB

1 Augie Lio, "It Could've Been Worse for Giants," *Herald & News* (Passaic, NJ), January 7, 1986.

2 Paul Needell, "It's a 28-Team Woe in Varying Degrees," *New York Daily News,* January 29, 1986.

3 Hank Gola, "LT His Own Worst Enemy," *New York Post,* February 17, 1986.

4 Vinny DiTrani, "Hero's Fall Irks Giants Watcher," *Record* (Bergen County, NJ), February 16, 1986.

5 Vinny DiTrani, "Taylor's Descent Traced to 1983," *Record* (Bergen County, NJ), February 16, 1986.

6 Frank Litsky, "Taylor Confirms 'Substance Abuse' Care," *New York Times,* March 21, 1986.

7 Peter King, "Giants' Taylor Avoids Media," *Newsday,* May 20, 1986.

8 Vinny DiTrani, "Parcells Comes to Defense of His Star Defender," *Record* (Bergen County, NJ), May 22, 1986.

9 Vinny DiTrani, "Parcells Optimistic on Taylor," *Record* (Bergen County, NJ), May 16, 1986.

10 DiTrani, "Parcells Comes to Defense."

11 Ibid.

12 Ibid.

13 Bill Verigan, "At 250, No Extra Work for Lawrence's Tailor," *New York Daily News,* May 23, 1986.

14 Bill Verigan, "Taylor Silent but Frisky," *New York Daily News,* July 22, 1986.

16 THE LOCKER ROOM PAY PHONE

1 Bill Verigan, "No Dough, No Joe," *New York Daily News,* August 6, 1986.

2 Hank Gola, "Irish DE looms as Jints Top Pick," *New York Post*, April 28, 1986.

3 Don Williams, "Dorsey Runs Like Dorsett," *Star-Ledger* (NJ), May 3, 1986.

4 Vinny DiTrani, "Giants Follow Their Guru of Sinew," *Record* (Bergen County, NJ), March 25, 1986.

5 Laurence Chollet, "Giants Kick the Meat and Potatoes Habit," *Record* (Bergen County, NJ), September 7, 1986.

6 Ibid.

7 Frank Litsky, "Morris Is Back with the Giants," *New York Times*, August 28, 1986.

8 Hank Gola, "Former Giant Tuggle Loses Cancer Battle," *New York Post*, September 1, 1986.

9 Frank Litsky, "Tuggle, Ex-Giant, Dies of Cancer at 25," *New York Times*, September 1, 1986.

10 Hank Gola, "McConkey Weighs Anchor," *New York Post*, September 2, 1986.

18 ROLLING

1 "Backtalk; L.T.," *New York Times*, January 24, 1994.

2 Frank Litsky, "Seahawks Beat Giants by 17–12," *New York Times*, October 20, 1986.

3 Lawrence Taylor and Steve Serby, *LT: Over the Edge* (New York: Harper-Torch, 2003).

19 FOURTH AND 17

1 Paul Zimmerman, "A Giant Step Forward," *Sports Illustrated*, December 15, 1986.

2 Lawrence Taylor and David Falkner, *LT: Living on the Edge* (New York: Warner Books, 1987).

3 "America's Game: 1986 New York Giants," NFL Network.

21 SEPARATION

1 Jim Burt and Hank Gola, *Hard Nose: The Story of the 1986 Giants* (San Diego: Harcourt, Brace, Jovanovich, 1987).

2 Christine Brennan, "All World's a Stage to Redskins' Manley; But On-Field Act Draws Greatest Applause," *Washington Post*, December 7, 1986.

3 Paul Zimmerman, "A Giant Step Forward," *Sports Illustrated*, December 15, 1986.

4 Ibid.
5 Ibid.

22 TAKING THE WIND

1 Frank Litsky, "Pro Football; Taylor Provides a Many-Faceted Self-Portrait," *New York Times*, January 4, 1987.
2 Michael Eisen, "LT Giants defensive superstar speaks out about his game, his lifestyle and his future," *Daily Record*, January 4, 1987.
3 Litsky, "Pro Football; Taylor Provides."
4 Peter King, "Believe It or Not, Giants Are Superstitious," *Newsday*, December 24, 1986.
5 Vinny DiTrani, "A Giants Coach Never Forgets," *Record* (Bergen County, NJ), July 27, 1986.
6 Ibid.

23 "NOT GOING TO HAVE A DAY ON ME"

1 Bill Parcells and Mike Lupica, *Parcells: Autobiography of the Biggest Giant of Them All* (New York: Bonus Books, 1987).
2 Tom Verducci, "Ouch! Bavaro Drilled by Media," *Newsday*, January 22, 1987.
3 Brad Benson and Frank Litsky, "Super Bowl XXI; Day by Day: Building Intensity," *New York Times*, January 26, 1987.

24 "WHAT IT WAS ALL FOR"

1 Bill Parcells and Mike Lupica, *Parcells: Autobiography of the Biggest Giant of Them All* (New York: Bonus Books, 1987).
2 Brad Benson and Frank Litsky, "Super Bowl XXI; Day by Day: Building Intensity," *New York Times*, January 26, 1987.

INDEX